China's Urban Revolution

China's Urban Revolution

Understanding Chinese Eco-Cities

AUSTIN WILLIAMS

Bloomsbury Academic
An imprint of Bloomsbury Publishing Plc

B L O O M S B U R Y
LONDON • OXFORD • NEW YORK • NEW DELHI • SYDNEY

Bloomsbury Academic

An imprint of Bloomsbury Publishing Plc

50 Bedford Square   1385 Broadway
London   New York
WC1B 3DP   NY 10018
UK   USA

www.bloomsbury.com

BLOOMSBURY and the Diana logo are trademarks of Bloomsbury Publishing Plc

First published 2017
Reprinted 2018

British Library Cataloguing-in-Publication Data
A catalogue record for this book is available from the British Library.

ISBN: HB: 978-1-3500-0324-8
        PB: 978-1-3500-0325-5
        ePDF: 978-1-3500-0322-4
        ePub: 978-1-3500-0323-1

Library of Congress Cataloging-in-Publication Data
Names: Williams, Austin author.
Title: China's urban revolution : understanding Chinese eco-cities / Austin Williams.
Description: First Edition. | New York : Bloomsbury Publishing, [2017] |
Includes index. Identifiers: LCCN 2017028071 |
ISBN 9781350003248 (hardback : alk. paper) ISBN 9781350003255 (pbk. : alk. paper) |
ISBN 9781350003231 (ePub) | ISBN 9781350003224 (ePdf)
Subjects: LCSH: Sustainable urban development–China. | Urban ecology
(Sociology)–China. | City planning–Environmental aspects–China.
Classification: LCC HT243.C6 W55 2017 | DDC 307.760951–dc23
LC record available at https://lccn.loc.gov/2017028071

Cover design by Eleanor Rose
Cover image © Getty Images

Typeset by Integra Software Services Pvt. Ltd.
Printed and bound in Great Britain

To find out more about our authors and books visit www.bloomsbury.com.
Here you will find extracts, author interviews, details of forthcoming
events and the option to signup for our newsletters.

To Martha

CONTENTS

ABOUT THE AUTHOR

Austin Williams, author, journalist and associate professor of architecture at XJTLU in China, has visited many Chinese cities and Eco-cities and takes an honest view of their progress and perils. From traffic pollution to the liberation of mobility; from the dangers of deforestation to the wonders of industrialization; from rural sanctification to urban globalization, this book explores how these cities are creating—and also attempting to resolve—China's fundamental contradictions of development.

Williams is the China correspondent for *The Architectural Review*, contributing editor, AR (Pacific Region), and writes occasionally on Chinese architecture for L'Architecture d'Aujourd'hui and Asian Age. This book is a development of the author's presentations made at CUNY (New York), the British Chamber of Commerce (Shanghai), University of Hawaii (Honolulu), Zhejiang University, Wuhu University, Anhui, the University of Hong Kong, Beijing University and the Battle of Ideas in London.

PREFACE

China is a country of contradictions. A place of rickshaws and space stations, of tropics and deserts, of dynamism and restraint, of yin and yang. Many have pointed out that China's social contradictions are inherently unsustainable, but the ultimate contradiction is that the Chinese state seems to be able to sustain them. How else can a country that seeks to be a player in the globalized world still blithely restrict access to ideas on the internet? How else might we explain the fact that its president celebrates China's 5,000-year-old civilization[1] even though the country had revolutions in 1911 and 1949. Or the fact that it is the world's second-richest nation that still self-identifies as an under-developed country. It's a liberalizing capitalist economy that has tightened the state ownership of giant corporations in order to ensure their "socialist direction of development."[2] And it is a patriotic and pious nation from which many people still seem keen to flee.[3]

This book is meant as a challenge to those who attempt to impose a Manichean worldview on China: who see it as either politically enervating or frighteningly authoritarian, an economic miracle or a historical tragedy, a Chinese Dream or a nightmare of conformism, because in reality all of these descriptions apply. Author Jonathan Fenby recommends that China watchers should be a little less glib in making immediate assessments of China and should not just take into account not just the China that hits the headlines but introduce a nuanced understanding of its underlying complexity.[4] This book hopes to reflect that attitude. As such it is neither a relativist celebration of Oriental difference nor a paean to contemporary Western superiority.

If there is one thing that people know about China, it is its urban revolution. China has built more shopping malls, hotels, office buildings, housing estates (as well as golf courses and theme parks) than any other country in the world.[5] According to some, it is building twenty cities a year for twenty years, having already urbanized the equivalent of the entire US population in the first decade of this millennium. However, as a result of this urban explosion in which China is now said to be nearly 60 percent urbanized (up from 17 percent in 1976), many people see China's cities as merely a euphemism for the dangers of unrestrained growth and the problems of the modern world. Indeed, Tom Miller, author of *China's Urban Billion,* contends that "China's rapidly growing cities will remain ugly, congested and polluted."[6] But less well known is that of all the new cities being created, the Chinese Ministry of Housing and Urban-Rural Development has declared that many of these will be "Eco-cities." But given that, as author Wade Shepard points out, "the words 'eco' and 'city' combined together seems like an unabashed oxymoron,"[7] for many this could be the ultimate Chinese contradiction.

China's thirteenth Five-Year Plan issued in 2015, laid down an unequivocal pledge that it would embrace a "green" development model over the following five years, leaving many Western commentators puzzled by China's ability to change course: one minute marginalized for allegedly polluting the planet, the next leading G20 talks on climate change. The resulting confusion led some to hail Chinese Eco-cities as either a fundamental change of heart in China's expansionist industrial policies or snipe that they are probably Chinese environmental cover-ups. Eco-cities are either overindulged or disbelieved. The Finnish environmentalist Eero Paloheimo calls Eco-cities "standard-setters,"[8] whereas ex-*Huffington Post* author Bianca Bosker says that Chinese Eco-cities are "the same sprawling McMansions under a different name."[9] American academic Julie Sze advocates "healthy skepticism (in) the eco-city"[10] debate.

After living in China I have come to realize that this country is more fascinating and nuanced than Western-centric and the Sino-centric bias normally allows. As an academic and journalist, I hope to cast some light on some of its hidden stories. In doing so, I do not intend to shy away from bias but equally attempt to seek out the facts fairly. The award-winning commentator Hu Shuli, founder of Caixin Media, says that it is "a good time to be a journalist in China, because there is more news than there are journalists"[11] and nowhere is this more true than with reference to China's urbanization.

The debate has moved on from simply building new cities. Nowadays, Chinese urban commentators talk of "mega-cities," "meta-cities" or even "hyper-cities" and of course "Eco-cities." Allegedly, China will have fifteen new "supercities" by 2025 (each of 25 million people) not to mention giant urban corridors, regional powerhouses and 200 new "ordinary" cities. Will these new kinds of urban development be good, humane, healthy places? Undoubtedly, they will be well planned, but the rise of the Chinese middle classes means that urban residents are looking at a better quality of urban life, and the poor too want a piece of the action.

China's urban condition is much pontificated, regularly criticized, frequently applauded but seldom (outside academic circles) openly investigated. The necessity for a political assessment of China's relatively new Eco-urban phenomenon—which undoubtedly bears upon China's place in a global environmental discourse—is the object of this book. It is a book that attempts to provide some insights, anecdotes and examples from which you, the reader, can make a more informed assessment.

That said, the subject of exploration may give rise to a number of contradictory viewpoints of my own, and I can only hope that these diverse observations, undoubted uncertainties and unresolved theories are accepted as part of an unvarnished critique of a vast, unfinished urban experiment. This book, like China, is a work in progress.

Notes

1   Jinping, Xi, Address at the Commemoration of The 70th Anniversary of The Victory of the Chinese People's War of Resistance Against Japanese Aggression and The World Anti-Fascist War, *Full text of Chinese president's speech at commemoration of 70th anniversary of war victory*, Xinhuanet, September 3, 2015. http://news.xinhuanet.com/english/2015-09/03/c_134583870.htm (accessed March 20, 2016).

2   Anderlini, Jamil, "Beijing Calls for Tighter Grip on State Groups," *Financial Times*, September 21, 2015.

3   Domenach, J-L., *China's Uncertain Future*. Columbia University Press, 2014, p. 117.

4   Fenby, Jonathan, *Tiger Head, Snake Tails: China Today, How It Got There and Why It Has to Change.* Simon & Schuster (London), 2013, p. xii.

5   Campanella, T.J., *The Concrete Dragon: China's Urban Revolution and What It Means for the World.* Princeton Architectural Press (New York), 2012, p. 14.

6   Miller, T., *China's Urban Billion: The Story Behind the Biggest Migration in Human History.* Asian Arguments, Zed Books (New York), 2012, p. 6.

7   Shepard, Wade, "China's Eco-cities Are Often Neither Ecologically Friendly, Nor Functional Cities," *The Great Debate,* Reuters, September 22, 2015. http://blogs.reuters.com/great-debate/ (accessed March 4, 2016).

8   Xiang, Li and Zheng, Xu (2011), "Eco-cities Are the Key to Conservation: Experts," *China Daily,* September 24, 2011.

9   Bosker, Bianca, *Original Copies: Architectural Mimicry in Contemporary China.* University of Hawaii Press, 2013.

10 Sze, Julie, *Fantasy Islands: Chinese Dreams and Ecological Fears in an Age of Climate Change.* University of California Press, 2015, p. 163.

11 Hu, S., Special Melbourne Lecture, Lowy Institute at the National Gallery of Victoria, July 11, 2016.

ACKNOWLEDGMENT

This book is my own work and hence the arguments, bias, errors and even contradictions are also mine. The ideas contained in this book have been fed by research undertaken at the Department of Architecture, Xi'an Jiaotong-Liverpool University, Suzhou, Jiangsu Province, PR China, and I would like to thank those close colleagues who provided me with intellectual succor over that period. In particular, I would like to thank Theodoros Dounas for his sincere friendship and robust intellectual challenges over the years; Achim Benjamin Spaeth for his professional candor; Kirsty Mattinson for her patience in Chinese language lessons as well as her passion for China and her willingness to inquire upon everything; Aura Istrate who is making inroads of her own to understand the specifics of livable Chinese cities; Xi Junjie who forced me on a mini-speaking-tour; Dong Yiping for answering interminable questions; and Chang Ying, Chen Chia-Lin, and Andy Wen for their fascinating practical insights.

I would like to thank the editorial team at the *Architectural Review* (London)—in particular, Catherine Slessor, Phineas Harper, and Manon Mollard for taking me on as China correspondent and encouraging me to visit weird and wonderful places and providing me with guest editorial space to polemicize about them—and Michael Holt, ex-editor at the *Architectural Review Asia Pacific*, for putting me on the masthead and demanding results. Similarly, I have learned a great deal from the various editorial colleagues at Masterplanning the Future, the first independent online architectural resource in China.

I have never before had so many exciting arguments about architecture and urbanism as I have had since coming to China in 2011, where those I have met have been supremely informed, eager to talk, and forthright in their challenges. For all the reports of (undeniable) censorship, I have predominantly encountered only the luxury of robust argument, dedicated inquiry and intellectual open-mindedness. I list here some of the most notable conversationalists: University of Tongji professors, Li Xiangning, Miao Pu, and Harry den Hartog; University of Hong Kong lecturers, Johnathan Lin and Joshua Bolchover, Professor Wang Yun at the Beijing University of Civil Engineering and Architecture, Maria Oenoto COP21 representative, Oxford University Professor Alan Hudson, Mary O'Donnell of Shenzhen Noted, and Future Cities Project director, Alastair Donald.

In addition, I would like to thank XJTLU and University of Liverpool professors David Sadler and Andre Brown who gave me the opportunity to help set up a new architecture department in China, and therefore to whom I shall always be exceptionally grateful for having changed my life. Of course, I must also thank my charges: the ever-attentive Chinese students, most particularly of my Urban Studies classes, who always pushed me to know more.

I have learned much from Kerry Brown's and Jonathan Fenby's writings and conversations. My thanks also go to Wade Shepard, author of the excellent "Ghost Cities of China," who unbeknownst to him, actually inspired me to write this book.

I would like to thank James Thompson and Claire Constable at Bloomsbury for allowing me the time to write, while having faith and patience that it would all turn out ok. I would also like to thank all the unsung heroes at Bloomsbury, especially copyeditors, designers, marketing and sales as well as Hao Wu for the Eco-city map and Hao Jiang for graphics.

And finally to the incomparable Claire Fox, who, while I was working happily in London, sent me a job advertisement for a six-year posting in China that began my adventure on the other side of the world. I am one among the many who have learned from her that difficult questions and unpopular answers are often the most important.

MAP 1 *A map of Chinese Eco-cities mentioned in this book.*

Daqing

Baicheng

Miaofengshanzhen   Caofeidian   Shenyang

Huangbaiyu

gsheng   Beijing   Qian'an   North Korea

Ordos   Tianjin   Dalian   Pyonyang

hina   Jinan   Seoul   South Korea   Japan

Xi'an   Zhengzhou   Qingdao   Tokyo

Rizhao

Hefei

Wuxi

Wuhan   Dongtan

Baoshan

Chongqing   Nanhui

Suzhou

Lake Eco-City   Thames Town

Yichun   Zhoushan

Wujiang

Guilin   Hangzhou

Gui'anNew Area   Xiamen   Tongling

Gongqingcheng

Zhongshan   Fuzhou

Huizhou   Nanchang

Shenzhen

Guangming

Pingdi

Zhuhai

Sanya

Vietnam   Manila

dia

Philippines

CHAPTER ONE

What Is an Eco-City?

Traveling the 65 km from the center of bustling Beijing, past the 6th Ring Road, is a rather slow experience. My taxi sped or, rather, trundled through industrial suburbia past pagodas and pylons, chimneys and cooling towers until all of a sudden, as if passing a physical boundary, we arrive in quasi-rural China. Winding our way through colorful countryside and scattered villages, we find ourselves in an area of forests, craggy mountains, rivers, dirt tracks, arbitrary construction projects, small-scale industry, and rural farms. It's a pleasant mess peppered with Chinese tour buses and weekend cyclists. This is Mentougou District, an area of cultural significance and a pilgrimage route to the Buddhist Temple on the top of the holy mountain of Miaofengshan ("beautiful peak").

Like the hundreds of other pilgrims crowded into the Huiji Temple and gazing out over the pines, I am looking for something. A sense of fulfillment. A personal challenge. Enlightenment. But this is not the same self-realization that many of my Chinese fellow travelers share. Indeed, I have come to seek out material rather than spiritual truth, to find what the *Huffington Post* described as the new "Ecological Silicon Valley," a place with "research institutes for modern science along with eco-efficient urban living."[1]

The images I had found online had been intriguing, comprising photomontages of fantastical buildings set in dense woodland: giant interlinked polyhedrons spilling down the mountain into a shimmering lake. As these space-age architectural shapes reach the water's edge, the buildings mutate into floating domes connected by suspended walkways. In 2015, one website wrote that the city has been "planned in collaboration with Finnish ecological experts...learning from both the successes and failures of other eco cities."[2] As part of this Eco-city's focus on residential needs, further into the valley, pristine modernist family residences are shown set among civic buildings—exciting parametric shapes—while other architectural forms are cut into the hillside. I had viewed many websites displaying images akin to an eco-nirvana. These were extraordinary visions from a science fiction movie balanced on the side of a historic Chinese landscape and unquestionably, unhesitatingly, it was well worth traveling to see.

So, here I am, standing in Miaofengshanzhen, a run-of-the-mill Chinese semirural townscape. The town and surrounding villages are in a reasonably unspoiled landscape with bog-standard housing packed into the valley and up the slopes. There remains only a few light industries, including quarries (many in the process of closing to reduce environmental damage) and agriculture (cherries, persimmon, and pears), livestock farming, and markets.

Searching high and low, from the bottom of the valley to the top of the mountain, it quickly becomes apparent that nothing much has changed here for some time. Even though the eco-polis project has been nominated for international awards, the proposed buildings exist only as drawings on the internet and in environmental forums, drawings which are still circulated by Eco-city campaigners as an example of what can be done.

Except of course it hasn't been done. It remains a fantasy. Not one of the eco-consultant's buildings has been built, not one stone laid, not one environmental objective reached. No "hip" geodesic domes.[3] The tranquil lake shown on publicity images remains the rather grubby Yongding River. Fair enough, as much of this mountainous region has long been praised for its environmental splendor, wonderful views, and surrounding natural beauty but that has nothing to do with an Eco-city. True, there is a little bit of development sprawl evident across the valley, but as far as a new city is concerned—"eco" or otherwise—there is nothing. Nada. *Meiyou*.

———

American ecological urbanist Richard Register is said to have coined the word "ecocity" to describe "an ecologically healthy city,"[4] a "non-violent city," and a place in which "to make peace on Earth and with Earth."[5] If this definition seems a little nebulous—if it sounds a little hippy—then don't despair. Register himself notes that "the term ecocity remains loosely defined,"[6] and US academic Mark Roseland states that "there is no single accepted definition of 'eco-cities' or 'sustainable communities'."[7] One European research paper concludes that, in practice, "many cities claim to be ecological cities but there are no non-ambiguous definitions,"[8] while US professor and author Julie Sze much more bluntly states that "these 'ecological' terms are often quite meaningless."[9]

Maybe that should be the end of that: end of chapter, end of book. No definition, no evidence. But there is a global discourse around this ill-defined concept that is worth looking into. After all, if no one really knows what the term "Eco-city" means, why is there so much money spent on it, and why is there so much demand for them? Indeed, there are armies of consultants, designers, advisers, and experts—foreign and homegrown—engaged in this ambiguous Eco-city industry in China (and across the world), each reinforcing the concept without explaining it. In fact, one global survey has suggested that "the absence of a strict definition has proven useful"[10] in that it has allowed the term to become popularized as a moral or ethical imperative[11] without anyone having to substantiate it (Figure 1.1).

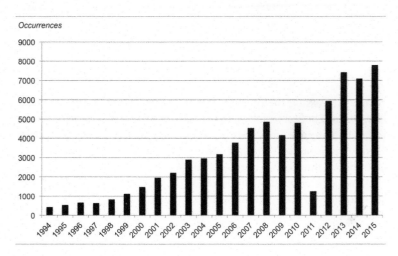

FIGURE 1.1 *Occurrences of Eco-cities in Chinese literature search*

China is certainly enamored with the concept. Simply by looking at the number of research papers published on the subject, we can see that there has been a creeping interest in Eco-cities over a number of years. (It is difficult to pass a construction site in any of the many major cities these days without seeing a hoarding plastered with party endorsements in big characters: "Creating the Eco-City with Green Energy," "Popularising Green Building," "The Tide of Eco-Cities Is Rising Up.") It is clear that in China, the Eco-city, whatever it is, has arrived.

Surveys by the International Eco-Cities Initiative in 2009 identified a total of seventy-nine Eco-cities around the world. That list included six Chinese Eco-cities. By 2011, the global list had increased to 176 and included 25 Chinese Eco-cities. Four years later, in 2015, China made its own list comprising 284 Eco-cities[12] out of a total of 658 major cities across its own country.[13] In other words, China claims that today 42 percent of all of its cities are Eco-cities. Anyone who has walked around a Chinese city lately will conclude that this is patent nonsense. Urban quality has definitely improved in the last decade, but for the most part Chinese cities are still the same vast, traffic-filled, pot-holed, shoddily built, uninsulated, congested, inefficient, wonderful urban sprawls that they have long been.

Notwithstanding the legitimate defense that Eco-cities are hard to define, what is their conception, function, and purpose that now allows China to portray itself as the Eco-city capital of the world?

What is a city?

Before addressing the question of what we understand by an "Eco-city," we ought first to ask: What is a city? On this too, there seems not to be such an easy answer as one might expect. Leo Hollis, author of *Cities Are Good for You*, suggests that "the city is too complicated for a solitary definition"[14] and, as such, its interpretation is something that has exercised the minds of demographers, geographers, and sociologists for many decades. Even though the city is simplistically associated as being the opposite of rural organization, this is not good enough for a detailed analysis.

Borrowing from research by the Organization for Economic Co-operation and Development (OECD), the European Union

(EU) is now fine-tuning its city typologies to incorporate the more inclusive descriptors such as "predominantly rural," "intermediate," or "predominantly urban" regions.[15] While many authors still legitimately identify urban areas as "those that are not rural," it is also the case that in many parts of the world, as industrialization and modernization increase and come into conflict with the agricultural areas, so the boundaries become blurred between town and country. As such, planners need to explain urban life in more specific or refined ways.

In 1820, Victorian aphorist Reverend Charles Caleb Colton wrote: "If you would be known, and not know, vegetate in a village; If you would know, and not be known, live in a city."[16] His pithy adage captured the progressive sense of the urban miracle in one snappy sentence. In a city, one can be socially networked and maintain independence and privacy at the same time, a contradiction that is not resolvable at the level of rural isolation. In this way, the city is distinguished more than just by its separation from rurality; it is a form of social organization that simply cannot occur in an agricultural economy.

Thirty years later, Marx wrote of the "idiocy of rural life,"[17] using the word "idiot" in its original Greek form to mean an unskilled or private person outside the social, educational, and political milieu of the group. Rural life could not provide the experiences and opportunities for personal flourishing that the city afforded. For a long time then, the urban condition was clearly linked to the idea of the urbane: it reflected cultural development, the promotion of the self, a celebration of social mix and, by the eighteenth century in Europe, the emergence of civil society. The great American commentator Lewis Mumford described the "theater of social drama" as one of the defining features of the metropolitan experience,[18] seeing it as more than the sum of its parts. However, urban statisticians clearly dislike ephemeral qualitative values and seem to prefer the quantifiable approach which results in cities being defined primarily in numerical terms: big and dense versus small and scattered.

However, the method of calculating the size and scale of urban regions is curiously vague and, in some ways, intentionally so. Across the world, official reports often tend to conflate the relationship between "urbanized areas" and "city" status. The United States defines "urban areas" as those places with a minimum population of 2,500. In Ethiopia, the classification for a city relates to conurbations of 2,000 people or more, in Benin the figure is 10,000 and in Botswana it is 5,000 (with the additional requirement that 75 percent of the economic activity is nonagricultural).[19] There are often other factors included in the definition, such as density or travel times, but population size is key. The United Nations is unabashed in stating that it classifies cities by population size primarily because a quantifiable number is easier to compare than a more qualitative assessment, but that doesn't necessarily mean that it is the best approach nor indeed that it is accurate.[20]

The OECD defines an "urban core"—an urban concentration within a metropolitan region—as having a population size of either 50,000 or 100,000 people, depending on the country, whereas the American government classifies a metropolitan area as a region with over one million people where up to 250,000 inhabitants live inside that region's principal city.[21] The more one digs into this topic, the more it becomes apparent that these pseudo-scientific numerical clarifications have a touch of *realpolitik* wrapped up in them. For example, the UN states that "if India's national authorities would classify populations of 5,000 or more as urban, the country would be considered predominantly urban and not rural." It stops short of saying: "and we can't have that." Remember, America is allowed to define urban areas as those with populations of 2,500 and over.

It seems that the city as a definer of development is quite clearly a biased reflection of the status quo and the UN has contrived a way of differentiating between urban areas in countries with vastly different levels of development so that everyone knows their place. The US government Census Bureau now talks more of "urban clusters," for example, to get over the embarrassment that in 2016 a single Chinese employer reportedly took an entire US city's worth of people—2,500—on a company holiday.[22]

Other departments of the UN have tried to oversimplify the morass of unfathomable statistical data in order to avoid complicated arguments. One such is the Population Division of the Department of Economic and Social Affairs of the United Nations, which offers a reasonably consistent definition of a city anywhere in the world as contiguous regions containing over 300,000 people. Coincidentally, this is the same number of people at one single factory in Longhua, Shenzhen, in south China,[23] run by the Chinese/Taiwanese company Foxconn. This single factory is home to the equivalent of the entire population of Pittsburgh and ten times the population of the city-state of Monaco.

The EU has recently increased the figure that they will accept as a designated city population to 500,000 and added caveats such as the following: "If 15 % of employed persons living in one city work in another city, these cities are treated as a single city." As you can see, this kind of number crunching is not intellectually sustainable, made all the more confusing by so many contradictory agencies vying for definitional supremacy. The UK sometimes sits above this bean-counting, relying on the magnanimous power of the monarch to confer city status, magisterially oblivious to demographics or measurables. In Britain, the royal prerogative—the ability of the king or queen to simply pluck a city out of the air—has been in place for 500 years. One of the more recent acquisitions has been the small conurbation of St. Davids in west Wales, inhabited by fewer than 2,000 locals, which has now been designated as a British city.[24] Remember, 2,000 people is the required population size for an officially designated city in Ethiopia, which may not flatter the Welsh Parliament's rural development ambitions, but certainly lowers the bar sufficiently for Wales to claim its seventh city, and the title of the smallest city in Britain. Coincidentally, St. Davids is also officially a world Eco-city.

Sadly, China's official data adds an entirely new layer of fog to urban statistics. It hasn't been helped by the director of the country's National Bureau of Statistics, who was arrested for corruption in 2016. One academic paper—admittedly written in the mid-1980s—notes that "the actual size of China's urban population remains a mystery"[25] but that didn't stop officials making grand definitive statements about it and such dubious claims continue to this day. Contemporary urban data is confused by the known and the unknown populations: the resident and the migrant populations, the latter category said to comprise up to 150 million people.

Shanghai is currently—officially—said to be the home to between sixteen and twenty-three million people, the former being official residents and the latter including migrants and unregistered peoples. One researcher jokes (but not without truth) that unlike any other country China has "a unique perspective for viewing the urban population … based largely on a combination of where people live and who is responsible for their grain needs."[26] Indeed, back in 1964, the national census recalibrated how it defined the urban population to make it more favorable to its internal political agenda with rural people designated as "grain producers" and urbanites as "grain consumers." More importantly, under the *hukou* registration system, by being denied urban status, agricultural workers were also excluded from education and welfare benefits. (There is more on the *hukou* registration system in Chapter 4.)

Paper cities

At the foundation of the People's Republic of China in 1949, there were 120 cities. By 1952, there were 159 cities (in other words, nearly 40 new cities had been created in three years). Five years later still, by 1957, there were a total of 176 cities. This certainly looks like a magical urban revolution, so it should be pointed out that it is, to a certain extent, smoke and mirrors. Even in China (where indulgent Westerners are prone to fantasize about China's inscrutable ability to work miracles), cities—that is, meaningful cities—cannot be created overnight. What actually happened was that China simply changed the designations of many rural towns into cities. Hey presto, urban growth.

A seldom-talked-about problem with this kind of urbanization-by-spreadsheet approach that affected the early days of Mao's rule is that if a city can just be written into existence, then it can just as easily be erased. In the 1960s, around twenty million urban residents were reclassified and moved to rural areas, accounting for nearly 18 percent of China's total urban population at that time, falling from 19.8 percent in 1960 to 16.8 percent in 1963. Urbanites were shipped from the cities back to the countryside as part of the rustication movement because, for Mao, transformative revolutionary potential lay with the laboring peasants in the countryside, not in the cities with the urban working class. In this conceit, the noble peasant was the instructor and the bourgeois urbanite the student. Cities became a materialistic indulgence. Mao promulgated a policy of "industrialization without urbanization" described by author Xuefei Ren as "a clear anti-urban bias in national policymaking in the socialist period."[27] So if we continue the time line started above, in 1957 China had 176 cities. By 1960, there were 208. But by 1965, there were 168 cities: 40 seem to have disappeared. Their continued existence as a bourgeois designation was simply politically unacceptable.

Five years later, by 1971, China still managed to accommodate a numerically larger urban population than the entire United States, even though it was clearly, and proudly, a predominantly agricultural nation. By 1978, the year of Deng Xiaoping's "Opening Up" policy (opening up to the world market), China had 198[28] (or 193[29]) cities but, miraculously, two years later in 1980, it had 229. Once more, the Chinese ability to create something out of nothing was invoked in a statistical flourish. More positively, this growth actually reflected the new government's rejection of the sanctification of agricultural life that had underpinned Mao's rule (that had ironically devastated so many rural livelihoods) (Figure 1.2).

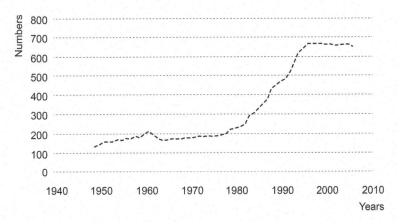

FIGURE 1.2 *The growth of Chinese cities since 1949*

This initial post-Mao reurbanization drive was carried forward under Deng Xiaoping's transformation of the economy from communist to capitalist (portrayed as "socialism with Chinese characteristics"). Under Deng, liberal reforms, especially in townships, provided the opportunity for new urban centers to emerge rapidly. By allowing capitalist incentives through the support of Town and Village Enterprises among other things, the average annual growth rate of rural industrial output from 1978 until 1994 was almost three times the national gross domestic product (GDP) rate.[30]

With this staggering growth came employment and migrant influx into many of these new liberalized urban centers. The coastal city of Quanzhou, for example (nowadays listed as an Eco-city), was the model of this kind of localized profit-driven urban development.

With a population of six million in 1995, it was the number one economic powerhouse in Fujian Province, helping to attract a large number of local rural residents but also a huge influx of migrant workers from inland China.[31] Today, its population stands at 8.5 million and is growing at 1 percent a year (when the national population growth is 0.5 percent).

Since the 1990s, the number of cities in China has soared, but such growth has been further confused by what the Chinese National Bureau of Statistics explains as "putting the rural counties formerly administered by the corresponding provinces under the administration of the relevant cities, changing the concept of the cities to an administrative concept."[32] In other words, entire provinces suddenly became cities. One example should suffice: Chongqing is regularly cited—here by Anthony Giddens—as "the world's biggest city" with thirty-one million residents,[33] but this hype is patently wrong as it fails to acknowledge that these numbers refer to the administrative area based on "city districts" and encompasses a vast area of farmland and small villages. Chongqing the province is the size of Austria, but the city of Chongqing actually comprises a population of *only* around 8 or 9 million. That's impressive enough, but, for some commentators, why let the facts get in the way of a hyperinflated one (Figure 1.3).

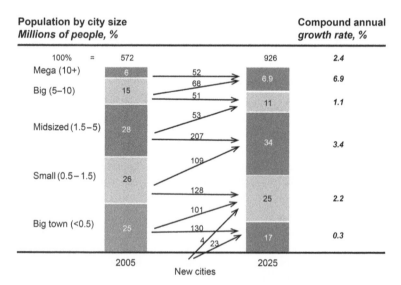

FIGURE 1.3 *Number of Chinese towns and cities to be created by 2025*
Source: McKinsey Global institute, in Woetzel, J. (2009). Preparing for China's Urban Billion, McKinsey & Company, p16

The exponential growth of China's cities since 1980 has been phenomenal: with, now, 658 cities nationwide. Many of these have been thrown up in haste, in the excitement of rapid development and wealth creation, but now China is pausing to think: to consider what it has done right, to experiment with other ways of urbanizing, and to put right many of the problems arising from the crazy splurge of construction over the last thirty years. Eco-cities are the new big idea.

China's first Eco-cities?

In many ways, Eco-cities, as they are commonly understood, could only happen in China: a vast country with large areas of notionally clear space (or the will to create large areas of open space), an erstwhile pliant population, an authoritarian regime, vast amounts of money, a positive vision of the future, local and national pride, a competitive spirit, a belief in change for the better, a blithe willingness to spend money and energy, and a casual disregard for the market where necessary. The fact that Chinese Eco-cities have long been proposed as *tabula rasa* solutions to the emerging problems blighting existing cities suggests that only countries with the room to experiment, in terms of space and finances, can play around with this model.

It was Abu Dhabi in the United Arab Emirates that got there first with what has been called the "world's first sustainable metropolitan development"—Eco-city of Masdar—that started on site in 2008. After a decade of branding, promotion, and construction, it is now reining in its zero-carbon claims. In fact, some of its more grandiose schemes have been put on hold. By late 2016, instead of the planned 50,000 permanent residents, the site housed just 300 students who seemed to wander around even more aimlessly than most students.

En route from London to Shanghai in mid-2016, I dropped in on Masdar to see how things were progressing. Journalistic reports had become a little confusing or contradictory, and many people possibly only know of this project from flattering or vitriolic articles, eyewitness advocates or critical bloggers, or the architect's seductive renderings. Designed by architects Foster + Partners, Masdar City is now cited as either the world's greenest city[34] or a non-Chinese ghost city.[35]

A short ride from the airport, one of the most shocking realizations is that the city, as so far constructed, is just 300 m × 80 m, that's the same size as Madison Square Park in New York (and one-sixth of the size of the Masdar's own solar panel farm). It took just ten minutes to walk around the entire perimeter of the existing city without fear of bumping into anyone (it was 46°C so everyone except me was indoors). I can report that Masdar is a perfectly pleasant business park with a very nice café scene, coffee shops, a few restaurants, and a library. But a city it is not.

Chris Wan, design manager for Masdar City, told me that within the next five years, with massive investment in emerging technologies and R&D, Masdar will construct a further 35 percent of the city (up from the 5 percent that I witnessed, completed in 2015[36]). However, the city brochures no longer talk extensively about the city's environmental performance (save for the Emirates' own "Pearl rating system," which is a mandatory energy-saving policy standard for all government buildings) and, instead, cite "ecosystems of research," which means something about engendering a "collaborative mindset and a spirit of entrepreneurship."[37]

Over the last decade, the hype around Masdar has been moderated downward, with more modest language. While Masdar's own Institute of Science and Technology suggests that everything is going according to plan,[38] there are evident problems. The euphemism "pedestrian-friendly" urban spaces, for example, excuses the reality that Masdar's hi-tech driverless car pods—a technological feature that had been central to its early press publicity—has been put on hold. You *have* to walk. The much-heralded natural cooling of the external architecture merely describes the warm breezes and shadows that alleviate the scorching heat, allowing people a paltry few degrees' respite as they scurry between air-conditioned buildings. There is seldom reference to sustainability or low-carbon issues, and it seems that even in empty, desert conditions, in the capital of the ruling elite and massively funded by oil wealth, Eco-cities are still not guaranteed to succeed.

———

New cities have the luxury of starting from scratch, usually avoiding planning constraints, but having to draw in the population from surrounding areas. Such ground-zero master plans don't need to fit into existing schema but have to plan for future capacity. In 1957, Lúcio Costa, the master planner of Brasilia, pointed out that "founding a city in the wilderness is a deliberate act of conquest…the city will not be a result of regional planning but the cause of it: its foundation will lead, later, to the planned development of the whole region."[39]

For China, at this stage in its development, building a new city is an act of architectural will, social engineering, political soft power, economic bravado, and a fundamental statement of modernization. In his book *Ghost Cities of China*, Wade Shepard described in great detail the process of building a new Chinese city, exploring the challenges, the successes, and the scare stories. In general, he concludes that they tend to succeed predominantly because China has the wherewithal to populate them and to structure their growth. Its Eco-cities have been planned since the 1990s but tentatively began construction only in the early 2000s. Quietly and steadily, China has been laying down twenty-year master plans for the construction of cleaner, greener urban areas with urban schema derived from a range of Western case studies. The early test beds are only now coming to fruition and, as such, the government has been hyping them up and beginning to carry forward some of the lessons into mainstream urbanism.

In the beginning, modernization in China tended to be shorthand for industrialization with scant regard for pollution and urban quality. But now, as affluence and expectations of a better life rise, fewer people are prepared to put up with it. The Party often ignores the populace, but clean air is almost a sine qua non of global engagement, a mark of statehood, civilized diplomacy, and international trade. As a result, new cities have to be better than the smoke-stacked, car-centric, smog-dominated existing urban centers. They have to be fitted with state-of-the-art infrastructure, be conveniently located, and offer aspirational cultural provision and impeccable facilities. They should be clean, amenable, and ready for a huge influx of residents.

A survey carried out by China's state news agency found that environmental protection is the number one concern of Chinese netizens. Although there are no details about the sample size or the academic validity of the test, it is an interesting snapshot of public opinion, with 86 percent stating that something must be done about ecological environmental standards and 74 percent stating that "environmental protection" was the most important issue.[40]

As Judith Shapiro argues in her paper "Mao's War Against Nature: Legacy and Lessons," all too often the parlous state of much of China's environment is seen to be the result of the rapid growth of the Chinese economy over the last twenty-five years or so. This is a convenient proposition for those countries for whom a slowdown of China's economy would be a good thing for their own competitiveness. For example, the closure of China's state subsidized steelworks—to halt its pollution—cannot come too soon to those who coincidentally bemoan the impact of China's cheap steel on the Western world. But Shapiro "seeks to challenge the received wisdom that China's environmental problems are attributable solely to post-Mao politics economic reforms and industrial growth."[41] Indeed, many of the seeds of its environmental problems were laid in the immediate precapitalist phase of China's development. This is worth remembering: that China is making great environmental leaps from a devastatingly low starting point.

According to the International Monetary Fund's World Economic Outlook Database, China's GDP (based on purchasing power parity as a share of the world's total) only really took off around 1992.[42] The subsequent 20 years of growth was, in many ways, the result of rapid industrial growth similar in scope to what, 150 years ago in England, Engels called "the juvenile state of capitalist exploitation." Consequently, this new phase of rapid growth compounded the prior damage done under Mao. New environmental hazards were produced but in a fraction of the time that most Western developed countries had endured. China's waterways became more and more polluted,[43] heavy metal adulteration of rice crops became a cause for concern in southern China,[44] and air quality in certain cities became a real health issue. This is undeniable but concentrating on environmental issues often blinds us to the concurrent social progress. For example, mortality rates for under 5-year olds in China have improved from 119.10 per 1,000 in 1969 (49 per 1,000 in 1980) down to 9.2 today, life expectancy has increased from 65 years in 1980 to 76 years today, and extreme poverty has dropped from 84 percent in 1980 to 10 percent today. Average calorific intake per capita has risen from just 125 calories in 1971 to 691 today.

But there are undeniable problems. Even though the data is contested, official Chinese sources show PM2.5 particulate levels to be around 300 µg/m^3 in 2013 in Beijing, which exceeds the EU emissions' daily average standards by a factor of six (and equivalent to the particulate levels in London in the 1960s). Other health indices are similarly stark, and there is a clear recognition throughout the Chinese leadership that China's rapid economic development over the previous three decades had exacerbated industrial accidents, affected mortality rates, and created a deficit in perceived quality of life.

What is more, inadequate regulatory standards have been slow to catch up, but in the last fifteen years or so, the state's environmental rhetoric has focused on urgent remedial measures to rectify the situation. With reference to the incontrovertible deterioration in air quality, the Chinese State Council issued an Action Plan for the Prevention and Control of Air Pollution whose aim was to reduce it by over 10 percent from 2012 to 2017.[45] It could have gone further and set even higher targets, but measures like this and many others are focusing toward the right direction and seem eminently sensible. In some ways, it is unremarkable that China would eventually begin to deal with its environmental problems.

China was one of the first countries in the developing world (as it classifies itself) to strategically introduce sustainable development on a national and regional policy level and has been using it as a way to promote a new direction for its urban development. The government announced in 2010 that 300 new cities would be built by 2025, of which approximately 20 would be Eco-cities. By late 2015, it announced that they already have at least 284 Eco-cities dealing, in some way or another, with a list of ecological problems. This is clearly spin and China has realized that the definitional vagueness of Eco-cities and performance criteria is an opportunity to milk the situation. But whether we believe the statistics or not, China's Eco-city program is a huge urban experiment that is improving air quality or life quality, or both, and needs unpicking and understanding.

Unsurprisingly, there are many Western activists and commentators offering advice. American consultancy Eco-city Builders (the organization initiated by Richard Register back in 1992 to promote the Eco-city message) is one of them. Register is the international consultant to the China Society for Urban Studies' Eco-Cities Planning and Construction Centre of China, a national nonprofit that seeks the "scientific development of our country."[46] Eco-city Builders points the finger at "the way we build (blamed for...)

promoting global warming, species extinction, loss of habitat and agricultural land, serious public health problems and even war."[47] With this litany of potential harms arising out of not building sustainably, it is hardly surprising that some Western environmental lobbyists are exasperated and insist that *something must be done*. With such high stakes for this self-assessed environmental agenda, many Western environmentalists have developed a sneaky regard for the nonnegotiable policy power of the Chinese state.

The London-based International Institute for Environment and Development writes that the "leadership of the central government in driving the green agenda is made possible partly by China's political system." This is factually true, of course, but there seems to be a tendency among Western environmentalists to revel in the unquestioned ability of the Chinese state legislature to "get things done." Indeed, many environmental advocates laud the strict penalties that China imposes on rogue officials or those engaged in polluting industries, somewhat oblivious to what Chinese justice involves. Indeed, China has introduced laws that may execute environmental offenders. When the OECD stated that "urban air pollution is set to become the top environmental cause of mortality worldwide by 2050,"[48] I guess that it didn't envisage that some of the deaths would be the result of complaints about urban air quality. Increasingly there is scant criticism of unelected technocracy, preferring instead to focus on the speedy results of Chinese planners compared to the interminable democratic process of planning in the West.

As American journalist Thomas L Friedman said a few years ago: "One party autocracy certainly has its drawbacks. But when it is led by a reasonably enlightened group of people, as China is today, it can also have great advantages(. It) can just impose the politically difficult but critically important policies needed to move a society forward in the 21st century."[49] Policy wonk Geoff Mulgan came to the same conclusion a few years earlier: "The one advantage of a one-party state, and a still substantially planned economy, is that when it moves, it will move fast."[50] The fact that Mussolini was reputed to make the trains run on time is another example of how the pure focus on efficiency can sometimes lead to acolytes being resigned—or oblivious—to the downsides. Indeed, when the environmentally credible future prime minister of Canada, Justin Trudeau, was asked which country he most admired, he answered:

"There's a level of admiration I actually have for China because their basic dictatorship is allowing them to actually turn their economy around on a dime."[51]

———

One of the most famous Western Eco-city advocates is Professor Eero Paloheimo, well known for planning a reasonably successful sustainable suburban town in Finland called Eko-Viikki. It is home to some 1,900 inhabitants and located just 8 km outside Helsinki, on 64,000 m² of vacant land. The early phases of the development were built between 1999 and 2003 as a solar panel demonstration project, with solar providing around 15–20 percent of all its heating loads. The front page of the Finnish government's assessment of the development, written in 2005, says that it is "a nice place, badly built."[52] A survey of residents revealed that most people live there because the housing is cheap—a not illegitimate reason—but only "10% said their reasons were environmentally based."[53]

Paloheimo, then a Green Party MP, had a long-held ambition to roll out a bigger and better Eco-town development somewhere in Europe but became disillusioned by the lack of buy-in by politicians and investors. Indeed, this is a common complaint with many environmentalists believing that even though they have the most important message to impart to the world, they feel that they are not taken seriously. All too often this expresses itself as a frustration at the pace of change and a cynicism about the potential for change, resulting in a desire to simply to do whatever it takes to get it done.

A Gallup poll in 2016 showed that environmental concerns took precedence over economic ones for the first time in America, between 2008 and 2014[54] (after which time they started to diverge again, when more people began to prioritize economic performance in the run-up to the presidential election). Similar disinterest—or the greater interest in wider pursuits—has affected many Western countries of late, and Western activists' environmental despondency has risen. Their desperation is summed up by environmental advocate John Vidal, who wrote in 2012: "We have never had so many environmental goals and objectives but (still) ecosystem decline is increasing, climate change is speeding, soil and ocean degradation continues, air and water pollution is growing." He asks whether this mismatch between what he sees as imminent threats and sluggish responses comes about because of "vain promises by cynical governments who only want to wave a piece of paper in front of gullible electorates? Or is there something else going wrong in the system of environmental governance?"[55] The implication is that a little more action by whatever means necessary is needed to counter what he perceives as public stupidity and government inaction. Environmental condescension, it seems, is a precursor to nudging people in what is deemed to be the "right direction."

Thirty years ago, the US political scientist Lester W. Milbrath highlighted the anti democratic nature of environmental activism, borne of frustration, saying that "environmentalists probably will continue to use direct action to influence policy as long as they believe that they are unable to affect change through normal political channels."[56] It is unsurprising then that there are some environmentalists with a sneaky regard for (what they see as) the benign authority of the Chinese state. Environmentalists after all have long argued for urgent action, and if the West won't listen, then the Chinese seem prepared to.

In a similar vein, over the first decade of the twenty-first century, many Western architects have emerged as willing developers of China and regularly talk about the country as an urban laboratory, excited by its fabled speed of development. They long to seize its opportunities: to give vent to their imaginations with few ethical questions asked. Sadly, many are blissfully detached from China's particular social, political, and cultural framework and treat it as a giant sandpit in which to play.

With this in mind, it was out of a curious mix of frustration and experimentation that Paloheimo found himself in China. Here, finally, he reveled in the opportunity to make his Eco-city happen with few nettlesome regulations or restrictions getting in the way. He says: "For 10 years I have tried to push this through in Europe (but) when I come here it takes one month to get the first one off the ground."[57] China is, he said, "a tourist attraction for designers."[58] Unsurprisingly, Paloheimo was thrilled to be offered a site in the beautiful Mentougou valley on the western edge of the Jiufeng National Forest Park scenic area outside Beijing.

So keen was he to build an Eco-city that he was prepared to construct a townscape on 28 km² of natural parkland in order to create a community of research institutes and a number of residential villages that would become an environmentally sensitive habitat for around 20,000–50,000 residents. In the process, the relocation of many hundreds of locals would be unavoidable, but their conditions would be improved.

His desire to promote his eco-vision became the subject of a 2013 documentary "Ecopolis" by filmmaker Anna-Karin Grönroos. This urban development in the pine forests of north China was recorded as an urgent, no-nonsense project "to save the world from ecological catastrophe."[59] "Mankind is causing this sickness. Mankind is the bacteria," he says at one point, echoing the rather condescending Malthusian claim that humanity is a problem and in need of the intervention of enlightened Eco-city saviors. It was environmental theorist James Lovelock who suggested that humanity is merely "a plague of people" and so where better to save the world than in the world's most populous nation.[60]

A Finnish-Swedish architectural firm (Tengbom) Eriksson—the original architects working with Paloheimo—have also provided their services to design a 160 km^2 Eco-city in Cheng Gong in Kunming. One Chinese article suggests that this Kunming project, if it reaches maturity, will be predominantly aimed "not (at) ordinary local citizens but at foreigners belonging to high society and the new rich."[61] This is not necessarily a criticism, because like many of the Eco-cities listed in this book, many of the local citizens and their regional politicians are supportive of Eco-city development precisely because it contains the word "development." "Gentrification" is not a dirty word in China. Yet.

The desire for economic development—or as some people see it, the less-principled reasons of personal financial gain—is a constant refrain across China. Almost everyone wants money to improve their living standards and quality of life. Ironically, Eco-cities have been known to fail in China because the eco-advocates are selling the opposite model: zero growth. As an intellectual movement, the environmental agenda developed in the West has a clear objective to saving the planet from man's alleged avarice through the restriction of excess and unsustainable behavior. The Western-influenced Eco-city is the physical representation of this culture of limits and proponents regularly advocate restraint. However, Eco-city advocates living in China—a developing country—haven't fully bought into this program of personal sacrifice, and, in several instances across the country, when Chinese developers realize that sustainable urban developments are often openly hostile to much-needed meaningful development, the partnerships often collapse.

In this instance, Paloheimo had to retreat defeated. His excitement at becoming midwife to a new city had blinded him to the red tape, local bureaucracy, and cultural context. Moreover, he seemed unable to recognize, philosophically, that his Eco-city was being supported in its initial phases precisely because it was meant to bring wealth and dynamism to investors, builders, party officials, and local villagers alike. In an interview, he told me that "a pilot project…cannot be realized profitably if the goals are purely financial….Central Government should support the first pilot project (…or) an idealistic billionaire or a very rich community. Roughly 5 billion dollars. That would be a real Eco-city with approximately 15,000 inhabitants."[62] In reality, the support for Eco-cities in China (or for any changes in land use) is often starkly self-serving—and understandably so. In an underdeveloped economy like China, people want to know what they are going to get out of it, especially if the consequence of building an Eco-city is that many of them will be forcibly evicted.

Therefore, with all the problems and contradictions that arise out of Eco-city developments, with all the domestic hassle and international cynicism, with all potential costs and social tensions, China has begun to change tack.

While the construction of entire new cities still continues in places like Tianjin, the Chinese government's 2015 *Green Book* provides Eco-Cities with a new definition and a new prefix. Eco-cities, it says, are "ecological cities with Chinese characteristics." They are not necessarily brand new cities, but new city brands.

Chinese Eco-cities are being ranked alongside indices that stem from President Xi Jinping's speech to China's National People's Congress in February 2015, known colloquially as "The Four Comprehensives." It outlined plans to "comprehensively build a moderately prosperous society; comprehensively deepen reform; comprehensively govern the nation according to law; and comprehensively strictly govern the Communist Party." The "comprehensive" prefix is deemed to imply a systematic approach to specific actions,[63] although it does allow a certain amount of flexibility in practice. The plans to build comprehensive Eco-Cities, for example, allow China to delve into a wide range of urban environmental objectives (resulting in a comprehensive spreadsheet of ecological concerns) while having the option to prioritize one and explore it in a deeper way. Somewhat antithetically, "comprehensive" doesn't mean that a city has to comply with all the strictures. Indeed, rather than being a thorough definition, the prefix has allowed regional party authorities to ensure that "ecological cities with Chinese characteristics" are considerably open to interpretation. The physical and moral restrictions of the Western model are not so appropriate here.

For example, an announcement in the *Shanghai Daily* newspaper in 2016 proudly boasted that Hangzhou in Zhejiang Province had become a national Eco-city. Having applied for this badge of honor way back in 2002, it finally achieved certification fifteen years later on the basis that its main sources of drinking water were shown to be "adequate," and that it registered 123 days with good air quality with the average being twice the World Health Organization's acceptable limits.[64] On this basis, surely there aren't many non-Eco-cities in China.

Notes

1　Anon, China's "Ecological Silicon Valley," *The Huffington Post*, June 19, 2011. http://new.www.huffingtonpost.com/2011/04/19 /chinas-ecological-silicon-valley_n_851112.html (accessed June 15, 2016).

2　Anon, "Eriksson Architects: Mentougou Eco Valley," *KA magazine*, May 6, 2015. http://kaonlinemagazine.com/eriksson-architects -mentougou-eco-valley/.

3　Bianca Bartz, B., "Ecological Silicon Valley in China's Miaofeng Mountains," *TrendHunter*, April 15, 2011. http://www.trendhunter .com/trends/ecological-silicon-valley (accessed June 12, 2016).

4　Fox, Jesse, "Ecocities of Tomorrow: An Interview with Richard Register," *TreeHugger*, February 14, 2008. http://www.treehugger.com /sustainable-product-design/ecocities-of-tomorrow-an-interview-with -richard-register.html (accessed March 20, 2016).

5　Register, Richard, *Ecocities: Rebuilding Cities in Balance with Nature*. Canada: New Society Publishers, 2006, pp. xiii and 5.

6　Register, Richard, *Ecocity Berkeley: Building Cities for a Healthy Future*. Berkeley, CA: North Atlantic Books, 1987.

7   Roseland, Mark, "Dimensions of the Eco-city," *Cities* 1997, 14(4), pp. 197–202.

8   van Dijk, Meine Pieter, "Measuring Eco Cities, Comparing European and Asian Experiences: Rotterdam versus Beijing," *Asia-Europe Journal*, January 2015.

9   Sze , J. *Fantasy Islands: Chinese Dreams and Ecological Fears in an Age of Climate Crisis*, University of California Press, January 5, 2015, p. 38.

10 Lian, Koh Kheng, Gunawansa, Asanga and Bhullar, Lovleen, Social Space, Lien Centre for Social Innovation, Issue 3. 2010,pp.84–92.

11 Holden, Meg, Li, Charling and Molina, Charling, "The Emergence and Spread of Ecourban Neighbourhoods around the World," *Sustainability* 2015, 7, 11418–11437.

12 Joss, Simon, Tomozeiu, Daniel and Cowley, Robert, "Eco-Cities—A Global Survey 2011," *University of Westminster International Eco-Cities Initiative,* University of Westminster, 2011.

13 Chinese Science Center of International Eurasian Academy of Sciences, Report on Chinese Cities 2014/2015, China City Press (Beijing), 2014, p. 9.

14 Hollis, L. *Cities Are Good for You: The Genius of the Metropolis.* Bloomsbury Press: London. 2013, p. 2.

15 OECD, OECD Regional Typology, Directorate for Public Governance and Territorial Development, June 2011.

16 Colton, Charles Caleb, *Lacon: or Many Things in Few Words; Addressed to Those Who Think*, Vol. I, 1820, # 334.

17 Marx, K. and Engels, F., "Manifesto of the Communist Party," in *Marx/Engels Selected Works*, Vol. One. Moscow: Progress Publishers, 1969. pp. 98–137.

18 Mumford, Lewis, "What Is a City?" *Architectural Record*, 1937.

19 Department of Economic and Social Affairs of the United Nations Secretariat, "World Economic and Social Survey 2013: Sustainable Development Challenges," *Department of Economic and Social Affairs*, 2013, E/2013/50/Rev. 1, ST/ESA/344.

20 Schnore, L.F., "Urbanization and Economic Development: The Demographic Contribution," *American Journal of Economics and Sociology*, January 1964, 23(1), pp. 37–48.

21 Ingram, D.D. and Franco, S.J. "NCHS Urban–Rural Classification Scheme for Counties. National Center for Health Statistics," *Vital and Health Statistics* 2013, 2(166): 2014.

22 Burgen, S. and Phillips, T., "Chinese Company Boss Treats 2,500 Employees to Holiday in Spain," *The Guardian*, May 6, 2016.

23 Demick, Barbara and Sarno, David. "Firm Shaken by Suicides," *LA Times*, May 26, 2010.

24 Dijkstra, Lewis and Poelman, Hugo Cities in Europe The New OECD-EC Definition, Regional Focus, RF01. 2012. p.5.

25 Quoted in Chan, K.W. and Xu, X., "Urban Population Growth and Urbanization in China since 1949: Reconstructing a Baseline," *The China Quarterly* 104 (December 1985), School of Oriental and African Studies, pp. 583–613.

26 Goldstein, S., "Urbanization in China: New Insights from the 1983 Census," *Papers of the East-West Population Institute,* July 1985, 93, p. 6.

27 Ren, X., *Urban China.* UK: Polity Press, 2013. p. 23.

28 Dunford, M., and Lui, W., *The Geographical Transformation of China.* Routledge, 2011. p. 148.

29 Li, B., and Piachaud, D., "Urbanization and Social Policy in China," *Asia-Pacific Development Journal*, June 2006, 13(1).

30 Wei, Z., "The Changing Face of Rural Enterprises," *China Perspectives* November–December 2003, 50. Online since April 19, 2007. http://chinaperspectives.revues.org/773 (accessed June 26, 2016).

31 Zhu, Yu , Qi, Xinhua, Shao, Huaiyou, He, Kaijing, *The Evolution of China's In Situ Urbanization and Its Planning and Environmental Implications: Case Studies from Quanzhou Municipality in China.* China: Centre for Population and Development Research, Fujian Normal University, 2007.

32 The National Bureau of Statistics of China, "Development of Urban Statistics & Data Exploitation in China," International Association of Official Statistics (IAOS)/SCORUS (Standing Committee on Regional and Urban Statistics), Shanghai, October 2008.

33 Giddens, A., *Europe in the Global Age.* Polity Press, 2013. p. 85.

34 Anon, Masdar, The World's Greenest City: The Project, Astrea Mideast, June 3, 2015 http://www.astreamideast.ae/masdar-the -worlds-greenest-city-the-project/.

35 DiStasio, C., "Masdar's Failed Sustainable City May Be Doomed to Become a Green Ghost Town," *Inhabitat*, http://inhabitat.com /masdars-failed-sustainable-city-may-be-doomed-to-become-a-green -ghost-town/ (accessed May 29, 2016).

36 Al Wasmi, N., "Masdar City Ready to Start the Next Phase," *The National*, April 3, 2016 (accessed May 29, 2016).

37 Innovative Sustainable Development: Investment and Leasing Opportunities at Masdar City, Masdar/Mubadal.

38 Mezher, T., Dawelbait, G., Tsai, I., and Al-Hosany, N., "Building Eco-Cities of the Future: The Example of Masdar City," *International Journal of Thermal & Environmental Engineering* 2016, 12(1), pp. 1–8.

39 Costa, L., "Report of the Pilot Plan for Brasilia," in Brasilia, Rio de Janeiro: Ministério das Relações Exteriores, Divisão Cultural, *1957* quoted in *Small, I.V.*, Hélio Oiticica: Folding the Frame, University of Chicago Press, 2016.

40 Shaohui, Tian (ed.), "Expectations for the 13th Five-Year Plan (2016–20)," Xinhuanet, November 28, 2015. http://news.xinhuanet.com/english/china/2015-10/28/c_134758508.htm (accessed June 13, 2016).

41 Shapiro, Judith. *Mao's War Against Nature: Politics and the Environment in Revolutionary China*. Cambridge University Press, Mar 5, 2001, p.xii.

42 Yang, L. *China's Growth Miracle: Past, Present, and Future*. Beijing: Chinese Academy for Social Sciences, 2013. p. 2, table 2.

43 Economy, Elizabeth C., *The River Runs Black: The Environmental Challenge to China's Future*, Cornell University Press, 2005.

44 Li, B., Shi, J.B., Wang, X., Meng, M., Huang, L., Qi, X.L., He, B., Ye, Z.H. "Variations and Constancy of Mercury and Methylmercury Accumulation in Rice Grown at Contaminated Paddy Field Sites in Three Provinces of China," *Environmental Pollution* October 2013, 181, pp. 91–97.

45 Andrews-Speed, Philip, China's Energy Policymaking Processes and Their Consequences, The National Bureau of Asian Research Energy Security Report. National Bureau of Asian Research, 2014.

46 China Urban Studies Introduction, China Society for Urban Studies. http://www.chinasus.org/chinasus/intro/leaders/ (accessed June 29, 2016).

47 "The Problem," Eco-city Builders, http://www.ecocitybuilders.org/why-ecocities/the-problem-2/ (accessed March 25, 2016).

48 New release, Environment: Act now or face costly consequences, warns OECD, Organization for Economic Co-operation and Development, March 15, 2012. http://www.oecd.org/newsroom/environmentactnoworfacecostlyconsequenceswarnsoecd.htm (accessed June 16, 2016).

49 Friedman, Thomas L., "Our One Party Democracy," *The New York Times*, September 8, 2009.

50 Mulgan, G., "China's Great Green Leap Forward?" *Times Online*, November 27, 2007.

51 Atkin, D., "Trudeau Admires China's 'Basic Dictatorship'," *Toronto Sun*, November 8, 2013. http://www.torontosun.com/2013/11/08/trudeau-admires-chinas-basic-dictatorship (accessed May 10, 2016).

52 Hakaste, H. et al., "Eco-Viikki: Aims, Implementation and Results," *City of Helsinki, Ministry of the Environment*, 2005.

53 Daniëls, A. "Life and Living in Low Energy Houses: Study of Technical Solutions in Low Energy Houses, Satisfaction, Lifestyle and Changes for the Residents," *National Consumer Research Centre*, Working Papers 2007, 102, p. 18.

54 Gallup, The Environment, http://www.gallup.com/poll/1615/environment.aspx (accessed June 15, 2016).

55 Vidal, J., "Many Treaties to Save the Earth, but Where's the Will to Implement Them?" *The Guardian*, June 7, 2012.

56 Milbrath, L.W. and Fisher, B.V., *Environmentalists: Vanguard for a New Society*. SUNY Press (New York), 1984. p. 90.

57 Paloheimo, E. quoted in Grönroos, A-K., "Ecopolis China," *Cargo Film & Releasing*, 2013.

58 Xiang, Li and Zheng, Xu, "Eco-cities Are the Key to Conservation: Experts," *China Daily*, September 24, 2011.

59 Paloheimo, E., Ecological Systems of Urban Planning: Eero Paloheimo's lecture in Binhai Forum, China, September 22, 2012. http://www.eeropaloheimo.fi/en/speeches-and-writings/ecological-systems-of-urban-planning/ (accessed June 15, 2016).

60 Lovelock, J., *The Revenge of Gaia: Why The Earth Is Fighting Back—And How We Can Still Save Humanity*. Penguin (London), 2007.

61 Chien Shiuh-Shen, "Chinese Eco-cities: A Perspective of Land-Speculation-Oriented Local Entrepreneurialism," *China Information* 2013, 27(2), 173–196.

62 Paloheimo, E. in private correspondence with the author. e-mail. June 24, 2016.

63 Kuhn, R.L., "Xi Jinping's 'Four Comprehensives' Show the Depth of His Leadership," *South China Morning Post*, July 30, 2015.

64 News, "Eco-City Status," *Shanghai Daily*, August 8, 2016.

CHAPTER TWO

Man Must Overcome Nature

FIGURE 2.1 *The loess mountains of Lanzhou*
Photo: Author

Lanzhou is the sprawling industrial capital of Gansu Province, located in the center of China. It's a rapidly expanding, increasingly prosperous city in a relatively poor province that has historically made its wealth on heavy industries such as oil refining, petrochemicals, textiles, and machine plant. It is a region of China whose topography has been effectively formed by the sedimentary silt deposits (loess) washed down by the Yellow River over many millennia: silt from which the river derives its name.

This is a frontier city facing onto the barren Qilian mountains to the west and the Gobi Desert further north and forming an unofficial boundary between the more developed eastern half of China and the underdeveloped regions to the west. It is now a major staging post on the new Silk Road and a significant transportation hub.

In 1999, *Time* magazine named Lanzhou as the most polluted city in the world.[1] In 2009, Gansu Province had the highest incidence of lung cancer in China. When I first visited in 2013, *The Economist* magazine was using World Health Organization data to describe Lanzhou as the second most polluted city in the world,[2] evident when I joined thousands of revelers taking the perilous cable car ride across the water to the White Pagoda Hill to enjoy the hazy views back, across the city. Remarkably, by 2016, Lanzhou was listed in the top 100 environmentally friendly cities in China (in sixty-seventh position). Such a miraculous transformation (or some might say "re-branding") is clearly laudable but an ecological turnaround of this magnitude in such a short space of time suggests that the data and criteria should, at the very least, be treated with caution. But if there is a change—from polluted nightmare to Lanzhou Eco-city status—what caused the improvement?

The recently created Lanzhou New Area (LNA), 55 km north of the old Lanzhou city, didn't exist in 2012, but that year it was willed into existence as a state-level new area. That simple shift in designation propelled LNA into the ranks of the other major global urban players in China such as Shanghai's Pudong, Tianjin's Binhai, and Chongqing's Liangjiang. With preferential treatment and huge amounts of money, it has taken just three years for LNA to emerge as an embryonic new city (although, admittedly, preparatory work has been ongoing since 2006).

With an investment plan of RMB32 billion and technical and financial support from South Korea, it is now a vast development zone that covers around 800 km^2 (roughly the size of Singapore) and already includes much of the physical infrastructure for huge telecommunications and high-tech industries as well as science incubators, data centers (and even a Great Wall media center and Dream World Tourism Park, currently under construction). Developer China Pacific Construction Group describes the scheme as a blend of the "best of Las Vegas and Venice."[3] LNA now boasts thousands of identical Soviet-style high-rise housing units in pastel shades anticipating the arrival of 100,000 workers to fill its rapidly expanding industrial capacity. From the sky it currently still looks like a huge building site patchwork, but on the ground it already has pockets of real urban life.

The LNA satellite city has already begun to influence the possibility for the old city of Lanzhou to reduce its reliance on heavy industries and provide a new direction for this region. In its ambitious development plan, LNA is developing what it calls a "green corridor" which will undoubtedly function as an additional boost to Lanzhou's overall regional claim to Eco-city status (as is its proposal for public parks and a decent use of the natural environment), but primarily LNA is claiming Eco-city status because of its improvements to air quality in the region. It has done this, in part, by reducing the old city's heavy industrial pollution and shifting lots of its manufacturing base to cleantech.

Notwithstanding these shifts brought about by the development of LNA as a gigantic free trade zone of development, the original city of old Lanzhou has also transformed itself in the last few years with a variety of mechanisms employed to improve the environment, including rather draconian clampdowns on Lanzhou's manufacturing output, on the use of coal, and on diesel-powered vehicles. Local officials describe an "iron fist" environmental strategy and an air pollution plan that resembles an authoritarian version of Britain's Clean Air Act from the 1950s. Professor Zhang Yuanhang of the Clean Air Alliance of China states that "the level of authority and the binding effect of this plan are unprecedented"[4] with severe penalties for evasion or noncompliance. As a result, the old city has replaced thousands of coal-fired heating boilers and thermal power plants with natural gas–fired heating systems; it is introducing a subsidized green car plan, dust suppression measures, and controls on unregulated outdoor fires.[5]

However, in addition to the environmental improvements in LNA, the main environmental improvements of the old city of Lanzhou are presumed to come from the proximity of Lanzhou New City (LNC), which is another separate development zone eight miles to the northeast of the old city. At the time of my last visit in late 2016, the groundworks were still under way, but things were moving at a rapid pace. Both LNC and LNA have been justified on the basis of an ecological strategy that is controversial to Western environmentalists' ears and represents what might be called "environmentalism with Chinese characteristics." Surrounded by vast mountain ranges, the authorities are carrying out a brilliantly drastic solution to provide room to build. They are removing the mountains.

In Gansu, Lanzhou, the loess is up to 300 m deep in parts,[6] and although mineral rich and extremely fertile, the ecological environment is rather fragile. But over the last few years more than 700 mountains have had their tops lopped off and the excavated loess material dumped to fill the valleys and create a plateau on which to build. The LNA extends up 800 km² and the LNC is creating a further 5 km² of new development potential. Both have been artificially created as elevated, flat plains to provide a base for construction: the former a new city in its own terms linking directly to the airport, the latter an extension of the old town. These are master plans that some say could happen only in China. Of course, similarly bold land-forming projects have been carried out before, such as Dubai's Palm Jumeirah, the coal mining mountaintop removal techniques of West Virginia, and the Netherlands where 17 percent of the land mass has been reclaimed from the sea, but there is something perversely casual about this Chinese project that is jaw-droppingly impressive.

Land-forming—turning what might be called unusable space into utilizable productive land—has been carried out in China for centuries (the tea plantation terraces of Hangzhou and the rice paddies of Yuanyang County in Yunnan, for example). Since the twelfth Five-Year Plan vowed to safeguard China's marine ecology, more contemporary versions have emerged. Zhejiang Zhoushan Eco-Island spent US$14.5 million reclaiming 4 km² of coastal wetlands from the East China Sea, for example.[7] But Lanzhou New Area's version is clearly a mega-scale master plan that has caused many eco-commentators to recoil in not-in-my-name horror.

So, just how has this alteration—some might say "destruction"—of huge swathes of natural mountain ranges helped Lanzhou convert itself from Silk Road Special Economic Zone status into the "Silk Road West International Business Tourism Culture Comprehensive Eco Industrial Zone"? What has landforming got to do with its Eco-city status?

Lanzhou old town is now eligible for the prized "Eco" label because the mountaintop removal project has consistently been justified as part of a grand plan to deal with the air quality issue. It is a city blighted by its location in a valley basin prone to the settlement of particulate-laden, stale industrial air as well as the air-borne sands from the Gobi. Thus, the removal of the mountaintops was originally proposed as a way of increasing the natural ventilation to the old city. In other words, by removing the pesky mountains—an encircling barrier to the free flow of air—invigorating natural ventilation breezes will have unimpeded access to blow away the irritating pollutants and create a cooler, fresher, cleaner city. A recent air quality indicator study notes that sulfur emissions in the old city have reduced by 49 percent between 2010 and 2015[8] and $PM_{10}/PM_{2.5}$ levels fell by around a third between 2014 and 2015. Before we get too carried away, there are only a small number of monitoring stations, statistical fluctuations are significant,[9] and a 2016 academic report concludes that Lanzhou is still "one of the most heavily polluted cities in China."[10] But I still find it exciting.

Curing cities of pollution through improving urban-scale ventilation has been discussed for years but not many countries have the luxury of trying it out. Beijing, for example, is proposing a series of "ventilation corridors"—areas of restricted development stretching tens of miles linking parks, lakes, and even highways— that will create open ventilation channels to blow away the city's irritating smogs. Whether Lanzhou's improvement can be attributed to the demolition of the mountain ranges of Gansu is open for discussion (although local officials maintain that it is patently true). But more importantly, the transformation of nature in order to create a better, more effective location for human growth, economic development, and social expansion is welcomed with a nonchalance that is absent from the Western discourse. One Lanzhou local told me simply: "These new areas ease environmental pressure and provide many more job opportunities."

It needs to be said that large numbers of local agricultural communities were also relocated in order to provide the land to facilitate the new area's development (I will discuss these kinds of clearances in Chapter 4), but many of them have been incorporated into the new city vision. Admittedly, they have been incorporated whether they like it or not. But speaking of relocation, Tom Miller, author of *The Urban Billion,* says: "There are lots of problems associated with this process but it is a very positive thing that millions of people who are living in west China, which until very recently was frankly dirt poor, are going to be living in much more civilised accommodation."[11] Miller's acknowledgment of human-centered progress is a welcome fillip to the commonplace Western condemnations of such urbanizing bravura.

In Julie Sze's book *Fantasy Islands*, she makes the point that Eco-cities, the very places that are intended to provide better living conditions for urban residents, very often simply prioritize nature over the human experience. She quotes a planner from the British engineering company Ove Arup who was actively engaged in the development of Shanghai's Dongtan Eco-city, claiming that "it is always 'about the birds'."[12] The alienation of people from such urban experimentation is characterized by architectural renderings and artists' impressions that are frequently produced to promote Eco-city developments that show empty green fields occasionally interrupted by a flock of migrating birds. Sze goes on to explain that when—rarely—humans feature in China's Eco-city artwork, they are Westerners enjoying the environmental good life with not a Chinese person in sight. In fact, humans of any nationality are seldom mentioned in the Eco-city discourse simply because to a large extent the Western concern over development tends to portray the sanctity of the natural environment above all else. The result is that some Eco-cities feel overpowering or alienating which is possibly the ultimate logic of environmentalism, a discourse that often privileges the natural world to the detriment of the human. As environmental activist James Lovelock once put it, when it comes to the weighing up priorities, "humanity comes second."[13]

Conversely, the Chinese government's evolving urbanization program attempts to concentrate (rhetorically if not really in practice) on putting "people foremost," placing greater importance on "humanism and social justice"[14] than on exploitative social and economic development. Often this means that growth has been prioritized with scant regard for the environment but even so the Chinese conception of environmental development could thus be considered to be a little more human-centered than the Western model to some degree. The contemporary Western concept of Eco-cities puts the environment first, whereas the Chinese model sees "people's natural health (as) the primal target of green development."[15] I concede that there are other examples that might be cited to challenge the Chinese government's own selective quotes, but the examples cited here are chosen as significant indicators of the real active trends in China compared to the West. The divergent uses of environmental concepts on either side of the world, and the contradictory tensions between the West's and the East's understanding of man's relationship to nature, have been clear for some time.

Contemporary Western fears that human dominion over nature is somehow harmful tends to infer that there is an autonomy in nature[16] and to despoil it is tantamount to an abuse of its "rights." The UK academic Penny Lewis writes: "Humanity's well-being is no longer understood to be provided by material progress and personal freedom, but on the idea of accommodation to natural constraints." It is a postcolonial narrative applied at the city level, whereby those who dare to treat nature as a utility—so common in China—are sneered at. In many ways, the West is using its newfound eco-consciousness as a moral stick with which to beat those who are acting—in its view—unsustainably and irresponsibly. Lewis makes the point that the new philosophical ideal known as Ecological Urbanism is a pragmatic framework dreamed up in Ivy League institutions in the West that "represents one of the first schools of thought to place environmental concerns at the core of its ideas,"[17] and she worries that it explicitly diminishes the importance and the audacity of humanity in the creative process. Indeed, humans are often seen as the problem.

Writing in the *Architectural Review*, Westminster University's professor of architecture Susannah Hagan describes her desire for the next generation of creativity to reflect "a more balanced relationship between obliterator and obliterated," a particularly ungenerous way of describing humanity maybe. Conversely, the Chinese Green Book lays out the government's plan for "adhering to the scientific outlook of people-oriented development, takes eco-city construction as a project for the most essential concerns— improving people's living standards, catering to people's demands and administering people-centered governance." It seems that while China retains a caricatured belief in "harmony" with nature, it is the West that truly believes it with Hagan, for example advocating for "adaptation rather than domination, 'living with' rather than 'living over'" nature.[18] In many ways, the contemporary Western discourse portrays environmental destruction as an inevitable consequence of hubristic human *over*development, whereas China tends to view environmental harm as an inevitable result of societal *under*development. China still wishes to transform nature; the West seeks an accommodation with it.

Indeed, the modern Western debate about the environment has tended to convey a sharp Malthusian divide between nature and the excesses of humanity, seeing too many people (or too much consumption and emissions by those excessive numbers of people) as a significant part of the problem. The first issue of the *Ecologist* magazine in 1970, for example, stated that man is "a parasite...a disease (that) is still spreading exponentially."[19] A generation later, James Lovelock complained that the world was suffering from a "plague of people,"[20] while by 2014 the environmental journalist George Monbiot had called humanity nothing less than "death, the destroyer of worlds."[21] Unsurprisingly, modern China—the most populous nation on earth—has tended to shy away from such an explicitly antihuman environmental angle and, unlike many Western Malthusians, is even relaxing its draconian one-child policy.

The one-child policy is one of those "well-known facts" about China: a coercive sterilization, abortion, and publicity campaign enacted in 1979 by Premier Deng Xiaoping (from a policy idea proposed in the early 1970s) to ensure that the population was stabilized, with heavy financial penalties for those flouting the rules. The one-child policy was an authoritarian, and sometimes barbaric, mechanism to increase the country's per capita economic growth and was undoubtedly a Malthusian attempt to link population to resource development.[22] But more importantly—for this chapter at least—the idea was, in fact, a Western environmental one. "The scientific rationale (for China's one-child policy)," says Harvard professor, Martin Whyte, "resulted from demographic projections produced by a small group of scientists headed by Song Jian, who were influenced by the Club of Rome's Limits to Growth and other Western doomsday writings in the 1970s."[23]

———

In an online lecture to Zhejiang University, Hangzhou in China, Peter K. Bol, Professor of East Asian languages and civilizations, compared two historical characters from the West and the East, drawing an analogy between the biblical representation of Noah and the parable of Yu, the founder of the Xia dynasty (circa 2100–1600 BC). Both mythic figures faced environmental catastrophe in their time, but each is reputed to have dealt with it very differently. Professor Bol's conceit is to examine the two figures as embodiments of the West and the East's relationship with nature.

The story of Noah's Ark is a staple Western Judeo-Christian narrative which celebrates Noah as a vessel for God's will during the great flood and thus a passive participant in the face of nature (God's wrath). Admittedly, Noah builds a boat to survive the rains, but essentially he sits it out. He is a victim of higher forces and can only batten down the hatches (comically portrayed in Julian Barnes' *A History of the World in 10 ½ Chapters*), emerging forty days later, safe and grateful for the mercy of fate. He has survived, as a humble servant of God's fear and dread. In many ways, this attitude is similar to the way that Judith Rodin, president of the Rockefeller Foundation and author of *The Resilience Dividend*, suggests that we accept hardship and simply pride ourselves on our ability to prepare for, withstand, and bounce back from a crisis.[24]

Conversely, in Chinese mythology (although a recent academic paper seems to provide evidence that this story is true[25]) Yu, when confronted by potential devastation, builds flood defenses, reroutes rivers, dredges channels, constructs canals, and tames those forces that threaten his community. Not only are the floods averted but the raging waters are routed to irrigate the fields, leading to agricultural plenty, so the story goes. It is a cheap shot, but here we have a hapless Western servant of fate contrasted to the active Chinese subject creating his own destiny. In the West, shit happens; in China, man overcomes nature. It is no coincidence that Yu is otherwise known in Chinese folklore as Yu the Great.

Professor Bol sums it up: "Man conquers nature, can overcome the greatest, greatest challenges. He can move mountains. He can move rivers. He can save humanity…This story of Yu is the story that goes right down to the Three Gorges Dam, which says, we can channel the rivers. We can move nature around to benefit humankind."[26] Ironically, through this positive humanistic reading, Bol is engaged in some mythmaking of his own, possibly constructing a set of dogmatic cultural stereotypes reflecting the contemporary times in which he is writing. The Bible does call for man to have dominion over nature, after all. Moreover, if he were to choose examples from the era of great British Victorian engineering, for instance, the British were not at all deferential or passive toward nature. Similarly, China could equally be characterized as holding contradictory views: a Confucian desire to transform nature versus Daoist respect for and protection of it. That said, caricatures often capture something essential, and Bol's humanistic differentiation does spotlight the reality of the conflicting or contradictory status of humanity versus nature, East versus West, today.

In the contemporary debate, the role of nature, the ability and the desirability of humanity to transform it, or the belief in environmental sustainability mean different things in China compared to the West. Even though the concept of sustainability emerged in China in the late 1980s, not too long after it was established in the West, one researcher pointed out that "the term appears to have been largely developed around agro-ecosystems" in China.[27] In other words, the association of sustainability with saving the planet that we find in the West's agenda in the 1980s was absent in the evolution of the word in China, which exemplified China's delayed integration into a global environmental discourse.

As the concept has become normalized on both sides of the world, it tends to convey different things to different people. One example should suffice. Recent research indicates that whereas Western students of architecture think of timber as the most sustainable material, their Chinese opposite numbers think that it is the least sustainable. (Given Professor Bol's earlier example, is it a coincidence that the world's largest timber-frame building is Kentucky's biblical theme park housed inside a gigantic Noah's ark?)

What has created this different approach to timber? What makes wood sustainable in the West and unsustainable in China, whereby the Chinese prefer to safeguard trees rather than seeing them as a resource to be chopped down?

While the United States and Europe have hugely increased the amount of forest cover as part of its managed timber reserves,[28] the historical damage to China's forests still troubles the national psyche. At the foundation of the People's Republic of China in 1949, tree cover had decreased to an historic low—less than 10 percent of the land area, and the following thirty years of Mao's reign didn't significantly arrest that decline.[29] China is now planting huge numbers of trees (increasing the forest cover from 17 to 22 percent of the country's land area between 2000 and 2015), but this intensifies the realization that trees are to be protected rather than felled and used for industrial purposes. In 2016, the Chinese president rolled his sleeves up and inveigled government ministers to plant saplings, reinforcing the message that trees are an essential tool of environmental protection. In typical Chinese fashion, such a patriotic rallying call has been taken up by peasants and schoolchildren alike and helps form the national character.

The ambitious plan to plant forty billion trees between 1981 and 2010[30] in order to absorb carbon emissions as well as to halt the encroachment of the Gobi Desert has led to a pride in safeguarding timber resources. Clearly timber is not considered to be a sustainable construction material in China, although Western sustainability advocates constantly reprimand them for refusing to understand that it is. (As an aside, China still needs to use timber and so imports New Zealand and Russian wood for its domestic use, thus preserving the sense that China no longer fritters away its own reserves.)

The academic survey that measured UK and Chinese attitudes to sustainable materials also revealed that whereas UK students think that concrete is the least sustainable material, Chinese students cite it as the most sustainable.[31] This counterintuitive inversion of what each perceive as a commonsense viewpoint, is proof, if proof be needed, that we are not talking the same language.

When it comes to city building, China clearly has something of a pragmatic love affair with concrete as a construction material. In his book *Making the Modern World*, Vaclav Smil reveals the startling statistic that China has used more concrete in three years, between 2011 and 2013, than America had used over the entire twentieth century.[32] To feed China's construction boom, the robustness and longevity of concrete is something to trump all other considerations, whereas the West tends to fulminate against the carbon emissions released in concrete's manufacture. On a recent visit to Tianjin Eco-city in 2014, it had almost completed 30,000 dwellings, all in concrete (walls, floors, and roofs). Some were made with prefabricated units delivered on diesel lorries from Beijing, 150 km away. The designs were unappealing, unoriginal but most problematic to Western eyes, they were unsustainable.

It reminded me of the time I attended UN Habitat II conference on Human Settlements in Istanbul in 1996 dedicated to the new "paradigm shift" toward environmental design. Delegates praised the small models of vernacular African villages; they smiled at New Urbanist communities in America; but they sniggered at the Chinese model of rigid, concrete high-rise towers. "We made these mistakes in the West already, and China has learned nothing," one exasperated British delegate told me at the time. It was very clear what message was being developed. While the noble Westerners were advocating small-scale, low-carbon, urban villages, the dumb Chinese were proposing high-density, business-as-usual cities. The

FIGURE 2.2 *Tangshan poster: "Man Must Conquer Nature"*
Source: Yang Peiming/Shanghai Propaganda Art Museum

underlying ridicule is still that China is on the wrong side of history and needs to get with the program.

It is worth taking a look at how the relationship between humanity and nature has evolved differently in the West and in China.

The (featured) poster is a classic socialist realist image of heroic workers, marching ever leftward (Figure 2.2). It was produced after the horrendous 1976 Tangshan earthquake that laid waste to 96 percent of all housing in the city (650,000 homes destroyed) and reduced 90 percent of all factories to rubble.[33] The central figure in the poster—the man with the word "Tangshan" written on his vest—rallies other public servants, citizens, and Chinese People's militia to help those in need. The utter devastation of this natural disaster is well documented in James Palmer's book *The Death of Mao*[34] and summed up in the prologue to the Earthquake Engineering Research Laboratory's survey report which coldly notes that "at 4:00 a.m. on July 28, 1976 the city of Tangshan, China ceased to exist."[35] Reports vary, but effectively, between 250,000 and 655,000 human beings perished in just fifteen seconds[36].

The Tangshan poster's slogan, 人定胜天 (rén ding shèng tiān/ man must conquer nature), is one of the most memorable—and sometimes misunderstood—of Mao's many slogans. It is a phrase here associated with the unfolding tragedy at Tangshan where it would be churlish to deny the anguish of the nation. In our era of environmental platitudes, we in the West who rarely experience the malignant force of nature sometimes forget that a legitimate response to a devastating earthquake might be a visceral hatred of the environment.

Over the years, we have become used to seeing earthquake survivors as victims rather than enraged agents of change. We have become resistant to the empowered active subject in some regard, with one writer suggesting that "long-term emotional consequences of a disaster are related to feelings of powerlessness and lack of control over forces bigger than oneself."[37] Indeed, there is a contemporary fad for resilience that counterintuitively seems to revel in a permanent state of frailty. Judith Rodin writes that "crisis is the new normal,"[38] exploring how resilience is a permanent state of risk management: a mechanism for making wariness of nature's dark forces into a permanent state of being. Compared to such fatalism, Mao's entreaty to combat and resist nature's barbarism seems challengingly heroic.

In China's troubled history, many millions have died as a result of nature's whim, and this 1976 poster was a rallying cry to the people to stand firm and unite against disaster. It was a statement of determination. The poster's equally irascible bottom line poses the question, "What fear we of earth being rent asunder?" and continues: "With just our hands we can build a new one." Admittedly the poster was a rhetorical expression of the Communist Party's demand for unity, for nationalistic cohesion, rallying the rescue efforts and nudging the population to a selfless act of assistance at a time when meaningful infrastructural aid did not exist. It was a significant campaign that may not be fully comprehended by people from the West living outside the imminent threat of earthquake or tsunami. It is a bold statement of humanity's resolve.

In some ways this poster was also a distraction from the fact that Mao was in no position to make rousing edicts. As this poster went into production, he was suffering from the advanced stages of Parkinson's disease and eventually succumbed to a heart attack later the same year. But even though this poster was clearly designed by committee, without his assistance, in order to rally the troops, these words were certainly Mao's.

The first recorded evidence of Mao's use of the phrase "Man must conquer nature" appears in the recollections of Bai Mei, the vice secretary of Hubei Province where, in 1945 after the devastation of the Second World War, Mao suggested it as a way of rallying the population to continue the fight for liberty. In this regard, man's desire to conquer nature was reflected in the need to have a revolution against the natural order: the colonial reality of foreign rule, China's subservience to world powers, and the barbarism of an eight-year war (in which twenty million Chinese had died),[39] in order to "build the new China."[40] Nature, meaning the natural social order and subservience to natural conditions, were in need of revolution.

By the 1950s, such was the wanton destruction wrought to ordinary people's living standards by nature and such was the lack of development by which people could overcome it that one author described how "sparrows were eating the people's grains and were outcompeting people for the dwindling food supplies." The frustrated response to circumstances often took on a form of quasi-Luddism lashing out against the immediate object of irritation. He concurs that "they had to go."[41] Thus began the Four Pests campaign of 1958, aimed at the extermination of mosquitoes, flies, rats, and sparrows. Over the course of the campaign, "1 billion sparrows, 1.5 billion rats, 100 million kilograms of flies and 11 million kilograms of mosquitos were killed."[42]

We have all seen the grainy black-and-white footage, I guess, of peasants compelled to stand outside and make so much noise that the sparrows could not rest, staying on the wing until they died of exhaustion. With hindsight—or maybe with a bit more forethought—the Chinese authorities might have realized that even though destroying the sparrows would help protect the grain stocks, there would be fewer birds to eat the other pests. Frank Dikotter points to the unintended consequences of such actions. The destruction of one immediate nuisance—the sparrow population— simply gave insects the opportunity to thrive. The immediate cause of concern for farmers had been chased to near extinction but without thought for the long-term results. With nothing to keep the insects down, the number of locusts expanded massively and crop yields collapsed. But this was not a conscious act of self-destruction, this was merely a clumsy response by pragmatic leaders and desperate peasants to imminent devastation. Wrong, yes. Stupid, maybe. Ideologically blind, undoubtedly. But it was also a practical, pragmatic, and critical remedy within reach of a fundamentally peasant economy.

Meanwhile, in the developed world of the early 1960s, a very different script was being enacted. While Mao Zedong was instructing people to conquer nature so that they might exert some semblance of self-determination on their lives, one relatively unknown American author was mobilizing everyone to see that "man is a part of nature, and his war against nature is inevitably a war against himself."[43]

Rachel Carson's book *Silent Spring* is a benchmark in Western environmental risk aversion, tackling the potential hazards that might lurk within agricultural processes and the dangers secreted in erstwhile innocuous products by the chemical industry. Published in 1962, at the same time when millions of Chinese were dying of starvation, it was the forerunner to the indictment of Big Pharma today. Her thesis was that the sounds of spring—the birds, the foxes, the cattle, the sheep—were all being silenced by pesticides. "Everywhere was a shadow of death," she writes blackly. In particular, she made great play of the possible harmful effects of DDT, a common pesticide used as an antimalarial chemical on crops and on humans. As a result DDT was banned in the United States in 1972 on the strength of her rhetoric.

In 2001, the UN Stockholm Convention included 100 national signatories pledged to eradicate the use of DDT as a precautionary measure, even though the link between DDT and ill-health is contentious. Many have suggested that a lot more people have died due to the continued prevalence of malaria in many developing countries (malarial outbreaks that would have been eradicated were it not for the ban, they say) than those who have allegedly been saved by withdrawing the chemical. Dr. Robert White-Stevens, a chemist at Rutgers University and a representative of the chemical manufacturing industry in the 1960s, wrote a critical article in the *New York Times* and appeared on TV as her staunchest critic, "If man were to follow the teachings of Miss Carson, we would return to the Dark Ages, and the insects and diseases and vermin would once again inherit the earth."[44]

Whatever the facts, Carson's book put humanity's harms against nature center stage. In many ways, this sums up the dichotomy. In the early 1960s, during the Great Leap Forward, the natural environment had been a casualty of the immense social turmoil by which rural China was "left with an environment ravaged by misguided Maoist era policies of massive relocations, dam building and land transformation for agriculture."[45] As we have seen. The environment was not high on the agenda when people were being forced to forage for survival. This period was "viewed by Chinese authors as a period of ecological disaster."[46] While China was concentrating on building a new country, the West had the luxury of pontificating about the environment. When Mao was forcing the population to slay pestilential sparrows, New York urban activist Jane Jacobs was forcing planners to promise that new urban developments would ensure that "not a single sparrow—shall be displaced."[47]

A decade later, the Western concept of an environmental "earth-consciousness"[48] was given real meaning by Apollo 17's famous photograph of the so-called "Blue Marble": the iconic 1972 photograph of the earth taken from space. For many in the Western world, this potent image strongly influenced (and reflected) the environmental discourse of a fragile earth in need of protection[49] and ignited the Gaia hypothesis in the West. "By changing the environment,"[50] Lovelock said, "we have unknowingly declared war on Gaia (earth)." Compare this to the late 1960s and the early 1970s, when China was going through a war of its own—a civil war—that has subsequently been called China's "decade of chaos." This was the Cultural Revolution—a period when tens of thousands of Chinese youth were sent down to the countryside to learn from a peasant lifestyle.

This celebration of the peasantry and a war against bourgeois Western capitalism seems to echo E. F. Schumacher's plea for Western societies to "disarm greed and envy."[51] But China was actually demanding that its people avoid greed even though there was no materialistic basis for such a concern. While Chinese students were being forced to work the land, students in Philadelphia were partying to mark the first Earth Day. It is hardly surprising that, for the Chinese, the sanctification of nature was, and is, a decadent nicety. Unsurprisingly, both the Great Leap Forward and the Cultural Revolution resulted in a generation who were less enamored by the sanctity of nature than some of their peers in the West were. At the start of the 1960s, absolute grinding poverty had generated levels of social degradation in China such that man was eating man, while by the start of the 1970s Chinese educated youth were forced to live like peasants.

For many Western commentators, the sanctity of nature and its despoliation under extreme conditions is what is worthy of comment. Ignoring the social realities confronted in this devastating period of China's history, one author condemns China's subjugation of nature in the 1960s, suggesting that it should have "attempt(ed) to live in harmony with it."[52] But in China, living in harmony with nature was the norm; it was called subsistence. For most people, nature wasn't bounteous and the reality (rather than the romantic myths) for peasants was driving them to despair. It is why even today, calls for "harmony" are ridiculed.

The collectivization of villages into bureaucratic communes had wrought terrible damage on the environment and the reality on the ground for ordinary Chinese people was a constant battle against nature to feed themselves. To ignore the socioeconomic misery for millions of desperate people is to miss much of the dynamics of twentieth-century China.[53] Films like Jiao Bo's *Village Diary* (2014) confirm that the struggle against subsistence continues to this day.[54] In such circumstances, there is no love lost on nature. It is red in tooth and claw. For many, it is still something to be beaten into submission.

Notes

1   Liang, C., "Most Polluted City on Earth," *Time* magazine, September 27, 1999.

2   Anon, "Choked: The Most Polluted Cities of the World's Largest Economies," *The Economist*, January 16, 2013.

3   Anon, "Build It and They Might Come," *The Economist*, May 4, 2013.

4   Xie, T., Bai, Y., Du, J., Kang, J., Zhao, L., Lin, Y. and Wang, X., "Air Pollution Prevention and Control Action Plan, State Council Clean Air Alliance of China, Secretariat for Clean Air Alliance of China Doc. GUOFA [2013]37," September 10, 2013 (English translation, Issue II, October 2013).

5   Lanzhou Air Pollution Emergency Plan, Municipal Environmental Protection Emergency Centre, December 22, 2015.

6   Derbyshire, E., Wang J., Jin Z., Billard, A., Egels, Y., Kasser, K., Jones, D.K.C., Muxart, T. and Owen, L., The Gansu Loess of China, Catena Supplement 20, Cremlingen 1991. pp. 119–145

7   Jiang, Gaoming, "Land Reclamation: Tread Carefully," *ChinaDialogue*, March 11, 2008. http://www.chinadialogue.net/article/show/single/en/1792-Land-reclamation-tread-carefully/ (accessed July 17, 2016).

8   Lanzhou, the successful completion of the "Twelfth Five-Year" pollution reduction targets and tasks, Municipal Environmental Protection Emergency Centre, March 18, 2015.

9   Lanzhou Environmental, Air Quality Monitoring Report, Lanzhou Municipal Environmental Monitoring Station, June 2016. http://hbj.lanzhou.gov.cn/.

10   Sun, L., Liu, Z., Wang, J., Wang, L., Bao, X., Wu, Z. and Yu, B., "The Evolving Concept of Air Pollution: A Small-World Network or Scale-Free Network?" *Atmospheric Science Letters* 2016. John Wiley & Sons.

11   Tom Miller quoted in Phillips, T., "From Sand to Skyscrapers: Inside China's Newest City as 400 million Move to Towns," *Daily Telegraph*, June 17, 2013.

12   Sze, Julie, *Fantasy Islands: Chinese Dreams and Ecological Fears in an Age of Climate Crisis*. University of California Press, 2015. p. 59.

13   Lovelock, J. *Revenge of Gaia: Why the Earth Is Fighting Back—and How We Can Still Save Humanity*. Allen Lane (London), 2006. p. 121.

14 Wang, M.Y., Kee, P. and Gao, J., *Transforming Chinese Cities*. Routledge (London), 2014. p. 49.

15 Liu, J., Sun, W., Hu, W., "The Green Book of Eco-cities: The Report on the Development of China's Eco-cities," *The Chinese Academy of Social Science*, June 26, 2015.

16 Heyd, T., *Encountering Nature: Toward an Environmental Culture*. Routledge, 2016. p. 35.

17 Lewis, P., "From Ego to Eco: Architecture's New Ecosophy" cited in Williams, A. and Dounas, T. (eds), "Masterplanning the Future: Modernism East, West and Across the World," *The Proceedings of an International Conference held at Xi'an Jiaotong-Liverpool University*, October 18–19, 2012, TRG Publications (London), p. 139.

18 Hagan, S., "Ecological Urbanism," *The Architectural Review*, March 16, 2015.

19 Goldsmith, E., "Living with Nature," *The Ecologist*, July 1, 1970. http://www.edwardgoldsmith.org/880/living-with-nature/ (accessed July 11, 2016).

20 Lovelock, *The Revenge of Gaia*, 2006, p. 3.

21 Monbiot, G., "Is This All Humans Are? Diminutive Monsters of Death and Destruction?" *The Guardian*, March 24, 2014.

22 Wang, F. and Mason, A., "Demographic Dividend and Prospects for Economic Development in China," United Nations Expert Group Meeting on Social and Economic Implications of Changing Population Age Structures, Population Division, Department of Economic and Social Affairs, Mexico City, Mexico, August 31–September 2, 2005. pp. 1–18.

23 Whyte, M.K., Wang, F. and Yong, C., "Challenging Myths About China's One-Child Policy," *The China Journal,* July 2015, 74, pp. 144–159.

24 Rodin, J., *The Resilience Dividend: Being Strong in a World Where Things Go Wrong*, Public Affairs, U.S., 2014.

25 Qinglong Wu, Q., Zhao, Z., et al, "Outburst Flood at 1920 BCE Supports Historicity of China's Great Flood and the Xia Dynasty," *Science*, August 5, 2016, 353(6299), pp. 579–582.

26 Bol, P.K., "Yao, Shun and Yu's story," China (Part 1): Political and Intellectual Foundations, Section 3, November 12, 2013.

27 Edmonds, R.L., *Patterns of China's Lost Harmony: A Survey of the Country's Environmental Degradation and Protection*. Routledge, 2012.

28 FAO, Global Forest Resources Assessment 2015 Desk reference, Food and Agriculture Organization of The United Nations Rome, 2015.

29 FAO, State of the World's Forests 2012, Food and Agriculture Organization of the United Nations, Rome, 2012, chapter 2, p. 12.

30 Eldred, C., "China Plants More Than 40 Billion Trees Since 1981," *Generation Progress*, August 10, 2010. http://Genprogress.Org/Voices/2010/08/10/15565/China-Plants-More-Than-40-Billion-Trees-Since-1981/ (accessed July 7, 2016).

31 Williams, A., "Understanding 'Sustainability' and Attitudes of Students to the Concept of 'Sustainable Development' in China and the UK," in *Proceedings of the International Conferences on Internet Technologies & Society*, ed. P. Kommers, T. Issa, M. Dantas, C., Costa and P. Isaías (ITS 2015), Educational Technologies 2015 (ICEduTech 2015) and Sustainability, Technology and Education 2015 (STE 2015), Florianópolis, Santa Catarina, Brazil, November 30–December 2, 2015. IADIS Press. pp. 99–112. ISBN: 978-989-8533-46-3.

32 Smil, V., *Making the Modern World: Materials and Dematerialization*. Wiley (London), 2013.

33 Spignesi, Stephen, *Catastrophe! The 100 Greatest Disasters of All Time*, Citadel (New York) 2004, p.48.

34 James Palmer, *The Death of Mao: The Tangshan Earthquake and the Birth of the New China*, Faber & Faber (London), 2012.

35 Housner George W. and He, Duxin (eds) The Great Tangshan Earthquake of 1976, Overview Volume, Earthquake Engineering Laboratory, California Institute of Technology, Pasadena, California, 2002, Prologue.

36 Spence, Jonathan. [1991] (1991). *The Search for Modern China*. W. W. Norton & Company (New York, London).

37 Bennett, C., "The Nepal Earthquakes Have Unleashed a Mental Health Disaster," *The Guardian*, May 15, 2015.

38 Moss, S. "Judith Rodin's Warning for the World: 'Crisis Is becoming the new normal'," *The Guardian*, January 27, 2015.

39 Mitter, R. *China's War with Japan, 1937-1945: The Struggle for Survival*, Allen Lane (London) 2013.

40 Li Yinqiao, *Fifteen Years by the Side of Mao Zedong*, Hebei renmin chubanshe, Shijiazhuang, 1992.

41 McKee, J.K. *Sparing Nature: The Conflict Between Human Population Growth and Earth's Biodiversity*, Rutgers University Press (USA), 2005, p. 86.

42 Lampton, D.M., "Public Health and Politics in China's Past Two Decades," *Health Services Reports* 1972, 87(10), 895–904.

43 Quaratiello, A.R., *Rachel Carson: A Biography*. Greenwood Publishing Group, 2004. p. 113.

44 Murphy, P. C. *What a Book Can Do: The Publication and Reception of Silent Spring*. Amherst, Massachusetts, United States of America: University of Massachusetts Press, 2005, p. 152.

45 Brown, C., Gonzalez, D., Medford, E. and Murray, A., "The Pressures of Industry on the Chinese Environment: A Tale of Two South China Cities," Final Research Paper, NSF/REU Program-Society and Environment in South China, 2002. p. 2.

46 Edmonds, R. L., *Patterns of China's Lost Harmony: A Survey of the Country's Environmental Degradation and Protection,* Routledge, 2012, p. 48.

47 Kanigel, R., *Eyes on the Street: The Life of Jane Jacobs*. New York: Alfred A Knopf Publishers, 2016. p. 242.

48 Jasanoff, S., "Image and Imagination: The Formation of Global Environmental Consciousness," in *Changing the Atmosphere*, ed. P. Edwards and C. Miller. MIT Press, 2001. p. 17.

49 Wuebbles, D.J. "Celebrating the 'Blue Marble'," *Eos*, December 4, 2012, 93(49), pp. 509–511.

50 Lovelock, J., *The Revenge of Gaia: Earth's Climate Crisis & The Fate of Humanity*. Basic Books (London), 2007.

51 Schumacher, E.F., *Small is Beautiful: Economics as If People Mattered*. Blond & Briggs (London), 1973.

52 Navarro, Peter, *The Coming China Wars. Where They Will Be Fought and How They Can Be Won*, FT Press, New Jersey, 2008, p.89.

53 Oi, J.C., *State and Peasant in Contemporary China: The Political Economy of Village Government*. University of California Press, 1989.

54 Jiao Bo (director), *Village Diary*. Central Newsreel and Documentary Film Studio, 2014.

CHAPTER THREE

Growing Pains

In the Western environmental canon, the mantra "Small is Beautiful" or the maxim "reduce, re-use, re-cycle" are among the many commonplace phrases that reflect what financial journalist Daniel Ben-Ami has called "growth scepticism."[1] In other words, this is an ideological contradiction or a moral indecision: a rhetorical support for growth, but one that coincides with a more dominant belief that growth must be subject to environmental, social, and moral limits. A recent conference on the consumer economy celebrates the variety of euphemisms for growth skepticism capturing the creeping renunciation of growth from some quarters: from "post-growth" economics to "prosperity without growth" or even "agrowth" or "degrowth."[2]

Conversely, over the thirty years that China has taken to emerge onto the world's stage, growth has not been such a cognitively dissonant concept. In 2001, General Secretary Jiang Zemin was unequivocal in his endorsement of "economic growth and social progress."[3] From Deng Xiaoping's exhortation that "to get rich is glorious,"[4] growth is a sentiment that chimes with a society that prefers to think that more is better than less. This perception has deep roots in Chinese history, but here we will explore some of the more relevant ones.

By 1960, all over China, Party cadres and overenthusiastic students were leading the push for industrialization to drive swift economic development necessary to compete with its capitalist rivals. One account from the city of Xi'an notes that patriotic youth held aloft banners proclaiming the Party's ambition: "Surpass England

and Catch up to America."[5] It was a slogan rather than a policy as there was very little material basis for such an ambitious sentiment save for the huge numbers of people that could be dragooned into China's rather backward manufacturing sector.

Growth was something positive to be willed into existence. It was a competitive mobilization toward a Western-style industrial economy carried out with heroic Chinese peasantry at the helm. In an echo of Britain's phoney war of the 1930s that was intended to provide a sense of solidarity behind a campaign to melt surplus metal for the British war effort ("Saucepans for Spitfires," read one wartime propaganda poster), China forced people to set up their own backyard steelworks in villages and towns to aid the much-vaunted modernization drive. It was equally phoney but on an entirely different scale (Figure 3.1).

Mao's demand that steel output had to double in twelve months resulted in bicycles, pots, pans, workmen's tools, doorknobs—scrap of any sort—being melted down into steel with no quality control and with a massive depredation of fuel supplies. Trees were cut down in their millions to feed the fires. In hundreds of thousands of local production units, peasant farmers with no understanding of industrial processes ended up smelting worthless pig iron, while at the same time burning vast amounts of timber and producing more pollution than products. Judith Shapiro writes that "erosion, sedimentation, desertification, and changes in microclimate followed hard on the heels of deforestation, resulting in a protracted loss of arable land."[6] Producing nothing of value, this mass lunacy engaged around 100 million people in a program of decimating forests, destroying craft tools and domestic utensils, and forcing people in target-driven, forced labor. It was a tragedy of epic proportions. The Great Leap had failed.

Within forty years, China was outperforming America in steel production by 20 percent.[7] Ten years later still and China has a steel production capacity that is now ten times that of the United States and is clearly the biggest steel manufacturer in the world, producing over half the world's crude steel stocks.[8] This seemingly exponential growth from nothing has typified many aspects of Chinese industrial production sectors over the late twentieth century: from steel production to manufacturing and technology. By 2016, it was officially recorded that China had overtaken the United States as the world's biggest construction market.[9] It is a remarkable transition

FIGURE 3.1 *"Long live the Great Leap Forward"*
Source: IISH / Stefan R. Landsberger Collections; chineseposters.net

for a country mired in rural communes, starvation, disease, and poverty just sixty years ago.

At the foundation of the People's Republic, Mao had stood on the walls of the Forbidden City and claimed: "I hope the day will come when all you can see from Tiananmen Gate is a forest of tall chimneys belching out clouds of smoke."[10] That day didn't occur and Tiananmen became infamous for other reasons, but it all points to the fact that this magical transformation has come at a cost. Whether in the industrializing zealotry of the communist years or in the juggernaut of China's capitalist phase, both have had social consequences. But from the 1950s to the early 1970s, the Party believed that "as a socialist state, it didn't have environmental problems."[11]

Xuefei Ren describes how China's urbanization under Mao was shaped by "the industrialization imperative" in which cities were solely manufacturing centers and rural areas were collectivized to become specialized only in agricultural production where "commerce, crafts and service industries were discouraged."[12] Hard to believe given the dynamic markets, shops, and malls of today, but Shanghai was once severely "punished for its colonial and imperialist past" and received particularly harsh measures to blot out its record of Western decadence. The city's biographer states that in the 1920s and 1930s "nowhere else did the population pursue amusement, from feasting to whoring, dancing to powder-taking, with such abandoned zeal…it catered for every depravity known to man."[13]

As a consequence of its bourgeois capitalist connotations, which Mao believed had created a "centre of despotic power,"[14] Shanghai was forced to endure thirty years of heavy industrialization and collectivization without any significant urban residential development or social improvement. Hong Kong academic Gary Pui Fung Wong notes that, from the 1950s to the 1970s, no new buildings were completed on Shanghai's "bund," the main warehousing and shipping dock along the Huangpu River.[15]

So one of the clearest outward signs of the transformation in the country's fortunes is in the physical environment, and Shanghai's skyline alone is testament to that transformation. Today, the urban landscape is unrecognizable from twenty, ten, or even five years ago and this urban dynamism is encapsulated in the graph tellingly titled "China: building Europe in 15 years" (Figure 3.2), which indicates that China has a size and speed of change greater than continents.[16] In 1998, for instance, the UK government announced that it was to build 4.4 million new homes by 2016, an ambitious twenty-year goal, whereas China completed that many new homes in the first eight months of 2012. This housing miracle (or dangerous bubble, depending on your interpretation) is ten times the rate of contemporary US residential completions, admittedly reflecting America's lowest rate of house building since 1946.[17]

The impact on how most people live has been equally radically altered in recent years, not only in their spending power but on their quality and quantity of life, with infant mortality just 10 percent of its 1970 level and life expectancy practically doubling since 1960, from 43 years of age to today's national average of 76 years. China has transformed itself socially and economically, and similarly Chinese people's physical surroundings have undergone a revolution, with villages disappearing and central business districts emerging in their place.

Growth has clearly been better than the alternatives, although admittedly it has been a difficult journey. For the older generation, there has been a certain sense of loss, which is well captured in a short documentary *Edge Town* by Jiang Hao, who interviewed residents of a part-demolished Jiangsu community. Their sense of resignation was clouded only by a palpable disorientation toward the future, especially by those who hadn't done so well out of contemporary economic changes. Simon Gjeroe, who cofounded Beijing Postcards—a shop that sells photographs and memorabilia of China's lost heritage from 1890s to the 1950s—recalls how when they first opened, they were attacked for reminding Chinese people of the poverty and colonialism of the past but after just five years, visitors, especially those from families not wealthy enough to own a camera, were more appreciative of the memories being captured. There are many elderly Chinese, like old people everywhere who appreciate the certainty of the past. This has a greater poignancy in a country like China, which is undergoing such frenetic change.

That said, there is little romantic allusion attached to the past. While Prince Charles once lionized the architectural purity of Shijia Hutong in Dashilar in Beijing and portrayed it as a locus of solid community values, many residents recognize it as a maze of decrepit alleyways and slum housing where 55,000 people live cheek by jowl at a population density six times higher than the Beijing average. Their accommodation resembles shanty houses with no running water where hundreds of occupants share communal toilets. Their community is one of tolerance and survival rather than choice.

Much of the area has subsequently been upgraded, much to the delight of local residents primarily because, upgrade or demolish, the criterion for opting for one or the other tends to be whether there is any money in it. Few were protective of their picturesque urban squalor. For many people, China's transformation has been so rapid that it is easy to forget that there are still more than seventy million people living on less than US$2 a day and with no other way of escaping poverty than to bargain hard for recompense when your house is razed to the ground. Some of the creatives and designers who helped prevent demolition in Dashilar have moved into the area, raising property values: a much-appreciated gentrification that is welcomed primarily as a mechanism for locals to improve their life chances and get ahead when they sell, rather than a victory of architectural conservation.

This chapter looks at the growth of the economy and its urban expression. It explores how the notion of growth is changing China but also how changes in China are altering the notion of growth.

––––––

In 1978, Deng Xiaoping's decision to end collective farming enabled farmers to sell their surplus produce in the marketplace. At the same time he opened up the country to foreign trade and investment, creating international joint ventures to bring in money and know-how. As a direct consequence, over the following thirty years, China's GDP grew consistently at around 10 percent per annum, rising from RMB36.5 billion to RMB24500 billion in 2007. Deng's dictum of "one country, two systems" for Hong Kong further welcomed the incorporation of capitalism alongside state socialism without any sense of it being an unsustainable contradiction. It was pitched as a pragmatic tension to be managed. Another tolerable duality was that of economic growth and urban expansion that grew in a dialectical relationship: each the precursor and beneficiary. Economic liberalization created the productive engine for the city's growth, but urbanization was necessary for efficient and profitable economic development.

Since China opened up to the outside world, effectively refuting the hard-line communist past and welcoming in certain aspects of capitalist enterprise, the nation's economy has been transformed at a speed and quality beyond any other country in history. In 1980, Shenzhen in Guangdong Province became the first special economic zone in China, the spark for one of the most explosive urban experiments in human history. It was here that Deng Xiaoping began his famous southern tour of 1992, introducing the economic reforms that would transform the region and the nation. From nothing (or a series of villages housing 30,000 people), Shenzhen has grown into a population of around fifteen million, reflecting an average population growth of 30 percent per annum over the last three decades. The new city of Shenzhen further benefited from the proximity to Hong Kong at the time of its transfer of sovereignty.

The early period of market reforms and relentless growth targets were characterized by the way that central government tended to use a "tournament competition" among local city mayors: promoting or demoting them on the key evaluation criterion of GDP growth.[18] For the decades since, it has been political suicide to downplay GDP. Indeed, many apparatchiks who might have wished to develop nonpolluting industries in their regions worried that they might destabilize the certainty of short-term growth and hence ruin the chance for political promotion. But there were a small number of political players who saw the wind changing and wanted to make a name for themselves. These risk-taking future leaders surely include Shenzhen's mayor, who announced in 2005 that he wanted the city to aspire to be a low-carbon Eco-city. His gamble paid off, and by 2010 the Ministry of Housing and Urban-Rural Development and Shenzhen's Municipal Government signed the agreement on China's first low-carbon eco-demonstration city to show that "low-carbon" and "development" are not mutually exclusive.[19] (Coda: Rather than guaranteeing his rise in the Party, ex-mayor of Shenzhen, Mr. Xu Zhongheng, was dismissed in 2011 for taking £3.5 million in bribes, sentenced to death, and reprieved.)

Academic Chen Jia-Ching points out that China is now using environmentalism "as a strategy for meeting goals of economic growth…with local state-led strategies for capital accumulation and expansion of territorial authority."[20] Indeed, the concept of high economic efficiency figures much more loftily in Chinese considerations of a working definition of an Eco-city than it does in Western models. Material and consumer growth is central to Chinese sustainability, but that seems to be anathema to Western thinking since the 1960s and 1970s, with one campaigner suggesting that we, in the West, have reached "peak stuff"[21] and journalist Monbiot suggesting that "economic growth is the problem, regardless of whether the word sustainable is bolted to the front of it."[22] In Europe and America, the focus of environmentalism has long been on "limits to growth," that is, reducing consumption or consumerism. Admittedly, the UN welcomes growth provided that it is "within ecological limits,"[23] whereas China, over the first sixty years of its existence, seems to have prioritized growth regardless of whether it pushed those ecological limits…sometimes to breaking point.

That said, China has not been as environmentally profligate as is sometimes assumed. One author notes that in 1984 the country was faced with a report that "the cost of environmental pollution…was about RMB 40 billion (US$6 billion) annually. The authorities were so shocked by this figure that they decided to make environmental protection a national policy."[24] China was the first country to publish a national-level "Agenda 21" strategy in 1994 arising out of the Rio Summit, and in the intervening thirty years, the State Environmental Protection Administration has issued 200 regulations and 500 national environmental standards, approved over five multilateral or international environmental conventions, and has overseen more than 1,600 regional or local environmental regulations.[25] Most of these policies reflected the need for enabling legislation, but many have set the scene for future environmental developments. It was in 1986—one year before the publication of the famous Brundtland Report that defined sustainable development in the West—that Yichun City in Jiangxi Province was the first to announce its intentions to become an Eco-city in China.

A recent documentary in China, *Under the Dome* (subsequently censored, but only after it had made a significant impact through Chinese social media), addressed what Cornell University professor Elizabeth C Economy has called China's "environmental crisis." But the film was making another point too, featuring scenes of the killer London's smogs in the 1950s and portraying them as an unfortunate but necessary stage of Britain's development. Indeed, America had to wait until 1970 for a Clean Air Act to "set an air quality standard based on a public health measurement."[26]

Challenging China's terrible air quality is important, but it is worth remembering that many citizens died across the developed world as a result of industrialization too. Fortunately history has shown that badly polluted cities could subsequently be cleaned up due to policy changes, technical advances, business opportunities, and public attitudes. China is keen to remind the West of its own history and global culpability but also to legitimize the fact that it is following most nations in this trajectory: first, growth-induced environmental hazards; second, cleanup operations; and, finally, the implementation of environmental regulatory standards and enforcement.

While China was being pilloried for its poor air quality and Beijing condemned as one of China's most polluted cities, the capital was activating plans to spend RMB18 billion (£1.8 billion) on environmental cleanup initiatives in Beijing alone. Actually, across China, this will mean closing hundreds of factories and throwing people out of work. The southern city of Ningbo, for example, proudly notes that since 2012 "568 backward enterprises were eliminated."[27] But before we criticize too roundly, remember that this is sometimes the brutal logic of environmental demands. After all, Britain's greatest carbon reduction policy was the closure of the UK coal mining industries with the destruction of 142,000 jobs,[28] albeit supplanted by imported coal.

In the middle of the nineteenth century, New York's local authority utilized "the power of eminent domain" (the government's right to compulsorily purchase land for public use), allowing it to clear away the existing poor, shoddy housing, and squatter settlements in order to take possession of almost 750 acres of land in the center of Manhattan. This vast area was to become New York's Central Park. Social benefits versus personal loss is a difficult ethical judgment but one that has been made throughout history. In 2007 China announced that Beijing would be building ten to twenty new city parks every year for the foreseeable future, with 100 hectares constructed within the city and 660 hectares of parkland created in the outer regions.[29] Who knows whether these parklands actually materialize is unclear, but if so people are going to have to move. The point is that environmentalism is not always benign and people's lives will be positively and negatively affected in the process.

Because of their geographical density, cities tend to be more productive and efficient than their more parochial rural neighbors. Greater proximity leads to energy saving and other environmental benefits. This is a reasonably uncontroversial statement, given that costs, time, and effort can be reduced across the production and distribution networks within cities. But in a recent United Nations Environment Programme (UNEP) document, the authors confuse this ubiquitous benefit of *any* city, with the specifics of Eco-cities.[30] China is happy to take advantage of any misreading in order to promote itself as an environmental leader. Coincidentally, it is legitimately making urban improvements to lead the field in environmental issues.

Beijing is already listed as the thirty-sixth environmentally healthy city in China; thirty-second for green consumption; the seventh most environmentally friendly city; and first on "new thinking on Eco-cities." Whatever these official titles mean, Beijing is setting out to change the face of urbanism and eco-urbanism in China. Currently, it is at the center of a process of creating a mega-agglomeration including plans for the brand new Xiongan New Area called "Jing-Jin-Ji" (shorthand for Beijing, Tianjin, and Hebei). This is an expansionist master plan that seeks to unite three regions in a transport network called "one core, two cities and three routes" with Beijing at the center. It will have an area of 220,000 km² and contain over 100 million people, making it equivalent to the official designation of a "large country."[31] It plans to create a new regional strategy for focusing on key industries, improved standards of living, and improving the links in between. The efficiency gains, the environmental benefits, and the growth potential are huge.

Once again, this is an urban form that has been written about for some time but seems to be working out in China in a more consciously planned and realizable way than similar attempts in the West. For example, while the unification of the mega-region of Northern California, Oregon, and Washington envisaged by Ernest Callenbach's novel Ecotopia didn't come to pass, Jean Gottmann's *Megalopolis*, written in 1960, was a much more serious and positive attempt to formalize the connectivity across the eastern seaboard into a supercity. That said, these fictional or theoretical approaches have been realized in real interlinkages that have evolved between neighboring administrations, say, between San Francisco, Sacramento, and San Jose or between the UK's pharmaceutical golden triangle of London, Oxford, and Cambridge.

China is following suit but on a much bigger scale and is also looking to its Asian counterparts to establish international technopoles[32]—linked cities across different countries sharing knowledge and authority. This kind of internationalization is already in existence in the West but now China is trying out efficient interurban partnerships for itself.

In many ways, Jing-Jin-Ji is the pinnacle of China's urban growth agenda. While China's Go-West trajectory is fundamentally important for the country's local internal trade and stability, Jing-

Jin-Ji's emergence in the East is designed not only to satisfy the needs of a huge population, providing a dense, developed, and an efficient high-tech center of innovation but also to grow its markets with Asian economies, such as Singapore, with whom it shares a desire to develop (unhindered, shall we say, by the need for open government).

Caofeidian Eco-city is located on the northeastern Hebei province coastline, southeast of Tangshan City and just outside the Jing-Jin-Ji zone. It is a substantial new metropolitan area being constructed a two-hour drive away—and on the opposite side of Bohai Bay—from Tianjin Eco-city.

When I first visited in mid-2014, it was an extremely difficult place to find, which is strange for a city, especially such a huge construction project that is said to be developing along 80 km of coastline. The first phase is claimed to be variously 30 km² or up to 74 km² depending on which newspapers you read, but no one living locally seemed to know what or where it was. Following his mobile phone GPS and yelling at passers-by for directions, my taxi driver took me to the tip of a vast dockland area, bristling with industrial cranes and delivery trucks, and told me that we had arrived.

Before setting off on this trip from Beijing, I had read the Western newspaper tropes about China's Eco-city pretensions and a number of other articles that provided evidence that this Eco-city phenomenon was overstated. The UK's *Guardian* newspaper, for example, carried a photojournalism essay that demonstrated that "Caofeidian eco-city was planned to accommodate one million inhabitants, yet only a few thousand live there today. It has joined the growing ranks of China's ghost cities." This is the common narrative adopted by Western commentators, who claim—somewhat gleefully—that China has overplayed its hand. Mind you, standing in a dust bowl, with a couple of bemused street-food stall holders grinning at me, it seemed like an eminently convincing observation. Here I was in the middle of a vast nowhere: a dusty, industrial outpost, the silence broken only by the rumbling of lorries churning out clouds of exhaust fumes. Not an Eco-prefix in sight.

Suffice to say, the Google map was out-of-date and I was in completely the wrong place. It was Caofeidian sure enough, but Caofeidian is a huge development zone. The taxi driver had simply taken me to the far southern tip of this gigantic man-made promontory to show off the industrial complex that had kick-started the new city project back in 2006. I was reminded of the time as a student, when I arrived in a caravan park outside Munich late one night—a miserable gravel pit with a standpipe for drinking and showering. The following morning I wandered into the next field only to find state-of-the-art bathrooms, top-of-the-range caravans, and cheerful holidaymakers and realized that I'd actually pitched my tent in an illegal Roma Gypsy squatter settlement in the neighboring field. Thirty years later, I was wandering around a grubby Chinese hinterland that should have been a new Eco-city. I flagged down a passing car and headed northeast.

The photographers who have posted all over the internet, showing Caofeidian as an empty urban undeveloped area, have made the same mistake as my taxi driver. The iconic photograph of a derelict entrance gateway (used time and again as a metaphor for Caofeidian's road to nowhere) is actually 3 km away from the entrance to the real Eco-city. The Eco-city was more than 15 km from where I had been dropped off.

But the industrial hinterland around Caofeidian, as around many proposed Eco-cities, represents one of the important challenges for its acceptance as an Eco-city. Caofeidian Eco-city, like Tianjin Eco-city, is situated in an enormous region of heavy industry, manufacturing and shipping at the very heart of China's coal, oil, and steel import and export ambitions. As we drove on reclaimed land, through subsistence farms, across pitted dykes, the horizon was crowded with nodding donkeys (oil well pumps) perpetually extracting crude from the ground. This quintessentially nonenvironmental zone, situated around the port for international shipping and trade in classically heavily polluting industries, is central to China's long-term goals to increase foreign trade. The idea that it can presume to associate any of this with eco-logic is symptomatic—to many Western commentators—of China's environmental charlatanry.

But China can point to the fact that it has already dealt with the most pressing environmental issue by relocating the original smokestack industries from their position around the urban fringes of Beijing, where they contributed massively to the decline in local air quality. These refineries and steelworks employed thousands on the outskirts of the capital. It was a reflection of China's commitment to reducing smogs, improving the conditions within the capital city at that time, and also providing an opportunity to restructure its industrial capacity that in 2007 it moved entire giant production processes, including Beijing's Capital Iron and Steel Group's steel plant, 200 km to the southeast onto the Hubei coast as "a model of China's environment-friendly industrial base."[33] There has been some disappointment among Chinese officials at the West's derision, missing the fact that the move has enabled technological upgrade in its hitherto out-of-date production facilities, and now it claims that 99.5 percent of the solid waste and 97.5 percent of the wastewater produced at the steel works are recycled.

An employment zone of the magnitude of Caofeidian New Industrial Area needs staffing, housing, and other infrastructure and facilities. Thousands of workers are being relocated in a matter-of-fact way, typical of no-nonsense capitalism, to populate the new factories, storage yards, smelting plants, and dockyards. If you believe the hype, over one million employees are anticipated here by 2020 and whether that many ever materialize, the necessary urban infrastructure is being master planned to facilitate the industrial growth potential. Admittedly, some workers do not have the choice and will have to agree to be relocated in order to maintain their jobs, but others are being encouraged with the offer of the Eco-city's provision of decent housing, clean facilities, clean air, and an improved quality of life.

Caofeidian Eco-city, which has been planned for some time in conjunction with a Swedish environmental engineering consultancy, is still at the early stage of development, and, at the time of my first visit, it was well behind schedule but still hoped to reach a population of 800,000 by 2020. However, one of the clearest indications that all is not well with its progress is that it is absent from Chinese academic research listings. The growth of the advocacy research phenomenon has driven university departments in China to tick the "Eco-city" box. But on Caofeidian Eco-city there is nothing. It is clearly not going smoothly. There is also no mention of Caofeidian Eco-city in BMI Research's China Real Estate Report 2017 (or 2016), confirming that there is no meaningful real estate available on the market.

Sadly, the recent property slowdown and the fact that Caofeidian is a nationally financed project (as opposed to Tianjin Eco-city which is a Sino-Singapore-funded scheme) have meant that the Caofeidian's development has been put on the back burner. It has stopped as the economy has slowed. As one research paper points out: "It is probable that for most of these projects (referring to Caofeidian and similar others), new efforts will eventually be made by different parties to re-launch the same projects, albeit often under a different label and with revised ambitions."[34] Currently, in Caofeidian there exists a rather forlorn police station, supermarket, and ubiquitous Ecomuseum containing an ambitious model of what the city should look like. There is very little else to show for ten years of work. Clearly, much of this time has been taken up with planning, laying smart infrastructure, and the invisible gains of land remediation—seizing land from the sea, desalinating the salt flats, and providing stable conditions for plants and structures to survive—but even so, Caofeidian is not as it should be.

The original plan was that it would eventually extend to 150 km². It was to have contained good quality housing (designated as first-class and second-class residential quality), high-tech industries and a science park, schools, hospitals, leisure and entertainment facilities (at the moment unspecified), as well as parks, farmland, green belt, light rail and monorail transportation systems. Had it gone to plan, there would be a residential harbor area, commercial services, and the obligatory "administration area" (sometimes known as "party headquarters"). Landscaping and the quality of spaces would be a huge improvement on what currently exists in urban Beijing.

The environmental master plan is still that the city will be powered by nonrenewal means: a 50 km² wind farm comprising 200 × 3500 kW wind turbines to generate 2.25 billion kWhours annually together with a refuse incinerator power plant. The public transportation is still scheduled to be via biogas vehicles and the solar panels will provide sufficient thermal power for individual homes instead of the quintessentially north China district heating system. (Note: Mao arbitrarily decreed that any location below the Huai River should be designated as "temperate," whereas homes constructed in the "cold" region to the north of the river are provided with centrally administered free district heating that kicks in mid-November in a cloud of coal-fired soot and sulfur.) Comparatively, the new city ought to be a generous improvement if it ever gets off the ground. But attention now, of course, is privileging the construction of the 2,000 km² Xiongan New Area a few hundred kilometers away from Caofeidian. As I write, Xiongan has received an initial kick-start fund of $19 billion from the state-owned China

Development Bank. This is a green megaproject that has greater likelihood of success than Caofeidian primarily because it seems to have the personal backing of President Xi Jinping. Watch this space.

With a little imagination, Chinese newly built Eco-cities like Xiongan could be likened to the New Towns movement in the UK, the postwar ambition that led to the creation of Milton Keynes in the mid-1970s. This was a new British city that reflected the futuristic urban ambitions of new technologies, new industry, and quality of life. It was designated as a "city in a forest" and proposed to take population pressure off London, evolving into a city of 250,000 people (although city status has never been granted). Irvine in California is another example of late 1960s urban development intended to improve the conditions and work–life experiences of residents. A strict comparison doesn't bear full scrutiny, but the fact that China has developed economically to the extent that it can now express its concern at the quality of urban expansion rather than simply the rate of expansion is an important connection.

Caofeidian Eco-city—if it ever restarts—is intended to be the lure for predominantly elite workers to live in a coastal region away from the congestion and stress, common aspects of many Chinese towns and cities. It claims to go beyond the "triple bottom line"—a phrase coined by John Elkington in 1994 to reflect the economic, environmental, and social impacts of sustainable development. Ever mindful of the developments in sustainability approaches in the West, and eager to please, China has utilized this rounded approach to environmental sustainability in its Caofeidian growth plans and says that the design will satisfy the seven stringent United Nations Sustainable Cities criteria of "physical, economical, biological, organizational, social, cultural and aesthetic" aspects (known as PEBOSCA). At the moment, at least, it is the economic aspects that are holding things up. But as the government eyes the environmental benefits of small-scale gains, of retrofit, of value and away from the idea of investment-heavy, high-technology, new urban formation, Caofeidian may prove to be a city whose time had gone before it had arrived.

———

Analysis of thirty-one second-tier cities (comprising provincial capitals, large commercial centers, etc.) and a further eighty-five significant smaller cities revealed that housing prices by 2013 had an average annual real growth rate of 10.5 and 7.9 percent, respectively, which "easily surpass the housing price appreciation during the U.S. housing bubble in the 2000s and are comparable to that during the Japanese housing bubble in the 1980s."[35] From food quality to air pollution, from adulterated medicines to the cost of living to creeping unemployment, the Chinese chattering classes are a little worried. At present they are more concerned with rising prices and political corruption than with pollution and food safety *per se*, but environmental fears continue to bubble under the surface.

The UN seems to reinforce this fear noting that "consumption patterns of urban middle- and high-income groups ... are responsible for the use of a significant portion of the world's finite resources and contribute significantly to the production of polluting wastes. Sustainable development should focus on better living and working conditions for the poor."[36] This all sounds reasonable and equitable, but has tended, in many instances, to romanticize poverty and to cultivate the poor as a cultural grouping, often referred to as "the precariat," who are groomed to be stewards of the environment. Whereas the Chinese government is adamant about creating a wealthy society and lifting people out of poverty and converting them into contented consumers, the UN seems to designate them as the new moral servants charged with cleaning up after the irresponsible consumption habits of the wealthy.

It seems eminently positive that the UN and environmental fellow travelers can claim to endorse growth, defending the idea that "the greening of economies is not generally a drag on growth but rather a new engine of growth."[37] However, while China still cites its GDP figures as evidence of its development—figures that are increasingly questioned in the West—the UN is quietly shifting the terms of the debate.

In its assessment of GDP, the UN's national economic performance indicators now includes "natural capital," that is, the value—in monetary terms—of forests, clean air, and soil (of "genes, species and ecosystems"). For example, economic development now includes a global assessment of the "contribution of insect pollinators to agricultural output" and concludes that this is US$190 billion per year,[38] a hefty boost to the GDP statistics by simply letting nature take its course. Similarly, conserving forests, according to the UN, contributes US$3.7 trillion to the world economy (equivalent to the GDP of Germany, the fourth largest economy in the world!) Even before the global recession, the value of calculating national economic performance on the basis of real economic growth and productivity has been an uncomfortable task and many Western economists have been eager to shift the frame of reference. While the desire to monetize nature, clean air, and happiness may be understandable, it is worth remembering that it is in productive industry, including industrial farming, that real growth happens.

But as real productive growth stalls in recessionary economies, characterizing a green economy as one which is "low carbon, resource efficient, and socially inclusive" (reminiscent of peasant economies everywhere) allows the UN to reformulate its concept of growth.

The Kingdom of Bhutan's gross national happiness (GNH) index has been seriously explored by the UN and other erstwhile sober economic commentators. GNH is a measure of "material and non-material" aspects of an economy, finding quantifiable economic benefit in the fact that "91.2% of Bhutanese were narrowly, extensively or deeply happy."[39] Bhutan's actual survey begins with the key question, marked from 1 to 10: "Taking all things together, how happy would you say you are?" Consequently, UN economists are revising Western monitoring standards in the light of such an open-ended and inclusive agenda, to the extent that the UN can now surreptitiously sneak in "human well-being" onto its own index of growth.

Adjusting some of the more unrestrained rhetoric of the past in order to satisfy some of its critics, China's twelfth Five-Year Plan called for "quality" growth as opposed to "growth at any cost." Even though this might look as if China is prioritizing intangibles, it is clear that downplaying economic performance, material growth, and infrastructural development and allowing simple pleasures, peasant nobility, and the value of insects to take its place is a step too far for China. China needs no lessons in romanticizing the peasantry, but even the People's Republic hasn't sung praises of the worker bee just yet.

By 2015, China's cumulative local government debt was alleged to be in the region of US$1.7 trillion, and with the economy slowing, production restraint was needed while bolstering the domestic economy. The Chinese economy had a GDP growth rate of around 6.3 percent in 2016 but economists predict further shrinkage to around 4.8 percent by 2020.[40] China still needs growth to survive and thrive but it is having to adapt to new ways of producing, accounting, and dealing with the consequence of change. President Xi Jinping has suggested that this new period of low growth is the "New Normal," in other words something that the Chinese people are going to have to get used to. Instead of high-speed growth, there will be a shift to "medium-to-high speed growth." Furthermore, Xi says that the economy needs to be "increasingly driven by innovation instead of input and investment." Jack Ma, CEO of Alibaba, the world's biggest retailer, suggests that "slightly slower growth"[41] might be a good thing after all. The immediate rush to wealth creation has now created the conditions for more focused attention on what next needs to be done in a classically stage-ist response to China's shifting economic fortunes.

There are nearly 145,000 state-owned enterprises (SOEs) representing a mere 3 percent of all businesses across China but which produce more than 43 percent of the country's gross value of industrial output. As such, "De-industrialization has been a particular challenge to the first generation of large cities that emerged with the growth of manufacturing ... Cities founded upon single natural resources or specialized industries have often faced the biggest difficulties of diversification and repositioning."[42] Even though China is having to artificially maintain the production output from many old polluting industrial sectors in order to attenuate the growth of unemployment, the *Guardian* newspaper reported Premier Li Keqiang as saying that "more environmentally-friendly development would be 'obligatory' for China to 'promote a restructuring of its national economy', currently experiencing its slowest growth in years."[43] In terms of its urban policy, Chinese businessman, developer, and sustainability advocate Yan Jiehe says, the next generation of cities should be "beautiful, but not plump."[44] In many ways, Caofeidian Eco-city represents the kind of acceptable, modern growth–oriented model that is essential for China's future, but also reflects the uncertainty, and maybe the impossibility, of achieving it. It is a city that was intended to be reliant on technology and is referred to in some literature as a "techno-city."[45] But within just a few years of Caofeidian rising and falling, other Eco-city models were rejecting its large-scale focus and proposing a more parochialist vision of what a good city should be.

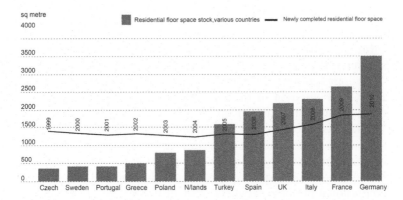

FIGURE 3.2 *Building Rome in a day: China's annual constructed floor space 1999–2010*
Source: © Economist Intelligence Unit's Access China service, www.eiu.com/ 2011, p2

Suzhou Eco-city in Jiangsu Province is located on the east bank of Tai Lake on a 6 km site and is the first phase of a 40 km² master plan. Drive directly west from Suzhou old town, past the American superconductor plant and the Panasonic factories, through the high-tech zone and you enter what the architect's brochure describes as a "New Eco-Town integrated with Nature, Mountain and Water." This is a low- or zero-tech Eco-city and the first phase already accommodates 50,000 residents (or at least that many homes have been bought). The full complement of five phases will create a total population of 300,000 people, making it the size of Cincinnati or, given its water-based pretensions, a city of the size of Venice in Italy.

The urban designers and government agencies that initiated the Suzhou project visited Caofeidian and Tianjin to see how those early-stage Eco-cities had progressed and to assess their modus operandi. The general conclusion was that they were too expensive and too reliant on technology. Instead, they resolved that Suzhou Eco-city would focus on emotional well-being through being "close to nature." This narrative has already encouraged the authorities to clean up the lake water that has always been dangerously contaminated (especially in the 1980s when it was the only drinking source for one million people). The result is a very nicely laid out, well-designed seminatural landscape with connotations of the simple life. The floodplains around Tai Lake have provided the opportunity to create a watertown enveloped by filtered lake water with electric water taxis ferrying people the long distances between places of interest.

Suzhou Eco-city is clearly a touristy and vacation-oriented resort, very different to the high growth, expanding market and urban master plan that many people have come to expect in China. This place is small and relaxed and provides a welcome break from China's stresses, prioritizing the boutique hotels and high-end teahouses, horse-riding stables, and an Eco-farm rather than the proximity to major production houses and high-profile international business networks. It is an Eco-City or an Eco-town for the well-heeled weekender. Of course, Eco-city propaganda is not really aimed at the poor and migrant workers, many of whom will continue to work in inadequate conditions around China for years to come, although the underlying message of sustainable restraint, or low growth and fewer opportunities promoted by Eco-city discourse, will undoubtedly impact upon them too.

The Urban Planning Bureau responsible for Suzhou Eco-town says that it is "life-orientated. It's low carbon, designed bio-climatically, and encompasses a slow movement strategy." When I visited in the scorching, humid summer heat, slow movement was a perfectly logical personal mobility strategy. But the political concept is taken from the Citta Slow Movement in Italy and is somewhat more contentious. One of the first Chinese cities to join this exclusive club was Yaxi, near Nanjing, a rural village of 40,000 people that has committed to cultivate organic produce in its fields. Residents have signed up to maintain "the sense of limits" and to work out ways to stop young people leaving the village.[46] Straightaway it is clear that Eco-cities have a philosophical basis in the culture of restraint.

The real aim of contemporary eco-propaganda seems to be to sell the benefits of the economic slowdown and inspire economic entrepreneurship, eco-business, and innovation. It is a call to arms that has contradictory benefits and drawbacks for the Chinese state. While Carl Honore (author of the classic book *In Praise of Slow*) argues that we should recognize the "grim toll on the environment"[47] that comes with the futility of growth, China still hangs on to the idea that environmental issues should be addressed in order to revamp productive growth. But here, by contrast, the Suzhou Eco-town project is toying with the Western restraint model.

The surrounding undeveloped villages—Xijingcun and Jinpu among others—have been captured within the boundaries of the Suzhou Eco-city resort but they have not been modernized. They are authentic run-down villages that have given themselves over to silk embroidery shops (a specialty of the region) so that any frustration at being left out of the massive investment in the area will have been counterbalanced by the promise that they will benefit economically from the hordes of tourists coming to buy their embroidery wares. These undeveloped enclosures fulfill the government's desire to help cultivate a low-impact way of life. This is done by not developing them.

As Shanghai-based Dutch Eco-city architect Neville Mars says, "We don't need many new buildings. The world is already pretty much built."[48] It should be noted that with 30 million Chinese people still reputed to be living in caves and a further 1.7 million "homeless and beggars," including 188,000 under 18-year-olds,[49] the idea of there being too much stuff still rings hollow. Furthermore, "limits to growth" is something that the Chinese working classes haven't heard for a long time, and confronted by the idea of having to forgo a new home in order to address the needs of environmental limits may throw the Eco-city program into starker relief than we usually find in the West.

The lack of "decent and affordable" housing in many urban, let alone rural parts of China, needs to be urgently addressed,[50] so the idea that there are limits to growth would be a philosophically interesting turnaround from rampant Chinese capitalism. But that doesn't stop China from trying, contradictions aside, to find its own version of limits to growth.

Notes

1   Ben-Ami, D., *Ferraris for All: In Defence of Economic Progress.* London: Policy Press, 2010, p. xi.

2   Chatzidakis, A., Larsen, G. and Bishop, S. "Farewell to Consumerism: Countervailing Logics of Growth in Consumption," *Ephemera Journal* 2016, pp. 753–764.

3   Anon, *China: President Jiang Zemin Handbook—Strategic Information and Materials.* USA: International Business Publications, 2015, p. 92.

4   Chong, Florence, "To Get Rich Is Glorious," *Asia Today International*, May 2005, 23(4), p. 5.

5   Kang, Z., *Confessions: An Innocent Life in Communist China*. W. W. Norton & Company, New York, 2007.

6   Shapiro, Judith, *Mao's War Against Nature: Politics and the Environment in Revolutionary China*. Cambridge University Press, 2001.

7   Stewart, T.P., Drake, E.J., Bell, S.M., Wang J., and Scott, R.e., *Surging Steel Imports Put Up To Half A Million U.S. Jobs At Risk*. Stewart & Stewart/The Economic Policy Institute, May 2014. http://www.epi.org/files/2014/Surging-Steel-Imports-05-13-2014.pdf (accessed June 26, 2016).

8   Worldsteel Association, Steel Statistical Yearbook 2015, Worldsteel Committee on Economic Studies (Brussels), October 2015, pp. 1–2.

9   Betts, M., Robinson, G., Blake, N., Burton, C. and Godden, D., *Global Construction 2020*. London: Global Construction Perspectives and Oxford Economics, 2011.

10   Zand, B., "The Coal Monster: Pollution Forces Chinese Leaders to Act," *Der Spiegel*, March 6, 2013. http://www.spiegel.de/international/world/chinese-leaders-forced-to-counter-environmental-pollution-a-886901.html (accessed August 2, 2016).

11   Yu, Hongyuan, *Global Warming and China's Environmental Diplomacy*. Nova Publishers (New York), 2008.

12   Ren, *Urban China*, pp. 23–25.

13   Dong, Stella, *Shanghai: The Rise and Fall of a Decadent City 1842–1949*. William Morrow (New York), 2001. p. 1.

14   Wong, Gary Pui Fung, "Shanghai, China's Capital of Modernity: The Production Of Space And Urban Experience Of World Expo 2010," Doctoral thesis, The University of Birmingham February 2014, p. 123.

15   Wong, "Shanghai, China's Capital of Modernity," p. 126.

16   Citterio, L. and Di Pasquale, J., *Lost in Globalization*. Jamkom, 2015, p. 158, 8.3.

17   Alderman, D., "Housing and Construction Markets," in *UNECE/FAO Forest Products Annual Market Review*, 2012–2013. p. 11, http://www.fs.fed.us/nrs/pubs/jrnl/2013/nrs_2013_alderman_001.pdf.

18   Zheng, Siqi, Kahn, M.E., Sun, W., Luo, D., "Incentives for China's Urban Mayors to Mitigate Pollution Externalities: The Role of the Central Government and Public Environmentalism," *Regional Science and Urban Economics*, Elsevier, 2013. pp. 1–11.

19 Song, L., et al. *China's New Sources of Economic Growth. Reform, Resources, and Climate Change*, Vol. 1. ANU Press (NSW, Australia), 2016. p. 329.

20 Chen, J.-C., "Greening Dispossession: Environmental Governance and Socio-spatial Transformation in Yixing, China," in *Locating Right to the City in the Global South*, ed. T. Samara, et al. New York: Routledge, 2012. pp. 81–104.

21 Goodall, C., "Peak Stuff" Did the UK reach a maximum use of material resources in the early part of the last decade? chris@carboncommentary.com, October 13, 2011.

22 Monbiot, G., "Consume More, Conserve More: Sorry, But We Just Can't Do Both," *The Guardian*, November 24, 2014.

23 Department of Economic and Social Affairs, "World Economic and Social Survey 2013 Sustainable Development Challenges," United Nations (New York), 2013. E/2013/50/Rev. 1 ST/ESA/344, p. 54.

24 Keeley, J., and Zheng, Y. (eds), *Green China Chinese: Insights on Environment and Development*. London: International Institute for Environment and Development, 2011. p. 15.

25 Kunmin, Zhang, Zongguo, Wen and Liying, Peng, "Environmental Policies in China: Evolvement, Features and Evaluation," *China Population Resource and Environment*, 2007, 17(2), 1–7.

26 Gardner, Sarah, "LA Smog: The Battle Against Air Pollution," *Marketplace*, July 14, 2014, http://www.marketplace.org/ accessed (accessed October 25, 2015).

27 Ningbo Municipal People's Government, "Ningbo: China: Overview," China Radio International, 2012. http://english.ningbo.gov.cn/col/col55/ (accessed June 15, 2016).

28 MacIntyre, D., "How the Miners' Strike of 1984–85 Changed Britain for Ever," *The New Statesman*, June 16, 2014.

29 Zhang, C. "Beijing Kicks Off Park Drive," *China Daily*, July 6, 2007.

30 Rode, P., Burdett, R., et al., *Cities: Investing in Energy and Resource Efficiency*. United Nations Environment Programme, 2011. p. 481.

31 Yao Ouyang, Y. *The Development of BRIC and the Large Country Advantage*. Springer, 2016. p. 35.

32 Castells, M. and Hall, P., *Technopoles of the World: The Making of 21st Century Industrial Complexes*. Routledge, 1994. pp. 8–11.

33 Hong'e, Mo (ed.), "China's New Development Zone to Takes Shape Near Beijing," www.chinaview.cn, January 28, 2009. http://news.xinhuanet.com/english/2009-01/28/content_10729346.htm.

34   de Jong, M., Yu, C., Joss, S., Wennersten, R., Yu, L., Zhang, X. and
      Ma, X. "Eco City Development in China: Addressing the Policy
      Implementation Challenge," *Journal of Cleaner Production* 2016,
      134, pp. 31–41.

35   Fang, H., et al., "China's Housing Boom," *Vox*, May 27, 2015. http://
      voxeu.org/article/china-s-housing-boom.

36   United Nations, "World Economic and Social Survey 2013:
      Sustainable Development Challenges," *Department of Economic and
      Social Affairs of the United Nations*, Chapter III, 2013, p. 61.

37   UNEP, *Towards a Green Economy: Pathways to Sustainable
      Development and Poverty Eradication—A Synthesis for Policy
      Makers*. United Nations Environment Programme, 2011. p. 3.

38   UNEP, *Towards a Green Economy*. Table 1, p. 7.

39   Anon, *Bhutan's 2015 Gross National Happiness Index*. Centre for
      Bhutan Studies and GNH Research, November 2015. http://www
      .grossnationalhappiness.com/ (accessed August 15, 2016).

40   Anon, China GDP Annual Growth Rate: Forecast 2016–2020,
      Trading Economics, August 15, 2016. http://www.tradingeconomics
      .com/china/gdp-growth-annual/forecast (accessed August 15, 2016).

41   Jack Ma interviewed in Gandel, S., "Alibaba CEO Jack Ma Says
      Slower Growth Is Good for China," *Fortune*, January 23, 2015.

42   Seeliger, Leanne and Turok, Ivan, "Towards Sustainable Cities:
      Extending Resilience with Insights from Vulnerability and Transition
      Theory," *Sustainability* 2013, 5(5), pp. 2108–2128.

43   Agence France-Presse, "China has 'duty to humanity' to Curb
      Pollution, Premier Says," *The Guardian*, Reuters, November 4, 2015
      (accessed March 19, 2016).

44   Chang, Liu and Haoran, Zhang, Launch Ceremony of "Exploring
      China's Charm City with Sustainable Development Potential," *Held
      in Beijing*, March 29, 2014. http://en.ss-ceo.com/down/2014-04/272.
      shtml (accessed April 20, 2016).

45   Wu, Fulong, *Planning for Growth: Urban and Regional Planning in
      China*. Routledge (London), 2015. p. 177.

46   Anon, "Yaxi (CHI)—It has been founded the Cittaslow China
      National Coordinating Committee," *Cittaslow*, August 6, 2016.
      http://www.cittaslow.org/article/yaxi-chi-is-been-founded-the-
      cittaslow-china-national-coordinating-committee-1 (accessed
      August 12, 2016).

47   Honore, C. "Recession? The Perfect Time to Slow Down," *The
      Guardian*, July 24, 2008.

48 Mars, Neville, "The Lowdown on Building Ecocities," speech at
    InkTalks, Singapore, published: August 15, 2016.

49 Li, Cao, "Strife on the Streets," *China Daily*, October 13, 2009.

50 Huang, Youqin and Li, Si-ming, *Housing Inequality in Chinese Cities*,
    Vol. 115, Routledge Contemporary China Series, 2014, p. 119.

CHAPTER FOUR

Industrial Heartland/ Rural Backwater

The train from Shanghai Hongqiao reaches speeds of up to 350 km/hr but still takes nearly six hours to reach Tianjin, one of the five great national cities in China, situated on the northeast coast. I arrived late one evening at Tianjin West Station, an iconic piece of architecture designed by von Gerkan, Marg and Partners Architects, the same architects who designed Nanhui Eco-city (see Chapter 6). Like many other Chinese stations this one too is designed at a colossal scale to cater for the frenetic human traffic in Golden Week when huge numbers take to public transport. The architects say that the design is a homage to "cathedrals of traffic" with a 60-m-high central barrel vault nave and platform aisles.

The so-called Golden Week marks the founding of the People's Republic of China on October 1, 1949, but it became an official part of the holiday calendar only in 2000. Since then, it has evolved into a one-week travel blitz. The second Golden Week is in January–February and marks China's Lunar New Year celebrations. In October 2015, during a mere seven-day period over 13 million tourists visited Beijing and an estimated 100 million people traveled by train. I last visited Tianjin in 2014 on one of the 350 non–Golden Week evenings of the year and the station looked cavernously empty. I jumped on the empty metro and was in my hotel by midnight, having seen almost nothing of Tianjin.

The following morning I was not able to see anything of Tianjin either, but this time it was predominantly because of the smog levels. My fellow hotel guests were advised to stay indoors where the views extended from the window to the edge of the pavement. I sneaked outside—into a sea of expectorating locals—but quickly sought refuge.

The hotel information desk explained that the new Asian Infrastructure Investment Bank (AIIB) was being launched in Beijing the following week and therefore the government had issued a Blue Sky (*lan tian*) directive. In other words, it had been decreed that there should be no air pollution while the foreign dignitaries were in the capital city, so, even though Beijing is 100 km away, the factories in Tianjin would be shut or put on reduced load for the duration of the conference for fear of a bad smell leading to a bad press. Several weeks later, in November 2014, the Asia-Pacific Economic Cooperation (APEC) conference added to the pressure. Many cities in the region banned cars, shut down steel production, and even told ordinary people to keep their household heating down to "the lowest acceptable level"[1] during the summit.

The real consequence of these diktats was that during my visit to Tianjin, which was a week before the first of these global events in Beijing, Tianjin's factories were working double and triple time to make up the difference: spewing out as much as possible to hit preproduction targets and to minimize the effect of the imminent manufacturing slowdown. Beijing would soon enjoy the clearest skies for many years. I was choking in the present so that bankers might breathe in the future. Subsequently, the phrase "APEC-blue" was coined by Chinese bloggers to mean something fleeting, something too good to be true.

Tianjin Eco-city is 80 km farther east, but if the smog could affect Beijing, then it can certainly waft over the Eco-city. Its problem is that it is a mere 10 km away from Bohai Bay, the industrial coastal region that includes several giant trade sectors including aviation, car production, petrochemicals, manufacturing, and electronics, as well as having the largest port in Northern China and an active shipbuilding industry. A quick tour around the area will give you a flavor of how hard the brand identity consultants have to work to sell the Eco-city, two hours' walk away. Aside from the Binhai Aircraft Carrier Theme Park, the city region boasts of 583 chemical companies including the giant Tianjin Bohai Chemical

Industry producing caustic soda, rubber, and plastic. Tianjin Heavy Industry is one of the largest steel casting plants in China, six coal-fired power stations (the largest producing 4000 MW—and all six producing the total equivalent of the entire power generation of Nigeria), the China National Coal Group, and the ailing Bohai Steel Group. Essentially, Tianjin Eco-city is on the outskirts of a massive industrial belt, so why is it there and how did it come into existence?

FIGURE 4.1 *Tianjin Eco-city*
Source: © Sino-Singapore Tianjin Eco-City Investment and Development Co. Ltd

Tianjin Eco-city is a Sino-Singapore venture that was given the go-ahead in 2007 (Figure 4.1). The eleventh Five-Year Plan (2006–2010) had made a big thing of the national need for a circular economy. Sometimes called a "closed-loop economy," it is an industrial strategy that proposes to link production, consumption, and reuse in a way that distinguishes itself from what McKinsey calls a linear "take–make–dispose economy."[2] It is about minimizing waste to improve efficiency but also to focus on designing products and processes that embed efficient ways of thinking. The Seventeenth National Congress in 2007 pronounced that cities must be efficient and that they would do this by developing a "scientific outlook." As a result of a literal interpretation, technology has become a significant feature of urban policy and practice from then on.

The Bohai region had been chosen against three others: Tangshan in Hebei Province, Baotou in Inner Mongolia, and Urumqi in Xinjiang, all chosen for their desperate need for an industrial cleanup and for improvements in water resource efficiency, the latter being an urgent issue for many of China's northern and western cities. China and Singapore agreed that they would have equal oversight of the plans and the progress of the final choice of the development. Because Tianjin had "greater prospects for commercial viability and long-term economic sustainability," Singapore preferred this location "for its residential housing market potential."[3] There were other reasons including its geographical industrial and distribution potential, and also it was to be sited on predominantly unpopulated salt flats requiring very few people to be relocated and not taking up precious arable land. One report describes the area as "an ecological wasteland comprising saline and alkaline land and polluted water,"[4] thus effectively keeping complaints to a minimum.

The environmental challenges though have been immense, with remediation and reclamation taking a considerable time. While many Western commentators have enjoyed criticizing Tianjin Eco-city as a ghost city, it has been quietly laying the basis of a real urban test bed. The once-contaminated land is now predominantly fertile (although I noticed a considerable number of dead and dying saplings on my officially sanctioned tour), and construction is well under way.

The initial design covers a land area of 30 km^2, with lots of green space, a central valley to give topographical interest, three distinct local neighborhood centers, and four residential areas. As I walked around, it was clear that the plans were already beginning to take shape; although the school was deserted, the offices were only partially occupied and the streets empty. However, these observations in no way refute the likelihood of the city reaching its planned population of 350,000 by around 2020 although, of course, it seems highly unlikely. In 2014, the Singaporean authorities confirmed that there were around 10,000 residents and over 1,000 registered companies already in situ, with many more commuters yet to commit.[5] Three years later and already a three-bedroom apartment costs US$190,000, although that may still hint that there are many more investors than inhabitants. In other chapters, I explore how many other cities are learning from Tianjin's mistakes and are trying to do similar things more cheaply. Consequently, Tianjin Eco-city is having to up the stakes and improve its quality-of-life offering.

In order to convince skeptics of its intentions, China has been forced to demonstrate its eco-ness through the quantitative measurement of its Eco-cities' environmental performance. In 2011, the Chinese Society for Urban Studies created the first checklist of Eco-cities' eco-criteria and formulated twenty-eight indicators in five categories. As anyone who has dealt with eco-labeling will know, it is a turgid tick-box culture of audits, indicators, measurement, and spreadsheets, and the checklisting of Eco-cities has exacerbated the bureaucracy to industrial proportions. The Bellagio Statement of 2012 (a commitment drafted by twenty-two international organizations under the watchful eye of the Rockefeller Foundation) asserts that "there is an ongoing need for research into the comparability of indicators, standards and frameworks," giving rise to a netherworld of consultants who oil—if you excuse the carbon—the cogs of yet more bureaucracy. Here's just a sample of the paper trails and rubber stamping required to attain Eco-city credentials:

The United Nations Habitat Programme has forty-two items on the checklist, including an "eco-civilization indicator system": each item needs to be monitored in order to demonstrate Eco-city compliance.[6] The global BREEAM measurement system includes six urban sustainability criteria; the United Nations Environment Programme has a huge list with twenty-three indicators concerned with native biodiversity alone; then, there are the World Bank's criteria and the ASEAN Model Cities spreadsheet. Since 2010–2011, China has joined in and created twenty-two indicators at the eco-county level, twenty-six at the Eco-city level, nineteen at the eco-garden level, and twenty-two at the eco-province level. For Tianjin Eco-city there are also the twenty-six specific China–Singapore joint criteria that take into account Singaporean national standards.[7] Everything is geared to certificating the eco-ness of Tianjin Eco-city.

The Chinese 3-star environmental monitoring system (similar to US LEED environmental rating) requires one year's operational data to be assessed before a building can be certified. I found that one of the Tianjin Eco-Business Park research centers had turned the heating off to provide a low-energy usage figure in the first year. Fortunately, there were many vacant offices in the building that also helped reduce the recorded energy averages too. Maybe after certification, the workers can finally turn the lights and heating on for real.

————

Aside from political shenanigans, the two criteria that China's emerging middle classes are most concerned about are air and water quality. Of the top ten most polluted cities in China recorded by Greenpeace in 2013, seven were located in and around Tianjin and Hebei Province. Even though China implemented a National Ambient Air Quality indicator system only in 2012, it still doesn't officially monitor PM2.5 (fine matter of up to 2.5 micrometers in diameter, such as soot, dust, and smoke) that the US Environmental Protection Agency considers significantly harmful to respiratory systems, especially among the young and elderly (Table 4.1).

TABLE 4.1 *The changing face of Chinese citizen's concerns*
Source: Pew Research Center, Environmental Concerns on the Rise in China, Pew Research Center's Global Attitudes Project, 19 September 2013, p2. HYPERLINK "http://www.pewglobal.org" www.pewglobal.org. Redrawn by author

| | % Very big problem | | |
	2008%	2012%	2013%	08–13 Change
Safety of food	12	41	38	+26
Quality of manufactured goods	13	33	31	+18
Safety of medicine	9	28	27	+18
Old-age insurance	13	28	30	-17
Air pollution	31	36	47	+16
Corrupt officials	39	50	53	-14
Education	11	23	24	-13
Water pollution	28	33	40	-11
Rich–poor gap	41	43	52	-11
Health care	12	26	23	-11
Worker conditions	13	23	23	-10
Traffic	9	18	19	-10
Crime	17	25	24	+ 7
Corrupt business people	21	32	27	+ 6
Unemployment	22	24	27	+ 5
Electricity shortages	4	8	8	-4
Rising prices	72	60	59	-13

One Hebei-born artist in Beijing made a name for himself in 2015 by wandering around with an industrial vacuum cleaner, sucking up the urban air, and collecting the floating $PM_{2.5+}$ deposits in the filter. After just 100 days, he had reputedly collected enough material to compress it and bake it into a housebrick-shaped object. Some online wags suggested that more pollution is therefore a good thing, as it enables the creation of building materials out of thin air.

But there are real cleaner benefits that derive from urban living. David Owen, author of *Green Metropolis*, notes the benefit of urbanism: "Population density…reduces energy use, carbon emission and waste in all categories."[8] Edward Glaeser, author of *Triumph of the City*, has calculated that an average household in forty-eight major Western metropolitan areas generates up to 35 percent less greenhouse gas emissions than the corresponding suburb. According to Glaeser, "To save the planet build more skyscrapers."[9]

One of the most influential books of recent times on China's pollution problems has been *The River Runs Black* by Elizabeth Economy. It documents with dramatic force the significant problems arising from Chinese industry's flagrant avoidance of pollution controls and health and safety checks and balances. Nowadays, China's water quality statistics—as opposed to the water itself—are some of the most transparent in the world (and ironically, the UK frequently requires a Freedom of Information Act request to access technical data on water quality). In other words, China is making an effort, and it might help for Western critics to be a little more tolerant of their gradual, year-on-year improvements.

For example, it will be 2030 before Chicago's "polluted rivers (are) so clean that people will be able to swim in them."[10] British standards reveal that 20 percent of all waterways are still classified as "poor" or "bad."[11,12] Over 170 years ago, Engels observed the water quality of the River Aire in Leeds: "Like all other rivers in the service of manufacture, (it) flows into the city at one end clear and transparent, and flows out at the other end thick, black, and foul, smelling of all possible refuse."[13] China has an industrial problem that is eminently curable and will surely take less time to resolve than it did in the West.[14,15] Already 15 percent of the dangerously polluted Yellow River, which spills out into Bohai Bay, has been removed. What is even more impressive is that it is investing in potable drinking water projects and in desalination plants to improve the quality and quantity of water available to all.

Air quality is a real problem in China but is also eminently resolvable. The authorities have identified PM_{10} particulates as the main pollutant, and by 2011 concentrations had allegedly decreased to 98 µg/m^3 averaged across eighty-six cities.[16] A 2015 survey showed that this had dropped even further (as a population weighted mean across 190 cities) down to 61 µg/m^3. However, this is still almost three times the World Health Organization-recommended levels, a standard only met by 1 percent of the 500 largest cities in China.[17] Coincidentally, it is about the level experienced in central London as I write.[18] The publicity brochures for Tianjin Eco-city says that it aims to meet these standards (as stipulated in China's new National Ambient Air Quality urban standards) for at least 310 days every year. Clearly, brochures tend to be aimed at a clientele that has the luxury of pontificating on environmental quality, but ironically this is the same class of potential residents that may not be content with the other fifty-five days of noncompliant air quality. Similarly, given that the Tianjin Eco-city website proclaims that the quality of watercourses will reach "industrial use" standards by 2020, it is still not a great advert for an environmentally friendly city.

In recent years, the issue that has most shaken the confidence of people choosing to move to Tianjin Eco-city was the huge explosion in the industrial quarter on August 12, 2015, that killed 173 people, mostly firemen. Even though it was a tragic accident that occurred 10 km away from the Eco-city, the authorities moved swiftly to close down the eighty-five companies that handled hazardous chemicals and to clean up the cyanide contamination. The ravaged ground has now been converted into a memorializing "Eco-park."

––––––

An increasing number of affluent, middle-class Chinese are following the environmental, antipollution logic and downsizing. It seems that we are witnessing the birth of the Chinese drop-out. Fleeing the alleged stresses of modern Chinese urbanism, theirs is a discernable shift to simplicity. In his paper on this relatively new phenomenon, Australian academic Gary Sigley interviews Chinese "lifestyle migrants," many of whom have opted to move from Beijing and live in the town of Dali in Yunnan Province, south China. This is a rural lakeside retreat whose remoteness is manifested by the fact that it was once a place of banishment under Mao. It is now a region popular with tourists precisely because of that remoteness (and presumably nothing to do with the natural marijuana crops). It is considered to be a sufficiently exotic destination that Chinese staycationers are buying holiday homes there. Many are escaping the city permanently for a better quality of life. One says: "I said goodbye to Beijing and goodbye to PM2.5"; another says: "We came for the clean air, sunshine, and relaxed way of life. We didn't come to Dali to live the high life."[19] A best-selling book by two downsizing Beijingers was entitled *Leaving Beijing for Dali: Do What You Like with Whom You Like.*

A romantic retreat to a simpler life has always been a thread running through Chinese philosophical and political thought. Even when, after the First World War, radicalized youth from the Mass Education Speech Corps flooded the countryside to educate the peasants, many students became transformed instead. The innocent youth went with dreams of science and democracy but became enamored by the noble simplicity of life in the countryside. This was the time when Walt Whitman was first being translated into Chinese, admired for his reflections "of the common people."[20]

In her excellent magnum opus, *All Under Heaven*, Jeanne-Marie Gescher writes that in the 1920s "Peking University's students received a lesson in what it meant to be a people...(the city) was less a citadel of omniscience, and more a corruption of the honest, hardworking, long-suffering farming man."[21] Of course, the long-suffering peasantry was actually an aggrieved political force which became the source of uprisings against "imperialists, warlords, corrupt officials, local tyrants and evil gentry,"[22] but still today many romanticize the peasant "traditions" and see them as a wealth of fresh, untainted ideas for the cultural elite. Pritzker prize–winning architect Wang Shu explains: "To live in the countryside with nature has always been an important theme in Chinese culture...regarded as cultural seeds, a source of intellectuals for the larger cities."[23]

In 2011, the Chinese government instituted a Village Beautiful movement—a subset of the Beautiful China project—which has three core objectives. First, ever worried about the revolting masses, China understands that it will not become 100 percent urban and so needs to provide social and infrastructural improvements for those who remain ruralized. Secondly, China's deep-seated belief in food self-sufficiency means that agricultural land and rural farmers are held in high regard and need to be protected in some ways. Thirdly, rebuilding or reconstituting the villages is one way of stimulating the internal domestic consumer economy through investment and tourism. It also should be added that significant numbers of people in rural China live in the most basic conditions and the overarching reason for government investment in rural affairs is to begin to provide for local village communities in a more sensitive manner than ever before. There are unsubstantiated reports that China had 3.7 million villages in 2001, which had been reduced to 2.6 million by 2010, and the research firm GK Dragonomics has estimated that 16 percent of the country's housing stock was demolished between 2005 and 2010.[24] Meanwhile, in urban areas there are 2 billion m^2 of new building space added every year, and in early 2016 there was reputed to be 720 million m^2 of unsold housing.[25] These mismatches need to be confronted.

The process of engagement in the Village Beautiful programs has become a testing ground in central government versus local governance. Local party bureaucrats are posted to remote villages for up to three years in order to determine the priorities and possibilities for economically efficient improvements in villages. After such an arduous secondment, a young Party member can expect promotional rewards. In many places, and on certain issues, there has been a shift from central Party spending directives toward participatory democracy whereby locals can voice their opinions about the primary problems to be resolved and where ordinary people believe that money should be targeted. Admittedly, "democracy with Chinese characteristics" tends only to relate to participatory budgeting—a transparent accounting process where finances are provided and locals simply decide where, and where not, to spend it.

While it is an organizational model that can potentially empower local people to decide on what gets built, it still tends to be an "an elite-dominated process"[26] made by the village head rather than the local people. In some ways this is understandable. Through this process many thousands of miles of rural road networks have been constructed, all villages will receive flush toilets and electricity by 2020; and between 2006 and 2010, 200,000 libraries were built in rural areas, clearly significant benefits that may not have been high on the priority list of the more immediate needs of subsistence farmers. So, benefits accrue, but it should be acknowledged that the democratic deficit in these rural councils—like in China itself—is a problem. In village councils, the parameters for the so-called open debate tend to have been made in advance and the democratic will merely resolves how to implement predetermined directives.

In Jiangsu Province alone there are 10,000 managers overseeing improvements in 198,000 rural villages. By calling this the New Socialist Countryside Movement, the authorities are playing with fire with visions of collective ownership, peasant councils, production teams, and other Red Cultural reminders. One councilor likened it to "mobiliz(ing) the masses." Sometimes the tensions between leaders and the led can become all too apparent. In Ganzhou, Jiangxi Province, officials noted "the importance of rural participation, provided it would not hinder policy implementation." But, of course, it remains for the national Party to be the ultimate arbiter in disputes between locals and errant officials over misdirected funds or unsuccessful projects, reinforcing the social structure in which a "benign" authority oversees the democratic rules of engagement. As a result, village representation is ironically an instrument for strengthening state power.[27] Even so, this experiment is still an interesting shift from the more blatant top-down ways that decisions are usually made.

Another shift is the way in which the Village Beautiful program represents a "conceptual shift from urban-orientated development." Professor Wu Fulong suggests that left-behind villages require improvements and that villagers have been ill-served by urbanism. Urban areas have drained villages of their working-age generation, who travel from the countryside to find work, leaving rural China peopled by the elderly looking after young children. These youngsters are known as *liushou ertong*, or "left-behind children." The resulting demographic (and social) problems have been compounded by the backwardness of many rural areas where farmers have been left to their own devices, creating what one writer called a "Rabelaisian appetite for fertiliser,"[28] leading to soil pollution and degradation. In recent years then, a renewed focus on the physical condition of villages has been to address their population flight and their infrastructural plight. It doesn't necessarily address their semifeudal status or their economic ambitions. Indeed, in some ways the Village Beautiful program is intended to maintain their unspoiled, underdeveloped way of life and to use it as a selling point.

For example, at the end of 2011, the Chinese authorities passed legislation protecting "Intangible Cultural Heritage" (ICH), that is, the rituals, practices and skills of local people in local areas. ICH celebrates oral traditions, indigenous knowledge, and even "practices concerning nature and the universe."[29] In many ways it also celebrates poverty and stasis and frowns on development as a threat to the purity of the local cultural experience. A great number of private museums have sprung up in remote rural regions of China to formalize local culture with over sixteen "ecomuseums" for the "protection of natural resources and the development of cultural identity." We will look at these in more detail in the next chapter, but let's explore a couple of examples here.

Xinzhang village in Yunnan Province hosts the Museum of Handcraft Paper designed by TAO Architects. Making paper has long been a skilled craft in this remote forested region and this provides the local peasants—those that haven't yet benefited from China's economic miracle—with plenty of labor-intensive cultural activities to keep them occupied. The Chinese culture minister, Ma Wenhui, claimed that "cultural legacies with China's ethnic communities are facing an onslaught from modern urbanization and civilization,"[30] but the danger is that some of these villages are becoming frozen monuments to the past. The architect proudly boasts that since every family in Tengchong is involved in papermaking, "the entire village functions as a living museum."[31]

Take Anhui Province in east China. It is one of the historically poorest provinces, and the local authorities are proposing agritourism as the way forward. It is selling the rural culture of a farming community as a marketable leisure commodity in 300 impoverished villages. The intention is that 400,000 villagers will be lifted out of poverty, and as tourists, attracted to the unspoiled nature of the area, will buy stuff. It encourages local people to hold onto their history and traditions so that they can educate a generation that hasn't known rural hardship.

Conversely, "ecological migration" policies in Inner Mongolia are having the opposite effect by breaking up many of the "last redoubts of Mongol community life"[32] in order to safeguard the environment from what is deemed to be (disputed by some) harmful farming techniques. In the Alashan District of Inner Mongolia, China, farmers' land is being returned to forest and animal breeding grounds are being converted to pasture lands to deal with decades of overgrazing, soil erosion, and creeping desertification. These farmers traditionally survive on low-yielding, poor-quality soil, working all hours for meager rewards. As a result, the soil has been further degraded and the authorities are now returning it to grassland or using it for the cultivation of fast-growing sand willow trees to prevent desertification. There are many sad stories of old people being asked to leave their crumbling homesteads and relocate to new cities like Ordos Kangbashi for example, a city built in the desert at such a grandiose civic scale that it is incontrovertibly alienating for people used to life on the prairie.

Adam Smith and Song Ting's 2014 documentary *The Land of Many Palaces* tells the story of Ordos Kangbashi and reveals how rural farmers like these are being taken off their land and corralled into high-rise urban enclosures with scant regard for acclimatization. It is a progressive social improvement in their access to services and for opportunities for the younger generation, but no less heartrending for that. In the film, one old man who has been relocated to a new apartment shows us around the fake Mongolian farm constructed in the middle of his residential complex (with a fake water well and "ducks raised by the exhibition hall people"). He announces proudly that "it's to show the next generation how life was like." What he means is, how life was like for him a mere one or two months earlier.

Ordos Kangbashi, an oversized urban area in the middle of nowhere, is undoubtedly trying to offer farmers a better standard of living while protecting a fragile environment. A similar motivation drives the Village Beautiful movement, seeking to improve rural conditions for farmers in a more nuanced way, retaining them *in situ* to reduce the pressure to construct new relocation apartments. However ham-fisted these attempts may be, critics of urbanization have tended to overromanticize the everyday reality of back-breaking farm labor in their desire to sanctify the environment. Critics of urban problems often bend the stick too far and praise the nobility of rural simplicity in a way that would make Mao blush.

Rurality is becoming so appealing in the minds of eco-advocates that UK-based architect CJ Lim has designed an Eco-city in Guang Ming, northwest of Shenzhen in Guangdong Province, where "lush grazing and arable land can be found on the roofs of the huge circular towers that make up the city." The architectural drawings of what this city will look like show farmers squatting among the crops while browsing laptops, implying that this is farming with a sexy techno-twist. To further emphasize the harmonious relationship with nature, Lim explains how lychee orchards will act as air filters and biogas buses will whisk people from crop to crop.[33] The international architectural and engineering company Arup has designed Wanzhuang Eco-city that also fetishizes the rural. Its website states that "preserving, utilising and enhancing the local knowledge and farming skills of Wanzhuang's residents is vital. The rural landscape promotes close contact with nature, a proven source of well-being."[34] Actually, these Eco-cities are attempting to capture the nobility of the peasantry and the so-called integrity of farm labor within a giant metropolitan setting. Architect Wei Yang is designing a "truly exciting, eco-friendly…series of farm park complexes" in Daxing, Beijing, not too far from Zaha Hadid's plans for the world's biggest airport.

I am prepared to eat my words, but Arup's city for 400,000 people modeled on agricultural production seems to be such a category error that it will probably never be built. CJ Lim's proposal for a city with farms on the roof prioritizes self-sufficiency, which is such a strangely insular agrarian reference point for a country that is aspiring to dispel references to its underdeveloped status that it too may just remain on the drawing board. Wei's Beijing farms are surely a juxtaposition too far. These and other imperious designs seek to change the terms of the debate away from China's love of materialistic consumption and toward a simpler coexistence with nature.

That said, back in 2004, the Communist Party of China adopted a document on agriculture that stated that "industry should nurture agriculture, and cities should support the countryside."[35] This statement refers to the New Socialist Countryside Movement that has subsequently become a big thing in urban policy circles, applied not just to villages. One Eco-city resident, when asked why they have chosen to live in an ecologically urban environment, is quoted as saying, "The gain for us is not monetary; it's about building a new socialist rural society."[36]

The Village Beautiful program exemplifies a similar—typically Chinese—contradiction: it is attempting to enhance "the quality of tranquil urban life" at the same time as promoting the "great market potential" of agricultural land areas. In the latter, it is common to see armies of electric sightseeing buses ferrying hordes of sightseers between agri-tourist resorts, and even though these are beginning to annoy many rural residents, they bring much-needed money and investment. Where it works, it is held up as a model, to dispel references to where it doesn't. The state well understands that locals can become mobilized by cash, and if enough villagers are keen to try out a Village Beautiful arrangement, then plans are actioned. Through this program, the government is exploring ways to upgrade failing communities and derelict community facilities rather than razing them and relocating people. At its most basic, Village Beautiful is providing much-needed improvements in infrastructure to some of those most in need while not tearing down existing homes and communities to build new. Fortunately, the peculiarity of Chinese fealty means that in some cases local farmers are even helping protect, maintain, and even add to the initial Village Beautiful physical improvements in the social fabric by working for free on upgrading communal properties.

Wu Fulong notes that this countryside beautification strategy represents "a more forceful shift from urban-rural dualism to urban-rural integration,"[37] hinting at a connection with Ebenezer Howard's late Victorian "Town-Country" dialectic. (Ebenezer Howard is often thought of as the father of the Garden City movement, and his idea of uniting the efficiencies of the town and the calm of the country kick-started a radical urban movement at the start of the twentieth century in Britain.) Since the turn of the twenty-first century, his book has been taught in most Urban Planning departments in China, and the concepts are finding their way into a generation of Chinese Garden City developments and Village Beautiful programs. So, in typical fashion, China is absorbing, reinterpreting, and refashioning ideas from the West and is trying to make them appropriate for its own conditions.

The parts of China's contemporary urban strategy that resonate with the UK Garden City movement and the American City Beautiful movement of a century ago are that it emphasizes a "sense of loss"[38] resulting from a period of rapid industrialization and the yearning for a more considerate phase of development. In America in the late twentieth century—contemporaneous with Ebenezer Howard's ideals—polluted, congested cities like Chicago recognized that they needed to reform and provide "the best conditions for living."[39] Demands arose for a better quality of life and a romantic attachment to nature and wilderness that was being lost in the rush to urbanize.

It forced the introduction of parks, gardens, and landscaping into the city. For some commentators, these urban gains were a consequence of a prevailing sense of pessimism with a dehumanizing city. Their optimistic response sought to make improvements: to make the contemporary urban world a better place.[40]

Late-twentieth-century American designers like Calvert Vaux and Frederick Olmsted and urbanists like Daniel Burnham were heavily influenced by the picturesque romance of Thoreau and John Muir, striving for an urban pastoral release from the noise and stress of the city. Instead of withdrawing to the countryside (as some Beijingers are doing in Dali), Olmsted, the designer of New York's Central Park, created man-made landscapes that could give ordinary city dwellers "greater enjoyment of scenery than they could otherwise have consistently with convenience within a given space."[41] Here was a human-centric and democratizing environmental gift to the city for ordinary people to enjoy. Across industrial America, these new urban park experiments formed part of the valuable infrastructural improvement that was necessary to lift American cities out of the squalor, pollution, and overcrowding of that period.

Fast forward 100+ years and there is something similar going on in China. The Chinese official news agency Xinhua announced the Bureau of Landscape and Forestry's plans to provide Beijing with ten new parks by the end of 2016. The grand plan is to create over 2,300 hectares of green space by 2021; that's the equivalent of seven Central Parks or sixteen of London's Hyde Parks. As part of the green spaces initiative, 85 percent of Beijing's residents would be able to access a park within 500 m of their home.[42] Already 30 percent of all green space in Beijing is publicly accessible. The historic capital city of Xi'an in Shaanxi Province has reportedly added 2,000 hectares of green space over the last few years.[43]

Sadly Chinese statistics like these are almost impossible to verify, especially as "green space" can mean trees at the side of the road rather than a dedicated park. Suffice to say that China recognizes that many of its cities are functional, gray, and grim and is seeking to beautify them somewhat. (The ubiquity of delightfully ivy-clad concrete motorway overpasses across China is something that urban planners the world over can surely learn from.) China does urban landscaping particularly well and has a huge reserve army of cheap maintenance staff. The point is that it is now designing and managing urban developments in a radically new way to include the provision of more green spaces, parks, and gardens as "an integral part of citizens' welfare."[44]

China has made a global name for itself as the home of the huge, the superlative, the hypercity but is now toying with the idea that it is "necessary to abandon image making, up-scaling and the construction of mega-urban projects…(instead) 'beautiful China' aims to develop a sustainable and ecologically friendly environment."[45] Clearly, China is still designing urban agglomerations, constructing many cities and towns, and building thousands of new buildings, so this is not to suggest that China has had a complete change of heart. It simply confirms that there are contradictory pressures acting upon it at this particular moment in its development.

The country of masterplanning, of the urban super-project, of the big, bold visions, of the *grand projects* and rapid city-building ambitions of just a few years ago is finding that many of them are not very good. When, in 2015, China featured Beijing as its most "liveable city," Weibo bloggers saw the funny side. "Best joke of the week," said one. "Perhaps the news should have been published on 1 April," said another. The reality of China's urban messiness has forced the authorities to launch a "National Plan on New Urbanization" that places "people-oriented urbanization as an essential value." What this means remain to be seen but the American version—the New Urban movement—predominantly fetishizes the reduction of traffic congestion, for example.

Secondly, President Xi Jinping's crackdown on corrupt urban vanity projects has also pushed local Party officials to approve more modest projects, not wanting to be held accountable for the next generation of white elephants and ghost cities. Thirdly, they have discovered that it is cheaper and easier to remediate an existing city than to build a pristine city from scratch. Fourthly, the wide open spaces and civic pomp of many new cities is believed to have the potential to ferment a sense of grievance at the disparities between the grandiloquent lifestyles of the wealthy and the everyday lives of many of its ordinary people. In hushed tones, Party bureaucrats worry about the Gini coefficient (a measurement of income disparity in which 0 represents social equality and 1 represents total inequality. It is said that 0.4 is the point at which unrest kicks in, although there is no theoretical framework for this assertion).[46] Of course, social stability remains the central Party's foremost concern.

The final aspect of China's interest in early-twentieth-century urban planning is the desire to experiment with more nuanced means of social control. In a single-party state, social control and authoritarianism lurk not too far under the surface but as we have seen, China is desperately keen to experiment with notional autonomy—within limits. The democratic compromise of the Victorian era, where laissez-faire policies were countered by strong social values, led John Ruskin (and others in the nineteenth-century Art and Crafts movement) to claim that "the art of any country is the exponent of its social and political virtues."[47] Such ethical resolve often found spatial expression in the illiberal work of early urban designers and their "community-building" acolytes.

A century or so ago, for example, Daniel Burnham sought in Chicago to build a city in which parks would be designed "for health and good order...preventing crime, promoting cleanliness and diminishing disease." American steel magnate Andrew Carnegie who was an advocate of "free libraries, parks, and means of recreation, by which men are helped in body and mind" argued against charitable spending that might "encourage the slothful, the drunken, the unworthy."[48] Many of the urban social reformers of that time, on both sides of the Atlantic, saw the city as a den of existing or potential iniquity and of vice and moral decline and proposed that the city should be metaphorically sanitized through social health initiatives.[49]

I am not saying that this is happening in the same way in China. The fact that by 2010 China laid claim to 118 National Hygienic Cities, 28 National Hygienic Urban Neighbourhoods, and 377 National Hygienic Counties[50] is not the same as the social hygiene movement in the UK in the late twentieth century. Far from it. Indeed, the recent hygienic interventions in Chinese towns and cities were vitally necessary physical and medical rather than social cleanup campaigns. We'll explore China's social interventions in the next chapter.

In general, China's urban health initiatives are related to its antipollution drive, while historically Western campaigners were engaged in a moral cleanup. At the start of the twentieth century in the UK, Patrick Geddes, deemed by some to be the first master planner of the modern age[51] (and a fellow Scottish influence on Ebenezer Howard), was interested in more virulent interpretation of social hygiene.[52] Geddes was an avowed eugenicist, as were many established figures of the day.[53] Howard's famous proposal for the first Garden City, for example, featured "Epileptic Farms," an "Insane Asylum," and a "Home for Inebriates."[54] I include this as a reference point—simply because it is worth remembering the social and political context from 100 years ago in Western history. It is not intended to inform a direct comparison between China and the West today and it doesn't disparage the very real benefit of these original Garden City urban design interventions. The authors of *The Urban Design Readers* point out that many urban reformers of the early nineteenth century were not overtly eugenic, racist, or social Darwinist but merely interested in the calming influence of social control. There lies the similarity with China today and indeed of environmental discourse everywhere. What was advocated in the City Beautiful movement was "not coercive…(but) a social religion." The environmental city as an ideological construct.

As such, there is a normative, behavioral, *and* coercive element to urban planning. In contemporary China its most obvious expression is the *hukou*. The *hukou* (pronounced *hoo-koh*) is a registration document that formalizes the urban/rural divide. Even though it is quite oblique to compare it to social Darwinism, it is the case that through the use of the *hukou* certain sections of Chinese society are condemned to live in an exclusionary status where they are denied access, or granted limited access, to the city, to healthcare, to accommodation and schooling. It is a geographically predeterministic system as opposed to a racial segregation (although others might argue that there is a close segregationist correlation with the racial treatment of minorities in China).

This chapter has explored the urban/rural divide, and, in China, the *hukou* is the formalized expression of that segregation. The *hukou* dictates one's social status at birth. It is an immigrant registration document in one's own country that can restrict access to services, provisions, and education, depending on *where* you were born.

Even though there have been great strides in liberalizing the *hukou* registration system in China in the last few years, migrant workers—those who have traveled from their hometowns to find work—are legally obliged to register in their place of temporary residence. This means that they are temporary residents. They have no automatic rights and their children will be required to register for education in their original hometown, which will undoubtedly have poorer facilities and standards than the big metropolitan areas. Consequently, there are many millions of hidden laborers evading the system.

The US ethnographer Mary Ann O'Donnell, who has lived in and documented the city and urban villages of Shenzhen since 1995 (the beginning of that city's startling metamorphosis), notes that its actual population size is still shrouded in mystery. She points out that while the Shenzhen Party Secretary Ma Xingrui says that the population of her adopted city is twenty million, the administrative population hovers at eighteen million, while the city itself has never admitted to more than fifteen million. Only four million people have Shenzhen *hukou*, that is, they were born there; another eight million have permanent residency, that is, they have obtained legal rights to stay by whatever means; and another five to eight million "float" unofficially within the city.[55]

The way that it is frequently explained—or excused—by Chinese themselves is that as more and more people crowded into the new cities in the 1950s, the concomitant pressures on the urban fabric caused by overcrowding and social tensions forced the government to invent a way of halting overcrowding. The *hukou* became the central institutional mechanism defining the city–countryside relationship.

In fact, the *hukou* has a dual role. As we have seen, it determines whether a person is designated urban or rural (and a new category of temporary or semiurban has since been added). But it also designates if the person is an agricultural worker or a nonagricultural worker. In an early paper by Cornell University East Asia specialist Mark Selden, the *hukou* was simply a "demographic strategy that restricted urbanization."[56] Moving within cities or between small towns has always been relatively easy but getting an urban *hukou* for a big city has only ever been easy for wealthy or educated migrants. Sometimes knowing someone in authority can grease the wheels and help a migrant obtain a *hukou* designation change. But for poor people, one's designation at birth can blight you for life—like the Indian caste system.

China has long boasted that the *hukou* has avoided the terrible kinds of squalid shantytowns that one sees around Third World cities, suggesting that this is what happens when you have unrestricted flow. In his highly readable account of street life in everyday Shanghai, American journalist Rob Schmitz hints that the *hukou* might be a "necessary evil," and perhaps the only way that the authorities had of protecting and raising the standards of living of the country overall.[57] But as a nefarious system that restricts freedom of movement, limits life chances, and restrains the freedom of the individual, it needs more forthright criticism, I think.

If readers are wondering how such exclusionary policies could happen in one of the world's leading economies, it has to be said that discrimination is a casual fact of life in China where many of the more politically correct rules don't apply. Many commentators argue for *hukou* reform, suggesting that it would be too disruptive to abolish—but abolition is surely the only legitimate demand from those who endorse freedom and favor meaningful democratic social engagement.

That said, reforms are obviously welcome, and since early 2016, official *hukou* policy now decrees that every city—not just the small ones—is obliged to provide residency status and thus access to basic public services to anyone who has lived, worked, or studied in that city for at least six months, regardless of *hukou* designation.

In China, urban land is owned by the state and rural land is owned by collectives (there is considerably more nuance in reality but this conveys a general truth). Under Article 10 of China's constitution, the government may, in the "public interest and in accordance with the provisions of law" take back land into its own ownership after compensating the occupier. Another way for the state to develop land owned by agricultural workers is for it simply to change the *hukou* designation of the farmers to "nonagricultural" (i.e., "urban") so that they lose agricultural property rights, but get paid off and gain city status. Just ten years ago, one-fifth of the urban population existed as a result of this kind of administrative paper reclassification.

This introduces a further complication or contradiction in the *hukou* debate. In recent years, migrant laborers working in urban areas have begun to show an active disinterest in changing their *hukou* status. Research indicates that fewer than half want to convert to an urban *hukou*, preferring instead to retain their historically privileged status on the land to protect their right to crops that they hold with their agricultural *hukou*. An article on *hukou* reform in *Migration Letters* journal states that "only 10.7 percent of rural Sichuan migrant workers are willing to transfer their residency and accounts to urban settings."[58] And why not? They enjoy their various legal entitlements if they remain agricultural *hukou* holders: the right to land and its management, the right to a homestead, the right of collective income distribution, as well as access to grain subsidies and often leniency in family planning quotas.[59] They don't get the education, healthcare, or housing quality that their urban *hukou* counterparts do, but they are making economically rational decisions. In their equation, the lure of city status is not enough.

To sum up, some farmers leave the land entirely and gain urban *hukou* and resettle in urban areas. Some give up their farmland for monetary reward but stay in their old homes, thus retaining their rural *hukou*. Others leave the land entirely but still retain their rural *hukou* precisely because of its potential market value, while the poorest and most unfortunate leave the land voluntarily or forcibly, lose their rural *hukou* but are not granted a full urban *hukou*. And many wealthy urbanites are looking at downsizing to smogless country retreats. The rich–poor and urban–rural divide is not as clear-cut as it once was.

Notes

1 Bloomberg News and Zhou, Xin, "China Goes from Supplicant to Power Player as APEC Host," *Bloomberg News*, November 7, 2014.

2 McKinsey & Co, et al., "Towards the Circular Economy: Accelerating the Scale-Up Across Global Supply Chains," *World Economic Forum*, January 2014, p. 13.

3 Chang, I-Chun Catherine, Leitner, H. and Sheppard, E. "A Green Leap Forward Eco State Restructuring and the Tianjin Binhai Eco City Model," *Regional Studies*, 2016, pp. 1–15.

4 UNEP, South-South Cooperation Case Study the Sino-Singapore Tianjin Eco-City: A Practical Model for Sustainable Development, UNEP, March 2013.

5 News release, Sino-Singapore Tianjin Eco-City Investment and Development Co Ltd (SSTEC) welcomes new Deputy CEO from the Singapore Government, March 20, 2014. http://www.tianjineco-city .com/en/NewsContent.aspx?news_id=13656&column_id=10349 (accessed August 22, 2016).

6 UNHSP, UN-Habitat Global Activities Report 2015 United Nations Human Settlements Programme 2015, p. 42.

7   Joss, S., Cowley, R., de Jong, M., Müller, B., Park, B.-S., Rees, W., Roseland, M. and Rydin, Y., *Tomorrow's City Today: Prospects for Standardising Sustainable Urban Development*. London: University of Westminster (International Eco-Cities Initiative), 2015. pp. 53.

8   Green, J., "The Urban Dream," *China Dialogue*, March 15, 2010. https://www.chinadialogue.net/article/show/single/en/3535-The -urban-dream.

9   Glaeser, E., "Green Cities, Brown Suburbs: To Save the Planet, Build More Skyscrapers—Especially in California," *City Journal*, Winter 2009 cited in Cities and Climate Change: An Urgent Agenda, *Urban Development Series Knowledge Paper*, The International Bank for Reconstruction and Development/The World Bank, December 2010, Vol. 10.

10   Kamin, B., "New Rivers Plan: Bold Strokes and Big Challenges," *Chicago Tribune*, August 17, 2016.

11   Defra, *River Basin Districts Surface Water and Groundwater Classification (Water Framework Directive) (England and Wales) Direction 2009*. Department of Environment Food and Rural Affairs, 1999.

12   Sara Priestley, "Water Framework Directive: Achieving Good Status of Water Bodies," *House of Commons Briefing Paper*, Number CBP 7246, November 27, 2015, p. 13.

13   Engels, F., *The Condition of the Working-Class in England in 1844 (Preface written in 1892)*, trans. Wischnewetzky, F.K. Cambridge University Press, 2010, p. 39.

14   China Water Risk, 2014 State of Environment Report Review, July 14, 2015, http://chinawaterrisk.org/resources/analysis -reviews/2014-state-of-environment-report-review (accessed March 26, 2016).

15   WEPA, *Outlook of Water Environmental, Ministry of the Environment, Japan*. Institute for Global Environmental Strategies, 2009. p. 18.

16   Wang, Litao, et al., "Assessment of Urban Air Quality in China Using Air Pollution Indices (APIs)," *Journal of the Air & Waste Management Association* 2013, 63(2), pp. 170–178.

17   Zhang, Yan-Lin and Cao, Fang, "Fine Particulate Matter ($PM_{2.5}$) in China at a City Level," *Scientific Reports* 2015, 5, Article number: 14884, pp. 1–12.

18 London Air Quality Network, PM10 Pollution Episodes, January 17–January 26, 2017. http://www.londonair.org.uk/london/asp/publicepisodes.asp?species=All&region.

19 Sigley, G., "The Mountain Changers: Lifestyle Migration in Southwest China," *Asian Highlands Perspectives*, February 2016, 40, pp. 233–296.

20 Li Xilao, "Walt Whitman in China," *Walt Whitman Quarterly Review* 1986, 3(1), pp. 1–8.

21 Gescher, J.-M., *All Under Heaven: China's Dreams of Order*. Kaduba House, 2015. pp. 348–349.

22 Tse-tung, Mao, *Notes On Mao Tse-Tung's "Report on an Investigation of the Peasant Movement in Hunan."* Peking: Foreign Languages Press, 1968. p. 11.

23 Dong, Yiping, "Will Wang Shu's Village Be Nothing But an Imagined Form of Rural Life for Urbanites?" *Architectural Review*, November 17, 2015.

24 The Economist, "Creative Destruction," *Economist Magazine*, November 30, 2013.

25 Li, Jing and Gan, Nectar, "China's Guangdong Province Turns to State Firms to Buy Up Its Large Inventory of Unsold Homes," *South China Morning Post*, March 6, 2016.

26 He, Baogang. "Civic Engagement Through Participatory Budgeting in China: Three Different Logics at Work," *Public Administration & Development*, 2011, 31(122–133), pp. 122–133.

27 Looney, K.E., "China's Campaign to Build a New Socialist Countryside: Village Modernization, Peasant Councils, and the Ganzhou Model of Rural Development," *The China Quarterly* 2015, 224, pp. 909–932.

28 Navarro, P. and Autry, G., *Death by China: Confronting the Dragon—A Global Call to Action*. Pearson Prentice Hall (New Jersey), 2011. p. 180.

29 UNESCO, *What Is Intangible Cultural Heritage?* United Nations Educational Scientific and Cultural Organisation, 2011. p. 3.

30 Zheng, Limin (ed.), "China's First Law for Preserving Intangible Cultural Heritage Passed," CCTV.com, February 27, 2011. http://english.cntv.cn/program/newsupdate/20110227/103995.shtml (accessed August 10, 2016).

31 Williams, A., "TAO's Museum of Handcraft Paper, Xinzhuang, China." *The Architectural Review*, March 27, 2012.

32 Atwood, C.P., China's Regional Ethnic Autonomy Law: Does It Protect Minority Rights? Rayburn House meeting, London, Monday, April 11, 2005. http://www.smhric.org/news_76.htm.

33 http://www.cjlim-studio8.com/mp-guangming-smart.swf.

34 http://www.arup.com/projects/wanzhuang_eco-city.

35 Looney, China's Campaign to Build a New Socialist Countryside, pp. 909–932.

36 Golomer, P., Guillaume, S. and Cassier, A., "Tongxiang, Ville Ecologique," 2007 quoted in Ghiglione, S. and Larbi, M., "Eco-Cities in China: Ecological Urban Reality or Political Nightmare?" *Journal of Management and Sustainability* 2015, 5(1), Canadian Center of Science and Education.

37 Wu, Fulong ad Zhou, *Lan Beautiful China: The Experience of Jiangsu's Rural Village Improvement Program, ISOCARP Review 09.* Routledge, 2013. pp. 156–169.

38 Wang, M., *Urbanization and Contemporary Chinese Art.* Routledge, 2015. p. 231.

39 Burnham, D. and Bennett, E., *Plan of the City of Chicago.* Chicago: Commercial Club of Chicago, 1909. p. 1.

40 Williams, A., *Enemies of Progress: The Dangers of Sustainability,* Societas (Imprint Academic), 2008.

41 Olmsted, F. L., *Frederick Law Olmsted Papers,* Manuscript Division, Library of Congress (Washington), 1996.

42 Wang Yamei (ed) Beijing to Add 10 Parks in 2016, Xinhua. February 24, 2016. http://news.xinhuanet.com/english/2016 -02/24/c_135127350.htm

43 Zhang B., Xie G., Xia B. and Zhang C., "The Effects of Public Green Spaces on Residential Property Value in Beijing," *Journal of Resources and Ecology,* September 2012, 3(3), www.jorae.cn.

44 Yang, B. and Zhao, C. (2008). *Urban Park: an Integral Part of Welfare for Citizens—A Case Study of Shangzhi and Qinbin Parks in Harbin Metropolis, China.* 3rd Asia Europe Meeting (ASEM) Symposium on Urban Forestry, in Guangzhou, China, November 12–13, 2008.

45 Wu, Fulong, "People-Oriented Urbanization," *China Daily,* February 26, 2013.

46 Tao, Yong, Wu, Xiangjun and Changshuai, Li, "Rawls' Fairness, Income Distribution and Alarming Level of Gini Coefficient,"

September 13, 2014. http://arxiv.org/abs/1409.3979 (accessed July 4, 2016).

47   Ruskin, J., *Lectures on Art, Delivered Before the University of Oxford in Hilary Term, 1870.* Lecture 1.27, 1870.

48   Carnegie, Andrew, "Wealth," *North American Review* 1889, 148, pp. 653–664 and 149, pp. 682–698.

49   Worpole, K., *Here Comes the Sun: Architecture and Public Space in Twentieth-Century European Culture.* Reaktion Books, 2000. p. 32.

50   Li, Bingqin, "Building Healthy Cities: The Experience and Challenges Faced by China," *Urban Age—Cities, Health and Well-being*, LSE Cities Programme, 2011. pp. 1–4.

51   Keynote: Nathanial, P., "Patrick Geddes—the First Masterplanner and How This Relates to Today," City Regeneration. Nottingham University. 2016.

52   Bell, Sarah, *Engineers, Society, and Sustainability*, Morgan & Claypool, 2011, p. 39.

53   Law, A., "The Ghost of Patrick Geddes: Civics as Applied Sociology," *Sociological Research* 2005, 10(2), pp. 4–19. Online, University of Abertay, Dundee.

54   Howard, E., *To-morrow: A Peaceful Path to Real Reform with commentary by Peter Hall, Dennis Hardy, and Colin Ward (1898; reproduced 2003).* Routledge, 2003 [1898]. p. 142.

55   Ann O'Donnell, Mary, "Thoughts on the Spatial Distribution of Shenzhen's Population," *ShenzhenNoted*, June 4, 2016, https://shenzhennoted.com/author/maryannodonnell (accessed, June 4, 2016).

56   Cheng, T. and Selden, M. "The Origins and Social Consequences of China's Hukou System." *The China Quarterly* 1994, 139, 644–668.

57   Schmitz, R., *Street of Eternal Happiness: Big City Dreams Along a Shanghai Road.* John Murray, 2016. p. 57.

58   Cui, Rong and Cohen, J.C., "Viewpoint: Reform and the HuKou System in China," *Migration Letters* 2015, 12(3), pp. 327–335.

59   Cui and Cohen, "Viewpoint: Reform and the HuKou System in China," pp. 327–335.

CHAPTER FIVE

Civilizing Mission

From Wuxi, my flight takes me over Xi'an to Lanzhou in the center of China, and then I take a connecting flight for the long journey westward. I am flying to Kelamayi, also known as "Karamay" in the Uygur language, 300 km northwest of Wulumuqi (also called "Urumqi"), the latter the capital of the remote western province of Xinjiang. On the first leg of the trip, the barren mountain ranges give way to occasional lush forests and the beautiful Qinghai Lake. And then the Gobi Desert is all that is visible for hour after hour. After changing planes in Urumqi and flying over nothing but sand, dust, and scrub for a few more hours, the airport and the city itself appear as an oasis set in a man-made geometric landscape.

FIGURE 5.1 *Looking west towards Karamay, Xinjiang Province*
Source: Author

Karamay, just 150 km from the Kazakhstan border, has a population of around 400,000 (Figure 5.1). The city is home to the ubiquitous Han Chinese community, but there are allegedly thirty-seven different ethnic groups here, including Uygur, Kazak, Hui, and Mongolian. The city name means "Black Oil" in Uyghur describing the immense oil deposits that were discovered here in 1955, and the city was built in 1958 as a Sino-Soviet production facility outpost. From these meager functional beginnings it grew to be an oil worker settlement and is now the biggest integrated oil and petrochemical project in China. Clearly, the perfect place for an eco-certificate.

Karamay goes by the name "Pearl of West China," but, more importantly, over the years it has earned a fistful of testimonials including the National Model Environmental Protection City, the Excellent Tourism City, the Habitat and Environment Example City, the National Community Construction Demonstration Site, the National Healthy City Award, and the National Model Double-support City (a double-support city is one that expressly demonstrates its support for the army on the one hand and the government and the people on the other). In Eco-city terms it has equally impressive Chinese credentials, being listed in China's "Green Book of Eco-cities": it is seventy-second in the Green Consumption index, twenty-fourth in the league of cities providing "new thinking" on environmental issues, and fifteenth most environmentally-friendly city in all of China.[1] It also came a creditable thirty-ninth in the Top Fifty Chinese Green Industrial Cities Index in 2015 (a green industrial city is one that "requires rational and efficient industry (and) encourages consumers to choose green products that are uncontaminated"). A recent international master plan sought to develop the region under the title "World Petroleum City," but this didn't fit with the trajectory of its environmental ambitions.

Lying in the Zhungeer Basin, the city has a reasonably temperate climate where, for millennia, the desert ecosystem has been fed from natural springs and melting mountain snow. In the last twenty years, however, this city has become truly a man-made environment, where life has become sustainable through taming the desert. Now a relatively spacious modern city surrounded by a fertile green belt emphasizes the extent of human dominion, the greenery denoting its separation from an arid expanse of nothingness. Even more man-made changes are on the way as the city plans to grow to a population of one million by 2025.

Between 1997 and 2002 a water diversion channel was constructed to draw water from the northern Eerqisi inland river over 300 km away to feed the city—with integral hydropower generation along the way—which radically transformed the quality of life within the city. With its urban population scheduled to double, the city's eco-agenda prioritizes the management and protection of its natural resources, in particular with respect to its scarce water supplies. Project 635 is the official name for the rerouting of water from the Irtysh River and the construction of new reservoirs. To celebrate the creation of this oasis city, Karamay now has an annual water festival that includes (proudly stated in the city's tourist brochure) a "water-splashing competition and a thrilling fill the bucket with water race."[2]

The two key reservoirs are those on the north and south of the city connected with the first artificial river in the Gobi. This river now laps against a concrete urban shoreline, helps irrigate bankside planting, provides an attractive backdrop to the city, provides faux seaside promenades, creates a cool environment in summer heat, and sticks two fingers up to the desert. Millions of square meters of forest cover, made possible only by irrigation networks, have been planted on the outskirts of the city to ease the desert winds and provide urban cooling. Standing in a city on the fringes of the Gobi Desert with children paddling in fountains is a remarkable indication of what Mao might have called man's triumph over nature, while others, from the West of course, have called it a "totalitarian gigomaniac monument … against nature."[3]

For many years, Karamay has been a hugely wealthy settlement, and by the 1990s, environmental quality was still being "squared with the Chinese state's desire for continued rapid economic growth."[4] In other words, economic growth came first and the environment was often an unfortunate but necessary casualty. But by 2012, Karamay's GDP per capita was the highest of all Chinese cities, providing the opportunity over the next five years to pay heed to quality of urban life and aim to turn itself into a pristine, modern, thriving city in its own terms. At the time of writing, Eco-city Karamay had just entered the certified ranks of an "Advanced City of Well-off Society in China."

Now, lots of cash is being splashed on tourist-centric firework displays (which cannot help cause a frisson of excitement as fireworks are lit in a city where oil literally oozes from the ground). In 2016, it opened its first university (the Karamay Petroleum University) showing that it caters for educational ambitions of its youth, although there are few students as yet. It has also built a slew of museums, parks, libraries, and sport facilities providing for more modern metropolitan-minded urbanites. The environmental condition in Karamay is now integral to its sense of itself. In some ways, contrary to the situation in the 1990s, Karamay now considers environmental protection to be the precursor to the next phase of economic development, not the other way around. Whatever happens to the oil, Karamay is making itself into a real city and amassing the certification to sell itself as an eco-tourist destination of note.

Karamay has had to battle against historically legitimate bad press especially that of a 1994 cinema fire (non-oil-related) in which 323 people, mostly children, died. It is a story that was covered up for years but detailed with heartrending clarity in Xu Xun's award-winning documentary almost twenty years later. It recalls how, as the fire started, children between the ages of six and fourteen were told to remain seated until the visiting Communist Party officials had left the building safely. As the film was winning awards in the Madrid Film Festival in 2011, so Karamay achieved the treasured "National Civilized City" status, making it the first prefecture-level city in Northwest China with the trophy awarded by the Chinese Communist Party Central Committee's Spiritual Civilization Development Steering Commission. Out of the 369 criteria in the civilized city assessment at that time, two stand out: "government honesty" and support for "the healthy growth of teenagers."[5]

Civilized city status should reflect the fact that the city has civilized nature, turning Karamay into an economically, socially, and environmentally sustainable city where just fifty years earlier it was a place with "no grass, no water or even no birds."[6] From nothingness to a metropolitan civilization in less than a lifetime.

At the Seventeenth Party Congress held at the Great Hall of the People in Beijing in October 2007, President Hu Jintao set out the national plan to build an "ecological civilization" (shengtai wenming, 生态文明). It was a statement of intent to remedy what the *China Daily* newspaper called "the perception of the extremely high price we have paid for our economic miracle."[7] Put simply, the demands for an ecological civilization, it said, were meant to herald a new epoch where social and economic development would continue, but there would be much more consideration given to its effects on its surroundings: people and planet.

Many sustainability advocates were delighted at the apparent theoretical drift toward more environmentally friendly policy initiatives but deputy director of China's State Environmental Protection Administration, Pan Yue, used the same expression— "ecological civilization"—and explicitly ruled out that it had anything to do with the conservation of an unspoiled environment. He said it was related to the "possibility of human transformation of nature in order to form a civilization."[8] In other words, "nature" was to be an instrument for the social renewal of the next phase of Chinese development.

The eleventh and twelfth Five-Year Plans (from 2006 to 2015) designate Eco-cities as the key mechanism to transform economic production and development in order that it might be seen as part of an "environmentally, economically and socially harmonious society"[9]. Not long after Hu Jintao's speech, giant slogans were being pasted onto walls around the country: "Construct an ecologically civilized city"; "Create a civilized society; build a harmonious society"; or, less poetically, but straight to the point, "Speak in a civilized manner, act in a civilized way, be a civilized person and build a civilized city."

So, ever since Hu Jintao's speech, the clamor for an "ecological civilization" has exercised the minds of those who have to interpret such confusing official pronouncements, not least because the Chinese language is sometimes abstruse even for the Chinese. The word *shengtai* (生态)—ecological—originates in scientific biology but has come into more common usage over the last ten years or so to refer to the mystical Chinese-style notion of the interdependedness of all things, from nature to culture to spirituality.[10]

A UK-based architectural researcher, Penny Lewis, reveals that vagueness has crept into Western discourse too. She notes how nowadays technical, regulatory, or standards-based solutions to environmental issues are also finding less favor in Western architectural discourse and instead the debate is moving toward a more ethical, all-embracing notion of ecological thinking.[11] The Chinese philosopher Laozi, founder of Daoism, quipped: "Not-knowing is true knowledge," and it seems that a similar quintessentially pseudo-fatalistic love of uncertainty-in-itself is permeating Western urban and environmental thought. This kind of ephemeral approach is essentially a celebration of unpredictability, described by one writer as acting within an "essentially unknowable larger system,"[12] while another writer suggests that ecological thinking puts humanity into a "web of nature."

These ecological thinking ideas chime with the decades-old theories of anthropologist Gregory Bateson—a firm critic of Western scientific hubris. Consciously or not, some Western environmental theorists are tending to ally themselves to a somewhat parodic Eastern mind-set, merely as a consequence of their rejection of what they perceive to be the environmental (or political) failures of Occidental rationalism. Ecological thinking embraces complexities without necessarily seeking to resolve things precisely because they are too complex. It speaks in the celebratory language of opposites, of humans as organisms floating in complex environments. It embraces contingency, fluidity, diffuseness, and uncertainty and wallows in the random and unknowable. It flirts too with a religious reverence for the environment, causing Fritjof Capra, founding director of the Center for Ecoliteracy in Berkeley, to call Bateson a Zen master.[13]

Consequently, as sustainability fades somewhat in the West, the variant concept of ecological urbanism has emerged to take its place: a vague amalgam of environmentalism, fetishized waste management, restrictive practices, mysticism, and academic bluster. Mohsen Mostafavi, dean at the Harvard Graduate School of Design and author of the key book, *Ecological Urbanism*, is a leading advocate. He proposes the "reformulation of the subject … that does not simply take account of the fragility of the ecosystem and the limits on resources but considers such conditions the essential basis for a new form of creative imagining."[14] In other words, not only should we celebrate humanity's fortitude and resilience in inauspicious circumstances (the ability to survive disaster, for example), but actually we should revel in those unstable circumstances as a necessary progenitor of creativity.

In China, by contrast, pragmatic Confucianism rather than spiritual Daoism has proven a little more relevant to China's political modernization. At the moment at least, China seems to be a little more certain about its future and is still learning from the practical, managerial, planned, and scientific ways of thinking. Legitimization of social hierarchies through scholarly traditions is an indelible part of China. It still sees objective knowledge and rationality as its chief modus operandi.

Confucian thought thus plays a useful role for government but has also proved incredibly durable and adaptable for the ecological agenda. Confucianism emerged as a structural model for the Han Dynasty imperial scholarly class as a way of organizing society through rituals and customs. It also formalized the stratification of Chinese society through its famous examination system, resulting in a rigorous rote learning tradition that, in some ways, continues to this day. Confucius's birthplace at Qufu, Shandong, and Daoist Lao Zi's resting place at Louguan, Louguantai, are both part of the Chinese Green Pilgrimage Network, but Daoism and Confucianism serve different constituencies.[15] The more practical nature of Confucianism's relationship to nature—in its modern iteration— gives priority to the social affairs of man and serves better the needs of modern China.

However, in the current era in which China's capital growth is slowing and issues of social cohesion are exercising the mind, Professor Kerry Brown points out that the Communist Party is looking to "moral capital formation"[16] to validate the role of the Party as a political arbiter. The state-backed *China Daily* newspaper doth protest too much when it announced that ecological civilization "is not a term the Party has coined just to fill a theoretical vacancy in its socialism with Chinese characteristics."[17] Presumably, we are to believe that it is merely a coincidence that the adoption of environmental issues just happens to be an ideal combination of global legitimization, Confucian traditionalism, and pseudo-nationalism, and a little bit of socialist egalitarianism thrown in for effect.[18]

Ecological civilization as well as New-Confucianism presents nature as the all-pervading backdrop to human self-discovery and moral understanding,[19,20] and the Chinese Communist state's dalliance with Confucianism—even though it is in an awkward balance with religiosity—is content to see it used as a native philosophy to rival the imported concept of sustainability. After all, the largest section within the National Civilized City assessment system document relates to encouraging the public's ecological awareness and is the work of the National Party's Spiritual Civilization Committee.[21] The official publication of "The Socialist Values" in 2015 talks about them "rejuvenating the soul."

By 2015, 9 books and more than 600 articles had been published in China about ecological Marxism.[22] But actually, nowadays, China's relationship to environmental issues permits the disavowal of overtly communist rhetoric, replacing it with the more nationalistic language of Chinese history, culture, and tradition.[23] In his 2007 article "Ecological wisdom of the ages," Pan Yue noted that China's adoption of the ecological agenda "(corrects) the errors of consumerism and nihilism that western industrial civilization has brought us."[24] In this way, the Party has begun to use the rhetoric of ecology and civilization (and other synonyms) to promote national renewal and to counter much of the West's moral high ground by developing its own variant of environmental soft power.

Unsurprisingly, those in the West disenchanted by Western values are keen to follow; but in China, this agenda is not plain sailing, even for a unitary state. For example, take Pan's claims that China "has maintained a nation state united by roots, language and ethnicity…possible only because of the deep ecological wisdom contained within the country's cultural ideals."[25] Even this cultural conceptualization of ecology isn't completely clear about which cultural heritage, artistic value, or traditional wisdom is being referred to, and how "intrinsic" are these cultural values. Let's take a look at one example.

The growth of the Intangible Cultural Heritage (ICH) movement across the world, but especially in China, is being officially sanctioned as a way of respecting the values of marginalized peoples and their cultures—their eco-civilization. In this regard, "Ecomuseums" have been a growing phenomenon in China over the last twenty years, designed for the "protection of natural resources and the development of cultural identity." An ecomuseum is not meant to be a specific building but an area of preserved cultural heritage: an open air museum, if you will. In the Western world, the few surviving ecomuseums concentrate on community engagement, but that is more difficult in China where locals are less in control of the agenda. While Chinese minority groups are undoubtedly pleased to receive financial payments and infrastructural investment as part of each ecomuseum project's largesse, there is no great clamor by them to be a part of this program. Even so, since 2008, the government has laid out plans for more than one ecomuseum for each of the fifty-six ethnic minority groups.[26]

The first of these ecomuseums was set up among the remote Miao villages of Suoga in Guizhou Province in 1999. In 2007, to coincide with Hu Jintao's ecological civilization speech, the first eco-cultural protection zone was launched by China's minister of culture, Zhou Heping, in Fujian, claiming that it would protect "architecture, historical streets…historical remains; and…oral traditions, traditional performing arts, folk customs, rituals."[27] Some observers are a little uncomfortable with eco-labels that preserve culture in aspic—especially the tendency to romanticize minority communities—when they know that the underlying dynamic is a way of raising tourist dollars. Many worry that it sanctifies or Disney-fies underdevelopment. Some researchers have also criticized ecomuseums because they are seen to preserve backwardness in order to demonstrate how far the rest of China has civilized itself in comparison. Anthropologist Williams Nitzky describes how these places display minority peoples as "past lifeways" that are deemed to provide a "continuity of the Chinese nation and its 'past', to legitimize the dichotomy of the perceived 'backward', 'primitive' ethnic minority and the 'modern' Han majority."[28] Best-selling author Martin Jacques's statement that "Han identity has been the cement which has held this country together" is certainly not without its detractors.

While Confucianism (i.e., neo-neo-Confucianism) serves the modern condition, Daoism seems to be regarded as appropriate among certain minority groups:[29] an appreciation of nature as the source of moral understanding. Such a belief that there is a continuity, a commune, between nature and human beings may be too abstruse for China's immediate industrial needs but seems to be permitted in regions that are still living in underdeveloped conditions.

Often the ethnic minority group's relationship with nature (i.e., its lack of development) is what some people find charming. As an aside, one academic writing about UNESCO's ICH programs in Morocco says that the reality is one of barely concealed contempt for the groups being protected by those charged with their protection.[30] Back in China, the Han Chinese—deemed to make up 92 percent of the population—are easily portrayed through these nativist projects as having a more civilized distance from nature compared to minorities who are somehow deemed to be predisposed to coexist with it.

———

Forty years ago, the media presentation of Deng Xiaoping's convivial meetings with President Richard Nixon in the mid-1970s were often censored—at China's request—because they were accompanied by Deng's habit of expectorating loudly into his collection of spittoons. Such behavior allegedly led Kissinger to call him "that nasty little man."[31] And UK Prime Minister Margaret Thatcher was reputed to have used the epithet "that vulgar old bugger."[32] These condemnatory references to Deng's peasant ways were hugely embarrassing for many Chinese, not because of the diplomatic insult by the guests, but because Deng's behavior was seen as symbolic of China's national underdevelopment. Deng's uncouth behavior represented a side of China that the national media advisers wanted to hide from public view.

The embodiment of a cultivated society is contained in the Chinese concept of *suzhi* 素质 referring to the civilized standards of behavior of "high quality people".[33] It was the centerpiece of Hu Jintao's speech at the Communist Party's Seventeenth National Congress in 2007. At the time of the Shanghai Expo three years later, the city made a special focus of *suzhi*, encouraging city dwellers—those who needed to be reminded—that they were not to embarrass the host nation, their comrades or the Party with slovenly or uncouth behavior. The slogan of the Expo was "Better City, Better Life," focusing on the need for a better city that would arise if peopled by those who had a better understanding of urbanity. It published a list of the "seven don'ts": "don't spit, don't litter, don't damage public property, don't trample the grass, don't dress untidily, don't smoke in public places, and don't swear."

The leadership's desire to create an eco-civilization relates to the targeting of individual behavioral change in order to encourage people to identify with a developed rather than an underdeveloped mentality. Back in 2003, President Jiang Zemin's desire to create a "well-off" society said that the new middle classes would be "educated, cultured, civilized and creditable."[34] The proposition was that economic advancement would cultivate more civilized behavior and encourage social refinement and environmental circumspection, all of which would freely emerge as the middle classes attained more leisure time and became more cultured.

The new middle-class society would be one in which, it was argued, some should be allowed to get rich first—a social experiment that would generate cultural pioneers whose wealth and cultivation would trickle down to those who wait. Speaking of trickle-down effects, toilets in China contain curatorial signs showing a man standing in front of the urinal; it reads: "One small step forward; one big step forward for civilization." Simply put, aim high if you want to help transform the image of China as an undeveloped pisspot.

Unfortunately, those who are not deemed to be suitably cultivated often become targeted as morally culpable in the problems that they face—trapped in an ethical catch-22. As one author explains it: "Poor environmental conditions in migrant communities (were…) taken as an expression of low suzhi,"[35] while the government in the early 1980s attributed "China's failure to modernise to the 'low quality' (*suzhi di*) of its population, especially in rural areas."[36] In other words, slum dwellers live in slums and the condition of their slums reconfirms their slum status. It is an argument most frequently heard in Western discourse as the "broken windows" theory of urban improvement that claims that dilapidated surroundings create dilapidated morals. In this mainstream Western view, upgrading properties generates self-respect that leads to occupants taking better care of their surroundings, which in turn leads to social stability and encourages inward investment for yet more improvements. British author Nick Ross[37] has forensically debunked this instrumental interpretation of the modern-day herd mentality, but sadly he is not well read in China and so the myth continues.

As a result, civility has become something of a battleground for competitive advantage between cities in China. Social media is ever-watchful for coarse habits despoiling the civilizational developments of individual cities or the nation. The government has issued guidance for Chinese tourists traveling abroad, reminding them not to speak loudly and always to queue politely. An advertising video for the new Suzhou tram system, released in 2015, states that those who ride the tram are "so civilized, that there is hardly any rubbish."[38] Conversely, one Western commentator describes "(having) *low suzhi* is to be backwards—to think and behave like a peasant."[39] So *suzhi* is less connected to wealth and more akin to "breeding" (in the old British imperial tradition). It is a nuanced ideal and refers to the "somewhat ephemeral qualities of civility, self-discipline, and modernity."[40] It has a similar connotation to the concept of "national stock" used by British ruling classes worried about the "degeneration" of the British population at the time of the Boer War.[41]

———

Ecological civilization is essentially a program to speed up the "cultivation of good social morals" by the inculcation of environmental education in schools, local communities, and government. This clearly resonates across the three distinct layers of Chinese society; that of the individual citizen, wider society, and at a national level that, until now, have been captured in China's twelve core socialist values (Figure 5.2). Since 2012, these socialist values have been part of a national campaign to reinvigorate a sense of political, ideological, and social purpose in China. They are taught in schools and seen on TV adverts and billboards everywhere, even in English, and workers are told to remember them lest an official should test them. President Xi has said that authorities should "make them all-pervasive, just like the air."[42]

These snappy core socialist values provide clear guidance to all layers of society and show that the government too should be held to account; that is, of course the officials within the government and not the Party itself. They state that the government should be democratic and harmonious, and promote civility and prosperity; that society should encourage freedom, equality, justice, and the rule of law; and that individuals should be patriotic and dedicated and promote integrity and friendship. Clearly, most ordinary people will tell you that this is all nonsense and they are not going to memorize the texts but that doesn't stop it being written into the school and university curriculum, workplace charters, and government contracts, so that the entire social framework is imbued with this kind of mind-set.

The latest guidelines on building civilized cities take these core socialist values and provides even greater detail, including details of the new mechanisms required to monitor, ratify, and reward compliance. They are outlined in the government's National Civilised City Assessment System that lays out an audit trail of

FIGURE 5.2 *Poster: China's 12 core socialist principles*

ethical behavior by which to obtain civilized city status. As a result, there is a long list of criteria from which cities are adjudged to have reached peak civility. The headline categories include the following: the education of Party officials, the rule of law, state security, consumer growth and product quality, cultural facilities, volunteering, and environmental quality. The document then lists around 100 subheadings that are all audited. Below I identify only a few taken from the *Civilised City Evaluation Work Manual* featured in the *China Story Yearbook 2013*.[43] Effectively, a civilized city is one that has the following recorded, assessed, and verified characteristics:

Official education

When assessing a civilized city's application to gain civilized status, primacy is given to whether its officials are drilled in Party theory and knowledge of policy promulgation. Party cadres, it says, must lead by example by living a low-carbon lifestyle. Environmental infractions and civility violations will affect an official's chances of promotion and eco-misdemeanors will stay as black marks on his or her work record for the rest of his or her career. All levels of government will be "educated" as necessary as a means of filtering this mind-set down to the people.

The rule of law

The civilized city should strengthen, it says, grassroots Party Youth Leagues as the ideological embodiment of civilized behavior. Even though the structure of the Youth Leagues is being dismantled to prevent power plays, the core cadre responsibility is to disseminate education. They are also one of the means by which errant behavior is reported. Attempts to encourage participation in these official administrative and management roles are often contradicted by the toleration of lay whistle-blowers because China needs information about wrongdoings from a range of sources. In general, snitching is permitted because it tends to reinforce the role of the Party as the arbiter of last resort. However, the terrible legacy of the vindictive denunciations of the Cultural Revolution generated by a network of citizen informants means that the Party also needs to contain such telltale tendencies.

One Chinese parent told me, "If teenagers start to rebel against their parents' authority, that is the end of China," meaning that social order depends on a delicate balance of filial pieties, respect, observance, deference, authority, and social stratification. Looking on the bright side, there could be something faintly positive arising out of rebelliousness and genuine, rather than vindictive, whistle-blowing. It might reflect a challenging level of autonomous action. Creating a civilized city might, in some way, ennoble the status of civic autonomy through personal responsibility. This would be an interesting development.

State security

As a counter to the previous point, the document states that a civilized city is one that establishes and regulates the internet and written publications.

Consumer experience

A civilized city is one that maintains a good proportion of shops "without counterfeit products," the official guide says. It is also one that organizes and succeeds in antismuggling and "anti-forgery" campaigns to help promote the rights of legitimate businesses.

Cultural facilities

Civilized cities must have the accoutrements of civilization, and by the end of 2015, China had constructed 2,052 performing arts spaces, 2,956 museums, 3,315 culture centers, and 3,136 public libraries holding some of the 8.1 billion books that have been published in China. Even though the average Chinese citizen owns 5.91 books,[44] the average Chinese museum sometimes contains not much more. But these cultural institutions are a tick-box exercise. After all, the state actually counts the square meters of sports facilities constructed per person, as an auditable measure of sporting excellence.

The remote city of Ordos, Kangbashi, in Inner Mongolia, has a population of around 100,000 residents. (As a city regularly pilloried as a ghost town, it is useful to register that it is currently more populous than the city of Bath in the UK, or Boulder, Colorado.) Created in 2007, the official website proudly boasts that the city has "one historical site." It has several cultural attractions though.

One of the first buildings commissioned was Ordos Museum designed by MAD architects and completed before most of the city was built or even fully imagined. The city now claims three museums and six cultural buildings, all of which have been designed by renowned architects. Former vice mayor Yang Hongyan says that through the provision of a "cultural landscape it is possible to elevate the quality of the city and to make a more powerful Ordos."[45] This is about window dressing. Many of these buildings tick the culture quotient box with scant regard for content or visitor numbers.

Volunteering

Many netizens are making comparisons between the recent call for more volunteers with Mao's Red Guards during the Cultural Revolution. Ordinary urban residents today are being asked to do good deeds and volunteer more diligently to build the civilized city. Lei Feng is the name of the fabled young PLA soldier whose selflessness, love of the Party, and desire to help others have made him a powerful Chinese brand, still seen on newspaper mastheads and railway station billboards. Even though Li Feng died in 1963 (if he ever lived, that is), Chinese people are still enjoined to "learn from Li Feng" to be a little less self-centered and a little more civic-minded.

The National Civilised City Assessment System stipulates that a civilized city will have at least 8 percent of residents involved in some kind of voluntarily work. For instance, Mudanjiang in Heilongjiang Province is striving diligently for the prize of civilized city status and claims to have 100,000 volunteers. It points out "one outstanding example…81-year-old Yang Fuxin, a retired official who has been voluntarily patrolling Binjiang Park since 2004 to look after the public facilities and admonish people for uncivilized behavior."[46] China has long been well placed to orchestrate and administer such social policy initiatives, having a unitary party state that brooks little challenge to its issuance of policy mandates, and a polity that is remarkably ordered.[47]

Environmental quality

This issue has been addressed in earlier chapters, but let's take a look at one example in Chongqing, previous home of disgraced Communist Party member Bo Xilai. Chongqing is a gritty, industrial city of around nine million people. It is a city that has seen better days and is one of the rare places where, when I last visited, I sensed that it was a Chinese city in decline rather than my general impression in most other urban areas of cities moving ever forward. In 2016, it was named the most congested city in China and has the highest health-related economic loss caused by the air pollution than any other Chinese city (approx. £170 million).[48] My 2013 *Rough Guide* to the city describes it thus: "Busy, shambolic, overcrowded, *grubby* and atrociously hot in summer, beauty is not one of Chongqing's assets."[49] Of course, there is no accounting for taste as many people love it.

As Chongqing sets out its stall to be a model city for ecological civilization, it demands a number of key improvements, among others it calls for 300 days every year be blessed with "moderate air quality"; and that 46 percent of its entire surface area be forested. Li Yong, economist at Chongqing Academy of Social Sciences, is quoted as saying: "If Chongqing can succeed in transforming into a green, low-carbon city, there is no doubt that the rest of Chinese cities will be able to make this switch."[50]

Of course, ecological civilization is as much about paperwork as it is about any tangible results, and there is enough bureaucracy to satisfy even the most hard-line Party member who might otherwise think that China is going environmentally soft. Indeed, the thirteenth Five-Year Plan contains five development goals that capture the framework for a new model city of ecological civilization: a comprehensive citywide strategy that integrates economic, political, cultural, social, and ecological development into a unifying "green" strategy that requires at least forty different government departments to deliver the process. This vast machine includes the Central Commission for Cultural and Ethical Progress, the Central Committee for Comprehensive Management of Public Security, the Central Commission for Discipline Inspection, and the Ministry of Education.

By 2015, there were at least eighty-five cities with the designation "Civilised" with Zhongshan Eco-city on the Pearl River Delta coming top of the list. It is officially "China's Top Ecologically-civilized City."[51] The prefecture-level city is actually named after Sun Yat-sen, the founding father of modern China, so the city has a ready-made political head start.

In 2015, The Central Commission for Guiding Cultural and Ethical Progress awarded the city of Hefei in Anhui province the coveted civilized city status. As a city of migrants—having grown from 0.5 million to 6 (or 8) million in the last sixty years—the local government has placed a great deal of focus on "mak(ing) the local residents behave in a civilized manner." Wu Cunrong, local Communist Party chief, says that "in order to stop people littering, the government of Hefei formulated a regulation in 2014 to encourage citizens to report to the urban management administrators by offering the informants cash rewards."[52] Perpetrators will be blacklisted and find that they have bad credit ratings when they come to buy a property. Such is Chinese civil society.

Notes

1   Liu, et al., "The Green Book of Eco-cities: Report on the Development of China's Eco-cities", China Academy of Social Sciences, (China), June 26, 2015.

2   Sun, Hui, "Water Festival off to a Splash in Karamay," *China Daily*, August 26, 2016.

3   Sievers, Eric W., "Transboundary Jurisdiction and Watercourse Law: China, Kazakhstan and the Irtysh," *Texas International Law Journal* 2002, 37(1), pp. 1–42.

4   Chang, et al., "A Green Leap Forward Eco State Restructuring and the Tianjin Binhai Eco City Model," pp. 1–15.

5   Zhou, X. and Shi, Z., "Karamay to Receive Inspection by Civilization Office," *China Daily*, November 17, 2014.

6 KDRM, *The Exploration and Practice of Urban Sustainable Development of Karamay*. Karamay Development and Reform Commission, September 2014, pp. 1–44.

7 Xinhua, "Ecological Civilization," *China Daily*, October 24, 2007, p. 10. www.chinadaily.com.cn/opinion/2007-10/24/content_6201964.htm.

8 Meinert, Carmen (ed.), *Nature, Environment and Culture in East Asia: The Challenge of Climate Change*. Leiden: BRILL, 2013.

9 Samara, T. R., He, Shenjing and Chen, Guo. Locating Right to the City in the Global South, Routledge, 2013. p. 85.

10 McCoy, Michael Dalton, *Domestic Policy Narratives and International Relations Theory: Chinese Ecological Agriculture as a Case Study*. University Press of America, 2003.

11 Lewis, "From Ego to Eco: Architecture's New Ecosophy," in ed. Williams and Dounas, *Masterplanning the Future: Modernism East & West & across the World*, pp. 137–142.

12 du Plessis, C., "Thinking about the Day after Tomorrow. New Perspectives on Sustainable Building," Paper presented at Rethinking Sustainable Construction 2006 Conference Sarasota, Florida, USA September 19–22, 2006, pp. 1–24. CSIR. https://www.researchgate.net/profile/Chrisna_Du_Plessis/publication/30509697_Thinking_about_the_day_after_tomorrow_new_perspectives_on_sustainable_building/links/54d355b50cf28e069728110c.pdf.

13 Capra, F., "Homage to Gregory Bateson," 2010. http://www.anecologyofmind.com/gregorybateson.html.

14 Mostafavi, M. and Doherty, G. (eds), *Ecological Urbanism, Harvard University Graduate School of Design*. Lars Müller Publishers, 2010.

15 Pan, J., *China's Environmental Governing and Ecological Civilization*. Springer, 2015, p. 39.

16 Brown, Kerry, "China's New Moral Education Campaign," *The Diplomat*, September 21, 2015.

17 Xinhua, "Ecological Civilization."

18 Jie, Li, "The Path, Theory and System: The Great Innovation of Socialism with Chinese Characteristics Frontiers," 2012, Issue 12. Academy of Marxism. http://myy.cass.cn/ (accessed October 4, 2015).

19 Tucker, Mary Evelyn and Berthrong, John (eds), *Confucianism and Ecology: The Interrelation of Heaven, Earth, and Humans*. Harvard University Press, 1998.

20 McBeath, G.A., McBeath, J.H., Qing, T. and Yu, H., *Environmental Education in China*. Edward Elgar, 2014.

21 Cartier, C., *Socialist and Post-Socialist Urbanisms: Critical Reflections from a Global Perspective*, ed. L. Drummond and D. Young. Toronto: University of Toronto Press, forthcoming.

22 Geall, S., "Interpreting Ecological Civilisation," *China Dialogue*, July 6, 2015. www.chinadialogue.net.

23 Jin, Zhouying, *Global Technological Change: From Hard Technology to Soft Technology*. Intellect Books (Chicago), 2013.

24 Yue, Pan, "Ecological Wisdom of the Ages," *China Dialogue*, November 1, 2011.

25 Yue, "Ecological Wisdom of the Ages."

26 Keun, Y.K., *Multiculturalism and Museums in China, University of Michigan Working Papers in Museum Studies Number 7*. University of Michigan, 2011. pp. 1–27.

27 Howard, Keith, *Music as Intangible Cultural Heritage: Policy, Ideology, and Practice in the Preservation of East Asian Traditions*. Ashgate Publishing, 2012.

28 Nitzky, W. "Mediating Heritage Preservation and Rural Development: Ecomuseum Development in China," *Urban Anthropology* 2012, 41(2, 3, 4), p. 405.

29 Kohn, L. and Roth, H.D., *Daoist Identity: History, Lineage and Ritual*. University of Hawai'i Press (Honolulu), 2002. pp. 23–38.

30 Bendix, R.F. and Hasan-Rokem, G., *A Companion to Folklore*. John Wiley & Sons, 2012. p. 511.

31 Rowan, R., *Chasing the Dragon: A Veteran Journalist's Firsthand Account of the 1946–9 Chinese Revolution*. First Lyons Press (USA), 2008.

32 McGregor, R., "Peking Order," *Financial Times*, April 22, 2006.

33 Sze, Julie, *Fantasy Islands: Chinese Dreams and Ecological Fears in an Age of Climate Crisis*. University of California Press, 2014.

34 Guo, Y. in Goodman, D.S.G. *The New Rich in China: Future Rulers, Present Lives*. Routledge (London), 2008.

35 Chen, Nancy N., et al. (eds), *China Urban: Ethnographies of Contemporary Culture*. Duke University Press (US), 2001.

36 Stafford, Charles, *Ordinary Ethics in China*. Bloomsbury Academic, 2013.

37 Ross, N., *Crime: How to Solve It, and Why So Much of What We're Told Is Wrong*. Biteback Publishing, 2013.

38 Jiang, Peizhi, et al., "SND Tram Was Operated Successfully," *XJTLU Echo*, 2015.

39 Hadas, Edward, "Why 'suzhi' Should Go Global," Reuters, April 18, 2012. http://blogs.reuters.com/edward-hadas/2012/ (accessed September 23, 2015).

40 Yan, Hairong, *New Masters, New Servants: Migration, Development, and Women Workers in China*. Duke University Press (US), 2008.

41 Hammal, Rowena, "How Long Before the Sunset? British Attitudes to War, 1871–1914," *History Review*, Issue 68, December 2010.

42 Mu, X., "Xi Stresses Core Socialist Values," *China Daily*, April 25, 2014.

43 Barmé, G.R. and Goldkorn, J. (eds), *China Story Yearbook 2013*. Canberra: The Australian National University, 2013. pp. 268–269.

44 NBSC, "Statistical Communiqué of The People's Republic of China on the 2015 National Economic and Social Development," *National Bureau of Statistics of China*, February 26, 2016.

45 Woodworth, M.D., Frontier Boomtown Urbanism: City Building in Ordos Municipality, Inner Mongolia Autonomous Region, 2001–2011. Dissertation. Geography Department, University of California, Berkeley, 2013. p. 62.

46 Zhou, H., "A Civilized Society is a Strategic Priority for Mudanjiang," *China Daily*, November 28, 2011.

47 Gescher, *All Under Heaven*.

48 Li, L., Lei, Y., Pan, D., Yu, C. and Si, C., "Economic Evaluation of the Air Pollution Effect on Public Health in China's 74 Cities," *SpringerPlus* 2016, 5(402), pp. 1–16.

49 Rough Guides, *The Rough Guide to Southwest China, Rough Guides*. Rough Guides (London), 2013, p. 326.

50 Liu, C., "Built in a Dirty Boom, China's Biggest City Tries to Go Green," *New York Times*, September 26, 2011.

51 Press release, Zhongshan wins the title "China's Top 10 Ecologically-civilized Cities," Zhongshan Municipal Government, July 21, 2015. http://www.zs.gov.cn/english/about/view/index.action?did=1259&id=165652

52 Zhu, Lixin, "Cities Win National Civilized City Awards," *China Daily*, March 1, 2015.

CHAPTER SIX

Getting There

Covering over 9.5 million km², China is the largest country in Asia but only the fourth largest in the world after Russia, Canada, and the United States. Its climate covers the southerly tropical zone through to the northern frigid temperate zone and from the snow-capped mountains of Tibet to the grasslands and steppes around the Gobi Desert.

Xinjiang Province occupies 15 percent of China's total area and is known officially as Xinjiang Uyghur Autonomous Province (*Xinjiang* simply means "new territory"). Its capital Urumqi is perhaps most famous for being the farthest capital city in the world from the coast, a landlocked oasis in many ways. A formerly agricultural region until 50 or so years ago, oil and petrochemicals now account for about 60 percent of its GDP. Natural nonrenewable resources, most famously the northeasterly oil fields, are one of China's biggest energy sources. Extensive coal deposits serve the power stations, ironworks, steelworks, cement works, and chemical and fertilizer plants, which still drive this region as an industrial workhouse of China. Unsurprisingly maybe, in the first quarter of 2016, Urumqi registered the worst air quality of any city in China. That same year it was also rated the fifty-seventh most innovation-based Eco-city in China.[1]

Some of the energy strategies are surprising for a region that has typically been thought of as typifying inhospitable desert conditions. Xinjiang is home to "570 rivers and 270 mountain springs with surface flow of 112 billion m³ and recoverable ground water of 25.2 billion m³." In other words, potential reserves for hydropower production have been assessed to be around 5.6 percent of the national total.[2]

Southeast of Ürümqi, in Dabancheng, is one of the largest wind turbine power stations in the world, extending for miles across the desert. Within just a few years, China has turned itself from fossil-fuel fiend into a wind-powered wonder, producing, by mid-2015, over half the world's wind-generated electricity. Now 26 percent of Xinjiang Province's total power generation capacity is from wind[3] and five of the top ten wind turbine manufacturers in the world are Chinese.

The fossil fuels are still there, of course, amounting to 20 percent of China's energy reserves. Xinjiang's twenty-four coal fields are still retaining reserves predicted to be more than ten billion tons; oil resources are around twenty-three billion tons, and gas resources are of about thirteen trillion m^3. With this kind of stock, experts predict that nonrenewables are not going to be commercially competitive for a while, but China is investing politically in these alternative renewable energy systems anyway.

Until fairly recently, Eco-cities were always located along the northeastern coastal region. Just like the general thrust of China's urbanization drive, Eco-cities are primarily located in the most populous Eastern third of the country. Of late, though, many are now intended for these inland regions. Turpan New Area located outside Turpan old town (a historic city whose population is currently 71 percent Uyghur) is earmarked to become a New Energy demonstration district featuring solar power, geothermal power, and green transportation, energy efficiency, and recycled water systems. It is designated as an "Autonomous Region Harmonious Ecological City" and a "New Energy Pilot City," graced as it is with relentless solar energy. As with many of these "New Area" developments—from Suzhou's SIP to Xi'an's Chan-Ba district—Turpan New Area is a satellite to the original old city that will provide decent conditions for the predicted emergence of the middle classes. Effectively, it is simply a livable, clean, energy-efficient suburb. Better city: better life.

To create these utopian settlements in the desert, long lines of gas-guzzling lorries ferrying wind turbine blades to the far desert reaches of China's troubled borders are a regular sight. Massive road networks, thousands of miles of railway track, and millions of tonnes of concrete, all in pursuit of eco-development. How does China square this circle? It can, simply because it is not a contradiction. For China, development comes first. Saving the planet will just have to wait.

———

Even though China is the most populous country in the world, over 91.5 percent of the population live in the Eastern third of the country. That is to say, 8.5 percent of the overall population reside on 60 percent of the land. Those westerly residents, in large part, are made up of minority groups and as a result, the western fringes of China are visibly more Muslim, Kazakh, or Mongolian and significantly less "Chinese." Towns like Kashgar and Hotan are closer geographically and feel closer culturally to Afghanistan and Kashmir than the bright lights of Guangdong, Shanghai, or Hainan.

Back in the early days of the People's Republic, Mao sought to show up the legacy and barbarism of the European powers' imperial heritage and America's racist legacy by celebrating China's racial and ethnic minorities and defending their rights within the umbrella of the one-party state. His rhetorical support for various oppressed underdeveloped nations that were casting off the yolk of imperialism and colonialism was one in the eye for America's Jim Crow laws and Britain's colonial legacy. Opposition to the capitalist West was reflected in an express defense of freedom for local minorities within China. Mongolians, Tibetans, Uyghurs, and other minorities who had been victims of the Japanese and British ensured that support for their plight was deemed to be revolutionary.[4] But this begged the question: Who were these minorities and where did they live?

To find out, in 1950 teams of "Visit the Nationalities" officials were sent out to document the ethnic, racial, and tribal groups in China. The mechanism for ascribing a "nationality" had been set down by Stalin years earlier (way back in 1913[5]) using four criteria that classify a historically constituted community of people as those that share a "common language, common territory, common economic life and common psychological make-up."[6] This, according to Stalin and then Mao, was how you recognized a legitimate minority. Mao, of course, was not looking for "nationalities" as this would undermine the unifying rhetoric of the single nation—the People's Republic of China. So, the search was on for authentically Chinese ethnic minority peoples.

Armed with this vague checklist it was hardly surprising that by 1953, Mao's bureaucrats had found at least 400 independent "nationalities" within the boundaries of the new China. This was too many, and the officials were told to go away and try again. It is from such pseudoscientific beginnings—the Stalinist criteria are still used today—that fifty-six ethnic groups have eventually been settled on and are written into the Chinese charter.

The largest group, the Han Chinese, is a category that has the greatest social significance, reputed to represent 91.5 percent of the population. It is hardly a coincidence that the Han Chinese are predominantly those who number highly among the population within the western third of the country. The 8.5 percent of the population identified as minority groups map—with exceptions of migration—onto the two-thirds of China's land mass: the fringes, the central regions, and the western borderlands.

China maintains a delicate balancing act with minority groups across China and Xinjiang in particular. In order to integrate this autonomous region in the greater China narrative, the Party is investing heavily to provide a purposeful role and opportunity for these groups offering the potential to open up trade through the West, making connections with the rest of Asia and beyond. It is a policy initiative fraught with risks as well as economic and political benefits.

In the remote regions of China, where substantial populations of Hui and Uyghur, Mongol, and Kazakh minority ethnic groups are frequently disenfranchised and discriminated against, there is a need for the government to provide economic hope. It is of course no coincidence that these western regions happen to contain much-needed energy and mineral deposits that are an integral rationale for China's Great Western Development Strategy. This proposal will bring substantial interconnectivity and local development through trade and investment. The recently completed Lanzhou–Xinjiang railway, for instance, is the initial phase of a track that connects Shanghai in the East all the way to Rotterdam and Madrid in the West.

From 2000 to 2009, the government spent around £250 billion on this kind of transnational railway project in the far western regions. HSBC's Asia Pacific chief executive, Peter Wong Tung-shun, predicts, "These railway projects may not make money in the near term but the development of property and other projects along the railway line would boost economic growth and cross-border trade."[7] Whether this brings stability is another question.

The latest and some say the most far-reaching plans include the new railway link to the strategic Port of Gwadar in Pakistan. After completing the 1,800 km route from Islamabad to Gwadar, there will be a further 3,000 km to bring the line through the inhospitable Khunjerab Pass to China's Kashgar, a city with 80 percent Uyghur Muslim population. Theoretically, this rail network will eventually extend to the southern Chinese port of Guangzhou. Kashgar will undoubtedly be transformed from a desert outpost into a regional locus for trade and international economic relations. It is hardly coincidental that it will also be an economic boost in an area in which China is desperate to stave off Uyghur minority separatism.

This economic shift will put market pressure on the east coast by encouraging skilled and unskilled labor from distant provinces to stay at home in the west and to take advantage of subsidized local employment opportunities. By so doing, this may also reinvigorate the East by minimizing migrant densities and employment challenges to the indigenous population in southeastern manufacturing centers like Guangdong. One thing is clear though: the Chinese state intends to ensure that the country is more unified rather than split asunder.

Nowadays, everywhere in China is a long way away. The distance between cities is huge, but those distances are being shrunk by the expansion of rapid transport infrastructure. Sadly, distances within cities are still annoyingly far and as cities grow, so the internal travel times increase. Some people have noted that China's huge urban transit networks (Shanghai's metro system is 588 km long) is actually a symptom of its inefficient planning rather than the result of sensible forethought.

China's suburbanization and urban sprawl was nonexistent until 1978.[8] Some researchers have legitimately pointed out that the spread of cities in the subsequent forty years or so has been driven by peculiarities of the land market, uneven land reform, and the local government's willingness to lease land.[9] But I would like to suggest that there is actually an ideological *ambition* reflected in the recent urban sprawl. China's proposals for wide open spaces result from civic bravado and a rejection of the crowded streets of yesteryear. China has broken free from the cramped poverty of the past, rejected boring postmodern Soviet urbanism, and is claiming the freedom embodied in "wide-open spaces."[10] It has happened before. Way back at the turn of the twentieth century, architect Daniel Burnham was commissioned to provide a new urban model of Chicago, a radical cleanup to show that the crowded, dark, squalid, sunless days were over and this was a bright new, airy, nonpolluted future.

He employed sketch artists, most notably Jules Guerin, to paint images of how this new future would look. Just as Chinese computer graphic artists tweak their 3-D models, so too were Guerin's images drawn to deceive (or "persuade"[11]) using watercolor paintings of wide streets, expansive pavements, and even fountains in the middle of streets but with the perspective distorted to maximize the sense of space. If the Americans could model their new urban renaissance on the grandeur of French Baroque, it is hardly surprising that China has modeled its aspirations somewhat on Burnham's utopian vistas.

In Robert Bruegmann's excellent book *Sprawl: A Compact History*, which could be seen as a "defense" of sprawl, he points to the historical character of physical movement and social churn within urban agglomerations and suggests that this follows roughly similar patterns across cultures and times. What has been called "suburban development" has two characters: the outward expansion—"growth like the annual rings on a tree" of the affluent escaping to the countryside; and secondly, of the industrial working class attracted by cheaper accommodation on the edge of the city. A different suburban expansion was created by the later emergence of commuter belts along railway lines or major arterial road networks. Bruegmann points out that urban growth happens unavoidably: "The single most important variable was not whether the cities were European or whether they were American but rather when these cities reached economic maturity."[12] China is certainly economically expansive.

One of the clear benefits of urban sprawl is that it reduces pressures on urban centers. Clearly, China is potentially facing a significant urban tipping point in the near future with the population of Shanghai reputed to be between sixteen and twenty-three million (or up to thirty million, depending on which government statement you read). The city has recently pledged to cap its official population at twenty-five million by 2020[13] (i.e., the population of the entire

Australian continent in one city), and while this makes Shanghai clearly a congested city, the impression walking around the city center today is no more cramped compared to five years ago, even though 3.5 million more people have moved there in that short time.

This seems to be because, as well as expanding its urban area to allow these huge numbers of *in*migrants to blend in, Shanghai's 2000–2020 city master plan has programed an array of new towns, peripheral developments, and new urban centers in order to attract or encourage people to stay in noncity center areas, thus taking pressure off the urban core. By 2015, Shanghai showed a population *decline* of 0.4 percent on the previous year.[14]

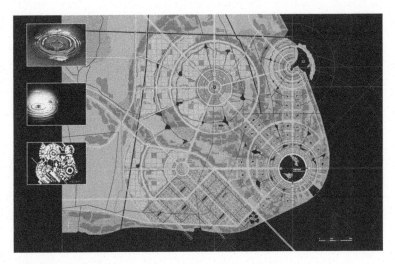

FIGURE 6.1 *Nanhui New City masterplan, Shanghai* © GMP, von Gerkan, Marg and Partners

One of the new Shanghai city regions is Nanhui New City (interchangeably known as "Lingang New Harbour City"), located on the southeastern tip of the Shanghai Pudong promontory. At the time of writing, Nanhui is an eerie ghost town, constructed around a giant circular lake. Nanhui officials reorganized the original design so that they could boast that the lake is bigger than the famous Xihu Lake in nearby Hangzhou. It is intended to be a new regional residential hub connected by the 32 km Donghai Bridge to the world's busiest Deepwater Port Area at Yangshan.

Designed with almost comical German precision by architects von Gerkan, Marg and Partners, it is said to be modeled on water droplets forming concentric and overlapping rings (Figure 6.1).

A considerable part of Nanhui area has been reclaimed using alluvial deposits to remake the promontory and it earns its Eco-city label from its "green city" status. In other words, it has generous strips of greenbelt "free from air pollution and traffic noise."[15] This is certainly the case while it remains an underused ghost town, and placing a lake at the very center of a city is a contrivance to *prevent* urban core construction and densification. But on a mundane level it also sets itself the relatively modest target of having 20 percent of all energy used from renewable resources.

Walking around in the otherworldly quiet of a deserted city, it is hard to believe that the area will thrive (presumably bringing traffic noise and air-quality issues). The government has relocated eight universities—starting with the Shanghai Maritime University—to force a sense of urban liveliness and youthful activity on the area, but as yet this seems to have been to little avail. In the summer months, the reputed 100,000 students are away and nothing is left to even suggest their prior existence. Admittedly, people are seizing the investment opportunity to buy up properties, but even port workers prefer to make an arduous 75 km journey, choosing to live in the real Shanghai rather than in the one-horse Nanhui. On a hot weekend in July, there is merely a trade in families who have traveled long distances to get some sea air along well-manicured promenades (Figure 6.2). It doesn't yet conjure the brochure-inspired hopes for "Copacabana-like relaxation on its shores."[16] Several migrant workers from Anhui who had relocated for the opportunities that such a new city brings were not happy with the speed of development. "It's very nice here, but too quiet," as they switch between selling ice-creams and organizing boat trips for the sparse numbers of tourists.

Actually, Nanhui is potentially a very pleasant green development *a la* Ebenezer Howard's Garden Cities model of 1898; and the circular pattern is a definite nod to Howard's schematic design. Howard's seminal work *To-Morrow: A Peaceful Path to Real Reform* had been a romantic socialist vision of humane, low-density living. In his circular schematic, he provided zones for industry, residences, education, leisure, and commerce mixed with generous parks and forestry. He wanted to blend the best aspects of the countryside

FIGURE 6.2 *Adminstration Center, Nanhui New City masterplan, Shanghai* © GMP, von Gerkan, Marg and Partners

with the benefits of living in a town into a hyphenated single entity, the "Town-Country." At its simplest then, the hyphenated Chinese Eco-city is simply meant to be a much nicer city than what went before.

Just as Howard wanted to improve the living conditions for a more civilized city than the polluted, overcrowded urban squalor that he was used to, so too Nanhui Eco-city is taking pressure off Shanghai city and proposing a new garden city for those who can afford it, or for those who can afford to choose. This Eco-city is merely China's interpretation of Britain's Victorian suburban satellites writ large. But more importantly, this new city has the advantage of accessible transportation connections that could make this a Free Trade development zone of choice. By tapping into the proximity of Shanghai's Pudong airport, this location is being reimagined as a potential Aerotropolis, originally propounded by John Kasarda: a city built around the airport giving instant access to the benefits of globalization.[17] If all goes to plan, Nanhui, which already has a subway link to Shanghai, will be connected to the airport with a superspeed Maglev monorail in order that it could pose a genuine alternate destination to the old town of Shanghai. That, at least, is the vision.

Indeed, China sees the publicity benefits of linking carbon-intensive transit industries (like an airport) to the so-called zero-carbon Eco-city centers, where one is intended to cancel the other out. One Aerotropolis has already finished construction at the Zhengzhou Airport Economic Zone in Henan Province (with consultancy advice provided by Kasarda) in the hope that, by 2030, two new terminals and five runways will handle seventy million passengers yearly—about the same as Heathrow in 2015.[18] It may come as no surprise that Zhengzhou, an urban area that contains the fastest-growing airfreight hub airports in China, still manages to be officially listed as an Eco-city.

For the Chinese, high-carbon airports in low-carbon cities are not the contradiction that appears to the West. While environmentalist George Monbiot has argued that long-haul flights are "as unacceptable as child abuse,"[19] here flying is a sign of globalization and ambition: that is, it broadens the mind, opens up economic opportunities, and is essential for development. China overtook America in 2016 to become the highest global spender on business travel, and this doesn't look like stopping. It is going to build sixty-six new airports by 2020.

———

With more people traveling than ever before, the Chinese maintain a delicate relationship with their house and home. The word "Jia" (家) means "home," "family" or "birthplace," as well as "hometown" and even "lineage."[20] Most Chinese imbue it with a meaning and emotional resonance that Western sensibilities can hardly comprehend. The pious duty of family respect is captured at Qing Ming Festival, where people are required to burn offerings and sweep the tombs of their dead relatives, thus paying respects to the elderly and the departed. That said, family duty is also a legal responsibility with families bound together in a peculiar contractual arrangement, meaning that children can be penalized by the authorities for not visiting their families on a frequent basis. Since May 2016, as per the law, the authorities can fine offspring, or provide them with a damaging credit rating, if they fail to look after their parents; and some elderly people have taken the opportunity to sue their own sons and daughters for their inattention. The Confucian mantra of filial piety that has stabilized Chinese society for many years has now been combined with a state-backed punishment system, leading to a more fraught relationship among the generations.

Sinophile researcher K.A. Mattinson has explored the relationships of ethnic, communal, regional, and provincial loyalties that exert duties—and confer benefits—on individuals in Chinese society above and beyond the legal jurisdiction of the state. She resolves that, at this particular moment in time, for the ordinary citizen, identity is profoundly local rather than national. In other words, for many people the protective lure (the *guanxi* network) of local identity provides a stronger web of meaning than an identification with the state. This is especially true of minority groups.

As we have already seen, the Chinese residence permit—the *hukou*—which determines where you stay and what access you have to resources has been described as "a de facto internal passport,"[21] emphasizing that within China's social organization there is a formalized exclusionary practice that breeds a sense of otherness, reliant on personal, familial, and local connections rather than on the state for survival. Indeed, for a notionally socialist state, society often seems more atomized, more self-defensive, more isolated than in the worst imaginings of Margaret Thatcher's dictum, "There is no such thing as society. There are individual men and women, and there are families."[22]

This is because, for over a century, China has suffered the vicissitudes of imperial rule, revolution, war, famine, cultural revolution, societal regimentation, and state capitalism, all of which have resulted in a self-protective and individuated society. Its communitarian pretensions are still very much in evidence on the surface but, actually, the individual's network is foremost. Such are the contradictions of a "modern socialist country,"[23] especially one that has given up the iron rice bowl. Individuals within close family units—honed through generations of survival, skepticism, and fear—look to each other to get on.[24] The better the network, the more likely one is to succeed and the easier it is to progress.

As a result, the Chinese home is a protective, cultural and emotional relationship as well as a physical one. However, even though the Chinese have a reasonably unique sense of place, of settlement, and of home, they have also been historically fated to up sticks at a moment's notice. All too often in Chinese history, forces outside and beyond their control have cast them adrift.

Pearl Buck's classic 1931 novel *The Good Earth*, set at the end of Imperial China, describes in wonderful and appalling detail the ever-present necessity of families to leave home to seek refuge from flood, famine, or skirmish. In the story, the protagonist is forced to flee his drought-ridden homestead to avoid starvation with his family and community. It is an epic narrative, which is even more degraded than Steinbeck's *The Grapes of Wrath*. *The Good Earth* is relentlessly wretched and vulgar, documenting powerlessness in the face of the destructive forces of nature and the heroic struggle against adversity. One character says: "In the town the dogs are eaten and everywhere the horses and the fowls of every sort. Here we have eaten the beasts that ploughed our fields and the grass and the bark of trees. What now remains for food?"[25] Refusing to sell or eat their own children—although others did—they marched southward but always with a recognition that their land retained family heritage, economic value, and personal sanctuary.

Chinese history is littered with similar tales. The Long March, the 10,000 km trek for political survival instigated by Mao in 1934–1935, has proven to be a "glorious foundation myth" of the Communist Party and of the People's Republic.

During the Cultural Revolution, detachment from home was inescapable for many people. Current premier, Li Keqiang, was withdrawn from education and sent down to Fengyang, a poverty-stricken region of Anhui Province in the mid-1960s, and President Xi Jinping was publicly denounced when he was just nine years old and forcibly removed to Liangjiahe in Shaanxi province, where he lived in a cave and worked the land. Aside from these high-profile examples, the other eighteen to twenty million youth sent down—some as penitents, some as willing volunteers—represented more than 10 percent of the urban population at that time. Taken predominantly from the main urban centers, this was a significant urban outflow of people who were still denied the right of return at the start of the opening-up period in China in the late 1970s. One American professor cites youth activists who traveled from Yunnan Province to Tiananmen Square in 1979 to demand that they be allowed to return home.[26] Remember, in 1955, Beijing's population was only four million; in 1975, just six million, so the returning eighteen million (although not all came back, and not all to Beijing) swelled the urban population greatly.

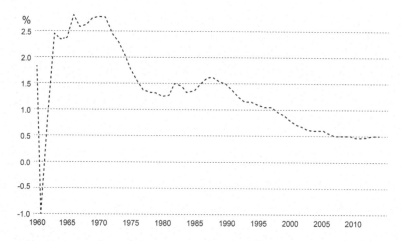

FIGURE 6.3 *Variations in the population rate in China*
Source: The World Bank Group, 2016

Fengyang in Anhui Province, Xi Jinping's place of exile, is also the town where award-winning filmmaker Jia Zhangke was born. Growing up in the Cultural Revolution in isolated, rural poverty has colored his narrative of a changing China. Like many of his films, his *Hometown* trilogy centers on marginal lives; one reviewer describes how "ruin is a recurring motif in Jia's films."[27] He documents the changing landscapes, broken lives and, moreover, the shifting relocation of humanity as demanded by China's historical and contemporary development.

In her book *Eating Bitterness: Stories from the Frontlines of China's Great Urban Migration*, Michelle Loyalka describes migrant workers as "people in transition in a nation in transition… stuck somewhere between their point of origin and their intended destination."[28] Free movement is not the same as freedom. Freedom of movement is an important right in the Enlightenment tradition but it is different than the commodification of people's mobility in a developing economy. Loyalka shows that many people have little choice but to leave their families to travel to a Shenzhen workhouse.

Since the mid-1990s, China has invested a huge amount in its transport infrastructure network—in comfort, speed, and convenience—and now has by far the largest high-speed rail network in the world. In 2004, the entire track length (including freight and slow trains) was 74,200 km. It is now twice as long. To put it in perspective, that's more than the entire Indian railway network constructed in just over ten years.

China's incredible social connectivity has been progressive and transformative but for many poor people it is still not available to them, and traveling is not an inherently enjoyable experience. For the poor, the old slow D-trains, with their hard-bed sleeping cars, ironically positioned with no chance of sleep amid the cacophony of family picnics and blaring video games, ferry migrants from the southeast to the northwest every Spring Festival.

The new infrastructure has undoubtedly increased connectivity. Professor Rana Mitter notes that "for centuries, the Chinese had experienced refugee flight...But the twentieth century allowed movement at high speed for the first time across the vast distances of central China, and this changed the way the Chinese people imagined their own geography."[29]

In its Go West campaign, the Party has invested massively in the central and western regions of China—away from its existing centers of industry and commerce on the East and southern coasts—in an attempt to spread the opportunities and to minimize discontent in the poor inland regions of the country. By increasing the amount of localized development, Chinese people can develop economically without the trauma of removing themselves from their families for eleven months of the year to find work in cities many thousands of miles away.

Clearly, there is still huge investment in these established free-trade cities that will continue to exert influence, from Shenzhen, through Shanghai and up to the newly revivified Bohai region, but China also wants to take advantage of the new markets and cheap labor in the interior of the country and around the western fringes. By developing the interior, the greatest concentrated annual migration of humanity every year will be significantly reduced. It will give people a chance to remain in their home regions, working to improve their lot without the wrench on their families.

One commentator notes that if only the big cities have "good job opportunities, housing, schools, stores and services, and cultural and recreational facilities, then of course people will want to live there. But if all these things are developed in small and medium-sized cities, people will be much more willing to live in these places and the population pressure on big cities will be eased."[30] It is a counterintuitive proposition, then, to invest massively in mobility in order to create more stable settlement.

In an unprecedented spending spree, the Chinese government is setting aside around US$6 trillion to create new and improved infrastructure over the next fifteen years or so. To put it in perspective, the entire world's GDP is US$74 trillion, so China will be spending one-twelfth of it—greater than the entire GDP of Japan—in physical infrastructure.

These huge sums will pay for the roads, the buildings, the industry, the railways, and the environmental preparation for the Chinese Belt and Road initiative (*yi dai, yi lu*), a mega project the like of which the world has never seen before. Admittedly the rhetoric taps into the proud history of an original Silk Road through central Asia during the Tang Dynasty and a Maritime Silk Route through the South China Seas, but this proposal is a greater order of magnitude. It will set the foundations for a major internationalization of trade and commerce, as railways and shipping lanes will increase connectivity across the globe.

And it will open up China from the center, creating new cities with access to and from hitherto landlocked regions providing the economic conditions, optimistic advocates say, for a new stability in the region. The investment in infrastructure will facilitate the relocation of over 400 million people from the countryside to newly created cities across China, but most significantly, the western regions—not only of business and industry but also of farmers and traders—will be reinvigorated as a potential place of progress.

This spending will facilitate trade in goods and services but ultimately, by unintentional default, it will enhance the flow of people and ideas.

Notes

1 Liu, J., Sun, W. and Hu, W., "The Development of Eco Cities in China," *Springer*, October 17, 2016, p. 293.

2 Duan, Jinhui, Wei, Shuying, Zeng, Ming and Ju, Yanfang, "The Energy Industry in Xinjiang, China: Potential, Problems, and Solutions," *POWER magazine*, January 1, 2016. http://www.powermag.com /energy-industry-xinjiang-china-potential-problems-solutions -web/?pagenum=1 (accessed August 5, 2016).

3   Shepherd, C. and Hornby, L., "Wind Turbine Maker Goldwind Looks Beyond Xinjiang," *Financial Times*, June 21, 2016.

4   Howland, D., "The Dialectics of Chauvinism: Minority Nationalities and Territorial Sovereignty in Mao Zedong's New Democracy," *Modern China* 2011, 37(2), pp. 170–201.

5   Stalin, "Marxism and the National Question," in *Works*, Vol. 2. Moscow: Foreign Languages, 1953. p. 307 (available on the Marxists Internet Archive, https://www.marxists.org/reference/archive/stalin/works/1913/03.htm).

6   Beckett, G.H. and Postiglione, G.A. (eds) *China's Assimilationist Language Policy: The Impact on Indigenous/ Minority Literacy and Social Harmony*. London and New York: Routledge, 2013.

7   Yiu, E., "'Belt and Road' to Need Up to US$6 Trillion in Funding over Next 15 Years, Says HSBC Head." *South China Morning Post*, June 19, 2016, http://www.scmp.com/business/mutual-funds/article/1977680/belt-and-road-need-us6-trillion-funding-over-next-15-years (accessed August 5, 2016).

8   Bao, B., "Literature Review: Urban Sprawl in China," *Economics*, 145. https://sites.duke.edu/urbaneconomics/?p=368 (accessed August 9, 2016).

9   Zhang, T., "Land Market Forces and Government's Role in Sprawl: The Case of China," *Cities*, April 2000, 17(2), pp. 123–135.

10 Davie, K., *The Rise of the U.S. Environmental Health Movement*. Rowman & Littlefield, 2013. p. 27.

11 Bruegmann, *The Plan of Chicago: 1909–1979 An Exhibition of the Burnham Library of Architecture*. The Art Institute of Chicago, 1979. p. 28.

12 Bruegmann, R., *Sprawl: A Compact History*. University of Chicago Press, 2005. p. 20.

13 Xinhua, "Shanghai Caps 2020 Population at 25 million," *China Daily*, December 24, 2015. http://usa.chinadaily.com.cn/china/2015-12/24/content_22797768.htm (accessed August 9, 2016).

14 Xinhua, "Shanghai Population Declines for the First Time," *China Daily*, February 3, 2016. http://www.chinadaily.com.cn/china/2016-03/02/content_23703777.htm (accessed August 9, 2016).

15 Reisach, U., "Sustainability—Challenges and Progress Made in China," Report on the Neu-Ulm University of Applied Sciences', Delegation Tour to Shanghai and Hangzhou, October 6–13, 2013.

16 Kim, J.I., "Making Cities Global: The New City Development of Songdo, Yujiapu and Lingang," *Planning Perspectives* 2014, 29(3), pp. 329–356. Routledge.

17 Kasarda, J.D. and Lindsay, G., *Aerotropolis: The Way We'll Live Next*. Farrar, Straus and Giroux, 2011. p. 6.

18 Anon, "Aerotropolitan Ambitions," *The Economist*, March 14, 2015.

19 Monbiot, G., "Meltdown," July 29, 1999. http://www.monbiot .com/1999/07/29/meltdown (accessed July 23, 2016).

20 Jie, L., "Shanghai Home, Excerpt: The Rise and Fall of Shanghai's Alleyways," *China Economic Review*, January 19, 2015.

21 Chan, K.W., "Migration and Development in China: Trends, Geography and Current Issues," *Migration and Development*, December 2012, 1(2), pp. 187–205.

22 Keay, D., "Margaret Thatcher: Interview for Woman's Own," *Woman's Own*, September 23, 1987, published October 31, 1987, Margaret Thatcher Archive. http://www.margaretthatcher.org/ document/106689 (accessed August 10, 2016).

23 Huaxia (ed.), "Full Text of Xi Jinping's Speech on China-U.S. Relations in Seattle," *Xinhua*, September 24, 2015.

24 Williams, A., "The Origins of China's Copycat Culture," *Global: The International Briefing*, 2014, Q1, p. 24.

25 Buck, P., "The Good Earth,", *The Albatross Modern Continental Library* 1947, 505, p. 65.

26 Yang, G., *The Red Guard Generation and Political Activism in China*. Columbia University Press, 2016.

27 Wu, Shu-chin, "Visualizing China in Transformation: The Underground and Independent Films of Jia Zhangke," *China Research Center*, August 4, 2010, 9(2).

28 Loyalka, M., *Eating Bitterness: Stories from the Frontlines of China's Great Urban Migration*. University of California Press, 2013. p. 243.

29 Mitter, R. *China's War with Japan, 1937–1945: The Struggle for Survival*. Allen Lane, 2013. p. 114.

30 Li, Mengbai, "Planned Urban Growth," *China Reconstructs*, November 1983, 32, pp. 7–9, quoted in Goldstein, S., "Urbanization in China: New Insights from the 1983 Census," *Papers of the East-West Population Institute*, July 1985, 93, p. 4.

CHAPTER SEVEN

Fake Eco, Failed Cities

In 2005, the Chinese artist Ai Wei Wei sent out an advertisement to the architectural press with an offer that many simply couldn't refuse. It was an open competition to design a community of 100 houses in a remote region of Inner Mongolia in northern China. The 2 km² site was modest compared to many in China, set in a desert the size of Switzerland. But for many of the chosen architects, this was a great opportunity to visit an exotic location, let alone to design a significant building in China. The architectural media were excited by their access to the world's most famous dissident and also by the fact that the invited architects were not the usual suspects but were all up-and-coming new practices. When the internationally acclaimed architectural practice Herzog de Meuron came on board to assist with the initial phase of the project, the stage was set for an architectural master class.

The project was the idea of the local developer, Jiang Yuan Water Company, with the intention to put Ordos on the map. It contacted Ai directly to develop the brief and "curate" the project. Phase I would be built by the end of 2008 and the remaining phase completed by the end of 2009, so there was no time to waste. In early 2008, the Ordos 100 International Architects Symposium was held where everyone turned up to be allocated their plot and explore their initial ideas.

The "Ordos 100" houses, it was decided, would have a floor area of 1,000 m². It is at this point that maybe alarm bells should have started to ring because this is inordinately big. It is big even by the standards of a large family home in an affluent part of Beverly

Hills. So for China, this is gigantic. (Australia has the largest houses in the world with an average floor area of 241 m²; the average new home in China is 60 m², the UK 76 m², and the United States 201 m². [1]) I visited the site in 2013 and explored the vast spaces, massive bathrooms, colossal entrance halls, inexplicably large garages, and enormous corridors.

These were architectural fantasies for nonexistent billionaires and each one was irresponsibly huge, monumentally fatuous, and completely empty. A mere five building shells had been created and lay derelict in the desert sun, succumbing to the windblown dunes. None of the projects were completed, no one lived there. A scandalous waste of time, money, and effort.

Ai filmed the initial process, and the documentary about the project is revealing because it is clear that there is an element of artistic irony about the entire venture.[2] One commentator has suggested that the whole thing might have been performance art with Western architects—from twenty-seven countries—arriving as innocent victims. The film documents the rise and fall of expectations as they scramble to collect their ticket to architectural celebrity. We see liberal designers putting environmental, social, and rational credentials behind them to create monstrous buildings. And Ai captures this on film. In an interview, Ai has said: "I am more satisfied with the anticipation of the architects, the interaction between sincerity and temptation."[3] It is certainly an interesting exploration of Western expectations and entitlement mixed with China's casual opportunism. Gullibility and guile? An example of China's cynicism or pragmatism? The clue, as they say, is in the title. Ai WeiWei's company is called "FAKE Design."

––––––

Things are changing, but for many years, being "original" has not been a socially acceptable form of self-expression in China. Quoting Chinese legal scholar Professor William Alford, one researcher notes that "because literati poets and painters focused on their interaction with the past, innovating 'within the bounds of orthodoxy' and the context of past forms, the idea of copyright never blossomed in China."[4] Copying is acceptable. It is in fact "'a noble art,' a 'time-honored learning process' through which people manifested respect for their ancestors."[5]

Even though Karl Popper recognized that "originality" was not essential to great art, he insisted that "creative self-criticism" was an essential component.[6] He possibly wasn't aware that in China the act of self-criticism had become an act of self-abasement, especially in the 1960s and 1970s. During the peak of the Cultural Revolution, Mao used his Red Guards to force the so-called revisionists to provide self-critical confessions to atone for their bourgeois sins. These were known as "struggle sessions," public humiliations of the individual where self-criticism amounted to documenting weaknesses, renouncing disloyal thoughts, enduring punishment, and committing suicide.[7] After such an Orwellian scenario it is no wonder that the concept of "criticism" opens old wounds. Hardly surprising too that resigned repetition of established mantras is built in to the national psyche.

After centuries of Confucian-esque rote learning, even today studying art or architecture in China often involves endless repetition of the canon. It is not unusual for students to spend hours literally tracing the masters of art and calligraphy to understand technique. It is hardly surprising that they see little wrong with plagiarizing someone else's ideas for their own ends. They are not plagiarizing, they will say, but copying with the utmost respect for the original.[8] Unlike those in the West who now seem to fetishize culture and cultural values, for many contemporary Chinese, cultural appropriation is not appropriation at all; it is simply an established fact.

Undoubtedly, appropriation can sometimes go too far, and in 2013, a school in Hubei was attacked by angry parents—smashing windows and overturning staff cars—to demand their children's right to cheat. One parent said: "There is no fairness if you do not let us cheat."[9] In some ways, for the last forty years, China has been cheating, nicking ideas from the West to fuel its own awakening. It hasn't reinvented the wheel, but learned from best practice. That is no bad thing. For instance, China developed a comprehensive urban planning policy only in 1989 borrowed, in some way, from UK planning guidance.[10] Since then it has been assimilating some good practice knowledge from Western cities and trying them out. Inevitably, on occasion, it makes a mess of things but it has been eager to learn.

Shanghai's Anting German Town, Thames Town in Songjiang, or Pujiang's Italian Town are but a few copycat city regions that have hit the headlines as urban parodies—or a smorgasbord (in the case of Luodian's Scandinavian Town)—of tick-boxed items from successful cities around the world. These various palettes of European urbanism have been thrown together in the vain hope that the urbanity of mature European cities will automatically arise. Thames Town, for example, is peppered with fake postmodern London's Dockland buildings from thirty years ago placed alongside Tudor Olde Englande half-timbered chip shops. It is all capped off with a Harry Potter statue. It's London through the eyes of an Instagram computer algorithm. On the most basic level it gives those who will never travel to London a taster, but more importantly it commandeers British culture in a similar way that British imperialists flaunted their trophies of colonialism. Owning, replicating, adapting, and then Chinafying various art and cultural forms from other shores is an expression of Chinese global confidence and, in some ways, its magnanimity.

We don't need to dwell on some of the more absurdist fakery in Chinese society—like the eco-tourism resort near Shenzhen built to resemble Switzerland's Interlaken (compete with Jungfrau railway) or the public toilet in Fuyang, Anhui, that is shaped like the US White House—to know that China has a tendency to take ideas from others and insert them into strangely inappropriate contexts. Since Deng Xiaoping's opening up of China and the economy in 1978, Chinese urban designers and policy wonks have spent a great deal of time learning from Western-centric city models of urban development, squirreling away details predominantly from European cities.[11] Look no further than Suzhou Eco-town in Jiangsu Province, apparently designed with "an understanding of local conditions and climate (but with the) principles of European Urbanism"; or Zhoushan Island eco-development off the mainland coast near Ningbo, where "the spirit of European urbanism," says the press release, "is convincingly interpreted for this Chinese seaside location."[12] The latter location, with a distinct whiff of artificiality, is now rated in the top ten environmentally friendly cities in China.

The celebratory endorsement of faux-Western urbanism reaches its apogee in the proposal for the ex-village of Dongcun outside Chengdu's fourth ring road, situated in an edge town that has all but been enveloped by the urban behemoth of Chengdu. Here, in the heart of China, on the outskirts of the provincial capital of Sichuan, local Chinese planners have been consulting with representatives of Letchworth Garden City Heritage Foundation—originally British Garden City that began construction in 1903 in quaint Arts and Crafts' style—in order to apply the design and livability lessons to China circa 2016. Even though a hopeful Letchworth representative says that "there are opportunities for clear synergies," the proposal to transplant the rationale for a Georgian English town of 30,000 people to the ever-increasing Chinese city of fourteen million sounds like wishful (or absurdist) thinking. It's hard to tell which side is selling the snake oil. In a telling article in *The Architectural Review*, urban researcher, Guy Trangos, argues that garden cities on the periphery of existing cities are "little more than commuter traps where the pull of the city far outweighs the market-town centers of these inauthentic and often nostalgic suburbs."[13] Whether this one is a genuine proposal is uncertain at this stage, but as the transactional garden city conversations continue, Dongcun and neighboring Tianfu are already building several un-Letchworthian skyscrapers by renowned architects like Adrian Smith and Gordon Gill for good measure.

This issue of authenticity in design, in architecture, and in culture is an important point of credibility in many Western countries. The tendency of China to indulge inappropriate, faux, and copycat designs arouses the chagrin of Western observers.

Authenticity is a significant talking point in modern China especially among architectural historians who regularly engage in a vibrant debate about its meaning, applicability, and merit. This is where the cultural differences between the Western and Chinese "ways of thinking" become apparent and profound. Western urbanists will ascribe the authenticity of a building to the experience of it being the original—even if that is a barely recognizable ruin—because it reinforces a perception of integrity: the honesty and the unadulterated freedom given to the artifact to speak for itself. It allows for imagination but primarily it serves to engage the intellect because it is deemed that one is in touch with real history. At Stonehenge, for example, these are the real stones around which real people stood: it brings history to life.

The guidelines issued by the Historic Buildings and Monuments Commission for England state that conservation interventions, that is, reparations of monuments are acceptable only if "the proposal would not materially harm the values of the place, (and...) the long-term consequences of the proposals can, from experience, be demonstrated to be benign."[14] With that in mind, "repair should normally be limited to what is reasonably necessary to make failing elements sound."[15] Delicate and minimal interventions have tended not to be the case in China, although it, too, aims to bring history to life.

It is not unusual to see history being created, unabashedly, before one's very eyes in China. In 2014, the reparations to Xi'an's fortress walls comprised reinforced concrete inner cores clad in freshly carved stone. It was done in full sight of the public. There was barely a fourteenth-century Ming Dynasty construction technique in sight but the resultant structure replicated the shape, form, and appearance of the original and therefore became, in many ways, authentic. This kind of Theseus's paradox is reminiscent of a classic episode of a popular British sitcom in which a road sweeper describes that after twenty years he still has his original broom, maintained with "17 new heads and 14 new handles."[16] Does the gradual repair and replacement of an object mean that the object is the same, or different? It's a dilemma that has exercised great minds since Plutarch and Aristotle. What if a building has one tile replaced, or two, or a hundred; at which point does it cease to be the original building, and if a second building is created using the original materials, does this become a replica or the original?

Take the historic walls of Pingyao city in Shaanxi Province, 12 m high and 10 m wide. These have been significantly repaired and rebuilt to reflect the city's history and are now described by UNESCO as a well-preserved example of a traditional Han Chinese city that "over five centuries of continuous evolution and development…(preserve) authentically the elements and features that reflect the Han cities from the 14th to 20th century."

The distinctions between copying and originality, between varying degrees of historical integrity, are sometimes less clear-cut than first we imagine. The delicate tracery of the Taj Mahal reflects the real hands that created it 500 years ago, whereas, by contrast, the delicate timber tracery of Xi'an's Temple of the Eight Immortals, originally built in the Song Dynasty (618–907), has to be replaced every fifteen years or so.

In one research project carried out with my students to submit photographs and details of the oldest building in their hometown, one submitted a 1,000-year-old town hall from Hangzhou; another sent me a photograph of a seven-year-old building in Chenggong, Kunming. This was the oldest building apparently! Growing up in a historic city center or growing up in a newly emerging urban landscape must result in a different relationship to authentic meaning: one stable and the other peculiarly transient. One Beijing prison is helping its long-term prisoners adjust to the astounding pace of change outside its walls by building a mini-city—supermarket, subway station, and internet café—so that they can acclimatize to a city that may not have existed before they went in.

In Zhou Hao's revealing documentary *The Chinese Mayor*, the cameras follow the mayor of Datong, Geng Yanbo, as he struggles to transform his city into a leading cultural capital. He does this with charming ruthlessness by evicting many thousands of people, demolishing their family homes, and reinstating the city walls and historic city core. The rebuilding is a traditional form but is constructed out of mass concrete which is clad in stone. His team collects salvaged artifacts from various bulldozed sites that he is keen to use throughout the new project. These recovered relics are merely used as decoration to impress visiting dignitaries of the cultural richness of Shaanxi and he instructs his team to "keep on buying," a belief that quantity equals quality. As a result of the regeneration work undertaken in Datong, one city guide remarks: "We can imagine, in the future, Datong will be an ancient city."

The architectural historian Robert Anderson, at Tilberg University in the Netherlands, suggests that an object, a building "if isolated from its cultural and historic context, can begin to feel meaningless,"[17] and the social construction of interpretation—whether of myths, culture, or reason—bring that meaning to life. In Europe, the meaning of authenticity is underwritten by the confidence with which people assert it; authenticity springs from cultures that have evolved a generally accepted narrative about their own societies over time. Professor Miao Pu of Tongji University has argued that "an authentic architecture must actively seek forms which plainly express the true conditions of its users' social, cultural, and economic life." He concludes that China displays symptoms of inauthenticity due to "the lack of strong beliefs or shared values in China today…beliefs shared by the whole society."[18]

It is not so much that authenticity is better understood in the West (academics have as much uncertainty in defining what it actually means as they do in China. After all, it was after a six-day conference in 1993 that the "Nara Declaration on Authenticity" meekly stated that "authenticity judgments may be linked to the worth of a great variety of sources of information"[19]). However, at least in European traditions, where history tends to have a long-standing, linear narrative, it is more confidently and universally upheld as a common good.

Ironically, China is always boasting about its unbroken historical continuity, so without going back over 5,000 years of alleged Chinese nationhood, in the next section I'll explore some of the historical prejudices and ideological principles that affect China's sense of history and authenticity.

———

In 1792, Lord Macartney set sail from Portsmouth on the first diplomatic mission to China. The envoy and his entourage were sent by King George III as an embassy intended to establish formal trade links with the Chinese emperor Qian Long. The British contingent took eleven months to reach Chengde (known to the British as "Jehol"), the mountain retreat north of Beijing (Peking) where the Manchu emperor lived during the summer months. The British hoped to improve trade relations and arrived offering technological gifts such as sextants, telescopes, timepieces, and other objects of contemporary Enlightenment rationality, even including a hot-air balloon and pilot. While these were meant to impress, the Chinese authorities rejected them as "gaudy ephemera."[20] While the British lobbied to trade with the Chinese, Qian Long dismissed the need for help or interference from "outside barbarians" and sent Macartney on his way. Writing to King George III shortly afterward, Qian Long said: "I set no value on objects strange or ingenious, and have no use for your country's manufactures." The British political cartoonist Gilray depicted Macartney's Far Eastern adventure as a hot-air balloon about to be punctured by a Chinese dragon (Figure 7.1).[21] Indeed, the British and French establishment had their own problems with Enlightenment ideas at that time, but history points to China coming off worse. Not long afterward began what China classifies as its "century of humiliation."

FIGURE 7.1 *James Gillray, "The Reception of the Diplomatique & his Suite, at the Court of Pekin," 1792*
Source: National Portrait Gallery Picture Library

China's refusal to engage with the wider world exemplified its splendid isolation, an isolation that had begun in Ming dynasty China in 1434 when a declaration was made forbidding foreign trade. It effectively destroyed its own shipping fleet and constructed the Great Wall as a symbol of its self-belief that China *was* the world. The story of Chinese isolation is often somewhat overhyped, but, in reality, China considered itself to be All Under Heaven (*tianxia*), meaning that China was, as far as it was concerned, literally "the Earth or all lands under the sky,"[22] and so the Qing emperor's contemptuous comments toward the British were merely the god-given aloofness of the Son of Heaven conveying a glorious sense of independence from other-worldly matters.[23] For the Chinese, Britain's gifts were unworthy tributes: the tributary system being a relationship of subservience rather than occasion for Macartney to pretend to equivalence or even flaunt Britain's advances. Sadly, such exclusionist complacency displayed by the emperor was one of the contributory factors in China's decline. Somewhat ironically, it is the dire consequences of *revived* trade in the nineteenth century and especially the trade with the East India Company that caused an even more terrible legacy several decades later. The East India Company represented the de facto architects of the Opium Wars (1839–1842; 1856–1860)—wars described by future prime minister William Gladstone as Britain's "national iniquity"—that caused China to suffer tragically under the yoke of the foreign powers throughout the nineteenth century.[24]

It was the erosion of China's self-determination during the British-Sino Opium Wars that was the spark for action in neighboring Japan across the East China Sea. During the second half of the nineteenth century, many in Japan's establishment had long monitored the situation in China and found it wanting. They had observed the unfair British imperial trade with the Chinese, the corruption of society through imported opiates, and the subservience of the native political class, and feared that the foreign traders would do the same to them. So, Japan found the urgent need to rouse itself after 250 years of relative peace.

Japan launched a fiercely nationalist political coup d'etat that threw out the ruling military Tokugawa Shogunate and reinstalled the Emperor Meiji. Even though a historically semifeudal imperial system had been relegitimated under the token authority of this new emperor, the consequences of the underlying pursuit of a nationalistic military power had been unintended. In order to fight off potential invaders, the need for greater clarity, rationality, planning, and scientific understanding—albeit in simple military terms—meant that Japan had disavowed its traditions and inexorably turned to Western-style thought. William G. Beasley, noted historian of Japan's feudal past, writes: "Confucian scholarship, no matter how vital to questions of moral behavior (was) militarily irrelevant."[25]

Chinese observers were watching the consequences of Japan's actions. Various Chinese political reformers and radicals were on the lookout for opportunities that might present themselves in order that they might exert their own national self-determination over the British imperialists. At the tail end of the nineteenth century, a significant number of nationalists, styled under the banner of the "self-strengthening movement" (1861–1895), demanded that China modernize—observing Japan's newfound economic independence—in order to improve its technological and military capability. It sent students overseas and translated Western literature as a way of opening minds to new ways of thinking. Ironically, as a result of years of subservience, the Chinese political class needed to ask foreigners for help, to provide technical answers and practical know-how, thus undermining its own self-declared autonomy. Sadly, throughout its thirty-five-year existence, the Self-strengthening Movement tailed off due to incompetence, collusion, corruption, compromise, and factionalism.

What had been missed by the radicals in China was that the essential criteria for Japan's success had been that it had been a *social* transformation—some might say, a revolution. It had removed feudal relations (retaining only a figurehead Imperial ruler). Conversely, China carried out a *practical* transformation that absorbed outside technological know-how but maintained the structure of society unchanged. One US military report at the time simply described China's version as an "effort to graft Western technology onto Chinese institutions."[26]

As China continued to battle for national identity and economic prosperity, the provincial government official, Zhang Zhidong, a man who had condemned the Western barbarians (as the foreign interlopers were known), came to a reformist realization. In his book entitled *Exhortation to Learning*, published in 1898, he put forward the maxim: "Chinese learning for essence, Western learning for use." In other words, China should take advantage of others to help advance its material and technical knowledge, but it should do so while still imperiously maintaining the traditional, hierarchical social, political, and cultural structure of society.[27] China should take whatever creative ideas it needed to improve its economic performance, but only in a technical sense, the social organization would remain wedded to the structures, pieties, myths, and narratives of the past. With limited exceptions, this approach has shaped China's thinking ever since. China didn't have the Enlightenment and therefore missed out on "modernity" centered "on individualism, rights, and science— (that) was a unique Western cultural experience."[28] Thus China was able to—it chose to—maintain many of its feudal, authoritarian, and mystical structures in place.

In order to rationalize this dilemma of its failed radical transformation, China has long placed great emphasis on pragmatism (ironically, a singularly American philosophy). Pragmatism can be characterized as follows: "If it works, Do it."

Pragmatism (as a defined philosophical school rather than just a workable reaction to events) originated in America in the late nineteenth century and came to prominence when William James gave a series of lectures in 1907 entitled "Pragmatism: A New Name for an Old way of Thinking." It included a dedication to John Stuart Mill "who my fancy likes to picture as our leader were he alive today."[29]

In truth it was Walt Whitman who had convinced James to become a pragmatist,[30] and alongside Charles Sanders Peirce and John Dewey, these three are acknowledged as the founders of what is reputed to be the only American-originating philosophical tradition. In essence pragmatism is a philosophical method that aims to reconcile the tensions between various ways of thinking, most notably the "dilemma," as James called it, between the "tough-minded" (empiricists) and the "tender-minded" (idealists). It was a way to reconcile scientific thought and religion, empiricism and emotionalism and reason and morals. In the context of the previous paragraphs, it could be characterized as offering a philosophical framework to understand Western learning for use, while accommodating to Chinese learning for essence.

John Dewey visited China in 1919, arriving on 1 May in the midst of radical fervor. Three days later, the revolutionary student-led protest known as the "4 May movement" marched in protest at the far-off Versailles Peace Conference that had assigned the German Treaty ports (the Chinese city areas effectively "owned" by Germany) over to Japan instead of handing them back to China. Students belonging to this 4 May "New Culture Movement" held aloft banners openly insisting that Mr Confucius be replaced by "Mr Science" and "Mr Democracy." This was a huge intellectual protest against the old order demanding Western-style democracy and modernization.[31] Caught up in history, Dewey stayed for two years traveling the country giving speeches and trying to understand the rapidly changing context.

In an interesting Stanford University essay, the essence of pragmatism is to suggest that "we do not need reasons for our beliefs when there are no challenges to them to be defeated." In other words, it is a philosophy of an easy life. Why engage in high-minded Cartesian doubt about the meaning of everything when there is no need to; we should doubt only when there is a reason to doubt. Dewey was now in the middle of a potential Chinese revolution where beliefs were being challenged daily but the pragmatic response was to lie low and see what happened.

Many years after being portrayed as a decadent agent of imperialist philosophy[32] Dewey's pragmatism was to reemerge as a defining feature of Chinese political ideology. Deng Xiaoping's catchphrase, "It doesn't matter whether the cat is black or white, as long as it catches mice,"[33] echoes Dewey's pragmatic dictum that we should address problems only on the basis of their practical consequences. In Deng's words, "Practice is the sole criterion of truth."

————

A fake city is one that hasn't convinced you that it is real. For example, everyone knows that the $8 billion replica Venice set in the frozen northern city of Dalian in Liaoning province, complete with 4 km of canals, is not real; and the replica of the Austrian UNESCO world heritage village of Hallsatt in Guangdong is not really heritage. But there are different levels of unreality. The Sino-Finnish Smart City (DigiEcoCity) in Gongqingcheng, Jiangxi (the name means Communist Youth League City) broke ground but immediately stalled even though it was a venture approved at the highest level.

As far as genuine Eco-cities go, environmental advocate Mark Roseland states: "Sustainable development strategies should favor bottom-up over top-down approaches; redistribution over 'trickle down;' self-reliance over dependency; local rather than regional, national or mega-projects."[34] This definition seems automatically to disqualify top-down China from authentic sustainable eco-construction practices, so we might conclude that China doesn't stand a chance of constructing anything that would satisfy Western environmental arbiters. But it would be a mistake to suggest that all Chinese Eco-cities are fake, or parodies, or unsustainable.

Undoubtedly, some are less believable than others, and this final section explores that category. Within China there are several types of unreal: the fabricated, the overclaimed, and the unsustainable. Let's take a look at each of these in turn as represented in the strange world of Chinese Eco-cities:

Fabricated

In 2010, Xinhua, China's state-owned media, reported on the failures in the construction of something called "The China Educated Youth Eco-city project." By the time the authorities intervened, the Eco-city effectively comprised a mere four or five multistory buildings with a grand entrance arch proclaiming its Eco-city status. A local developer had sold apartments to elderly couples in the area on the basis that this eco-development would provide them with excellent care facilities and an environmental setting. He brandished a certificate that confirmed that the Educated Youth Eco-city was approved for its "ecological health (by) Yunnan Center of Soil and Water Conservation." Eventually, the police found that this was a standard statement confirming that the project complied with normal soil and water conservation laws and regulations but "did not mean that the project (had been) approved for construction." In the words of the state-owned media, this project was a "scam" by a developer who illegally occupied the land, erected a grand sign, forged documents, and operated a fraudulent construction site. It was a good old-fashioned criminal act, ripping off the frail, elderly, and gullible.

Under Ministry of Finance guidelines, real estate developers can enjoy preferential rates if they have an "ecological" development plan. For example, they can get 45 RMB/m² subsidy for green construction methods and for small-scale developers this is sufficient reason to flaunt a fake certificate. Fleecing a number of pensioners was almost incidental. In this instance, the developer was prosecuted for "the lack of sound eco-city procedures" and the buildings were demolished. Sadly, there are many such examples of dubious construction practices or processes across China, tempted by environmental rewards.

On a different scale (and with no suggestion of malpractice), Changsha in Hunan Province is home to a project by the eco-developer, Zhang Yue, billionaire founder of Broad Sustainable Building. In 2013, he caught the world's attention with plans to construct the tallest building in the world at 838 meters, which would be built in record-breaking time. Sadly, we are still waiting. While Zhang blames intransigence and the authorities blame a lack of permits, some level-headed people saw it coming. Professor Yin

Zhi, head of Tsinghua Urban Design Institute in Beijing, said, "The technique that Broad Group uses has no precedent in the world, and the cost they promised is very low. So they either have some record breaking techniques or it's a lie. They are gambling. If they win, they will change the history of world architecture, but that's one chance in a million."[35] Far be it for me to comment on whether it is real or imagined technology.

Overclaiming

The overclaimed Eco-cities come in three different sizes: those that purport to be cities when in fact they are villages, those that claim simple everyday improvements to be of earth-shatteringly ecological importance, and those that insist that things are happening when the reverse is true.

The first is Huangbaiyu. It is called an Eco-city in *National Geographic*,[36] but actually is not even a village, merely an estate of 400 homes in a remote outpost in Liaoning Province. The project was first mooted in 2002 and carried the imprimatur of Deng Nan, daughter of Deng Xiaoping, and architectural eco-guru Bill McDonough. Agreements to proceed were signed in 2005, forty-two houses were built by 2006, and not much has happened since. None have ever been completed. My taxi driver, on the trip from neighboring Benxi, found it difficult to locate the site for two reasons: first, when asked, no villagers knew what an Eco-village was, and, secondly, the incomplete, dilapidated houses were completely hidden from view behind overgrown foliage. When we eventually located them, it was a scene of total dereliction: half-finished bungalows in a forest of weeds. Locals had squatters' rights to the gardens and used them as additional space to grow crops.

This project was a disaster from start to finish and has been well documented by American anthropologist Shannon May, who was resident in the village for the duration of the project.[37] She recounts how the straw bale construction system failed, the roofs leaked, the solar panels weren't connected, the biogas generator was undersized, and productive arable land was bulldozed and how a naïve local developer's mismanagement allegedly matched the architect's poor knowledge of local materials and labor capabilities.[38,39] The price of each house rocketed from $3,500 to $12,000, well beyond the pockets of the intended residents of this remote farming community.

My only reservation about the justifiable criticism leveled at the architect is Shannon May's suggestion that the project was unsuitable because the houses didn't need garages because none of the farmers had cars. Tellingly, between the end of her stay in the village in 2007 and my visit six years later, many farmers and villagers had cars and garages and the local authority was metaling the roads for heavier traffic. Maybe May was a little too embedded in parochial village life to notice the impact (and speed) of material progress. Garages aside, the key point is that this was a project that was lauded to the hilt by many Western sustainability advocates and environmental commentators and yet it was, and is, a disaster. Subsequently, as one bemused commentator notes, "All references to the site have been scrubbed from McDonough's website and that of the China-US Center for Sustainable Development."[40] All that remains is a purpose-made slum using up valuable arable land right in the middle of a picturesque, underdeveloped village. (Figure 7.2)

FIGURE 7.2　*The derelict reality of Huangbaiyu, Liaoning province*
Source: Author

A second variant of overclaiming is where commonplace urban improvements are often overinflated in importance. For the small town of Luoyang in Henan to be designated an Eco-City, for example, the authorities propose a landscaping project that sets out to increase urban green space, plant trees, and protect against invasive species that might damage planting. Unquestionably it will be an improvement in the quality of the urban experience, but not enough, surely, to result in an Eco-city badge?

Many suburban towns in China are now regularly being reclassified as "low carbon cities," precisely as China learns to deal with the massive global political pressure and national economic demands to cut carbon emissions. The twelfth Five-Year Plan calls for carbon emissions per unit of GDP to be reduced by 17 percent (the first stage in compliance with President Hu Jintao's commitment to a 40–45 percent reduction by 2020 [relative to 2005]). Eco-cities alongside major industrial sites will tend to disregard the emissions outside their backyard and merely monitor within their urban boundary in order to keep pollution statistics down. The Ministry of Housing and Urban-Rural Development (MOHURD) has set a number of key indicators for low-carbon developments that include: population density; pedestrian and bicycle lanes; public transit's share of total trips; proximity of transit stations; availability of public facilities, housing, and jobs; block size; average commuting time and distance; and regulation of parking lots provision.[41] Actually there is nothing intrinsically environmental about these points and, in fact, they are commonsense transport initiatives.

Trial cities for these transport proposals include Turpan New District in the middle of the desert and Beichuan, a city utterly destroyed by the Sichuan earthquake, both quintessentially *tabula rasa* planning projects that can accommodate new transport infrastructure more of readily than an upgrading of an existing city. The essential need to rebuild these cities allows for a more rational and efficient plan but surely it is overstating their eco-credentials, merely based on implementing an urban transport improvement and comparing it to what went before. Otherwise, surely any new transport system could legitimately earn the label Eco-city to its urban location.

The third variant of "overclaiming" relates to the overreliance on data, which is often to the detriment of the real lived experience on the ground. Chinese urbanism is not exactly "human scale" at the best of times but planners' concentration on nature and the environment in eco-developments often seems to be to the detriment of the everyday user experience and built quality. In some cases, the infatuation with monitoring buildings' environmental performance, and their air quality, energy rating, carbon emissions, and so on, leaves many researchers oblivious to the qualitative side of the urban experience.

The Chinese Green Building Council was set up in 2008 by the Ministry of Construction to establish an environmental rating system that would rival (or harmonize with) the American Leadership in Energy and Environmental Design (LEED) system and the British Building Research Establishment Environmental Assessment Method (BREEAM), which determine the classification of buildings' environmental credentials. The later invention of the national "China 3-star" system provides yet another environmental standard for construction and promoting carbon-neutral development. (These standards are discussed in Chapter 4.) MOHURD has set a target of 30 percent of all new constructed buildings to be green by 2020.

This national benchmarking system is a source of national pride, with one student noting that even though it "was only introduced in 2006 it has grown to become one of the most popular green building standards in China."[42] Whereas the Western systems rely on computer modeling of the design to determine the classification of the performance of the building, the "China 3-star" system relies on physical modeling of the building after one year in practice. While this sounds eminently practical and accurate, in fact it is open to abuse and manipulation. As previously noted, once the one-year monitoring period ends and the certificates of low-energy use and minimal carbon production compliance have been earned, it is very easy to turn up the lights and the heating to a comfortable, but unmonitored, level.

Unsustainable

Dongtan, China's first Eco-city development, was to have been built on Chongming Island near Shanghai, situated in the Yangtze River Delta. The first phase, comprising a city of 25,000 people, was due to have opened for the Shanghai Expo in 2010. By 2030, it was intended to house 500,000 residents. In reality, nothing happened.

Dongtan was the first Eco-city to reach international attention and international acclaim, feted by environmental advocates as well as urban specialists across the world. When things started going sour, people looked the other way. Environment writer Fred Pearce, one of the cheerleaders for the project, claimed that everyone had been "hoodwinked" by an elaborate deception: "Shanghai milked the media well," he said.[43] But in fact many commentators walked into this project with their eyes wide shut, as in Ai WeiWei's prank in Ordos. Dongtan's fall from grace was spectacular, but even five years after the project had officially been canceled, there were online stories hailing Dongtan as a model for success. Now, like Huangbaiyu, incriminating (supportive) evidence has been effectively expunged from the internet.

I first heard of the project in the early 2000s from environmental campaigner Herbert Girardet, when we met—for some unfathomable reason—at a meeting of the Soil Association in London. He piqued my interest in the Chinese Eco-city, telling me that he was regularly flying to Shanghai to act as a consultant to the "world's first eco-city" as he called it. As we all called it. I eventually visited in 2015, crossing the Yangtze by ferry and returning along the Shanghai Yangtze River Tunnel and Bridge to mainland Shanghai.

Chongming Island is formed by alluvial deposits and has grown into the second (or third, if you include Taiwan) biggest island in China, doubling in size by natural accretion from 600 km² in 1950 to 1,300 km² today. It has natural wetlands for migrating birds and is predominantly farmland. Life is hard for many on this island, and it feels like nothing has changed for centuries. Dongtan is in a remote location on Chongming Island that once served as a military base for the occupying Japanese forces, where syphilitic soldiers committed unspeakable horrors on local people.[44] Thirty years later during the Cultural Revolution, many Chinese youth and older intellectuals were sent here to work the Chongming Island farms to atone for their politically incorrect views. Thirty years more and British prime minister Tony Blair and President Hu Jintao were shaking hands over an Eco-city proposal that was to entrap the local population once again.

After the obligatory search for the famous Eco-city, I found a vast derelict wasteland interspersed with building rubble, some street signs, and a road that faded out into undergrowth (complete with a traffic light that had been eerily blinking red and green for six years with no traffic to control). Dongtan Eco-city is a huge patch of scrubland leading onto the bird sanctuary.

Julie Sze's exposé of the project in her 2015 book *Fantasy Islands* is illuminating, outlining a mixture of corruption, naïveté, and stupidity that ran through the project from its inception. The plan was to create an environmental city in which a "construction of nature draws on particular notions of wilderness in which people are largely absent."[45] Sze says that "one reason eco-cities resemble one another is that they share not only ideologies but also builders," noting that Western consultants are commissioned from a list of usual suspects who sit on pedestals as remote from the masses as the central Party. Sze quotes a promotional article describing the Dongtan Eco-city as if it was a bourgeois central London farmer's market. It reads:

> appreciat(e) this beautiful vista, as relishing the local fruit, vegetables, locally produced sausages, cheese and beer and hearing oral music, visitors will find themselves back in the good old days of the past, as well as in the 21st century.

With the collapse of this project, Shanghai officials had a light-bulb moment for their conception of Chongming Island. They learned that the fundamental tension between ecological conservation and the formation of an urban agglomoration can be resolved by doing nothing much at all. Why spend billions building an Eco-city that protects the environment when you can simply allow local farmers to continue working the environment for free? The islanders' desire for material modernization was never part of the Dongtan venture, but, now, given the failure of the project, for the time being nondevelopment is a cheap and easy way to save face and promote Chongming's ecological credentials.

————

There are many examples of Eco-city administrators bluffing their way to success, many examples of Eco-cities that have not progressed further than the drawing board, and many examples of the so-called Eco-cities that are no better than a collection of low-energy buildings, or farmland recultivation branded as ecological intervention (such as the "Returning Farmland to Grassland" project in Batou Eco-city).[46] But it would be disingenuous to suggest that this is the norm. In fact, the general tendency within China now is to make an effort to provide decent environmental conditions—whether by constructing new, creating satellite cities to a higher standard or by refurbishing old urban areas to modernize and hence improve the quality of life for its population. It is an open question whether these are Eco-cities or just "nicer cities," but even those that have failed to deliver are generally held to have provided valuable lessons in how to do it better next time. This is the subject of the next chapter.

Notes

1 Kane, A., "Think Small: Architects Shrink Homes and Apartments as House and Land Prices Soar," *The Guardian*, March 31, 2016.

2 Ordos100, https://www.youtube.com/watch?v=LLL72t_bHVo.

3 Wellner, M., "Talk with Ai WeiWei," in Ai WeiWei, Fake Buildings, Fake Village, Fake_Architecture, 2011. p. 85.

4 Ocko, J., "Copying, Culture, and Control: Chinese Intellectual Property Law in Historical Context," *Yale Journal of Law & the Humanities* 1996, 8(2), Art. 10, pp. 559–578.

5 Yu, P.K., "Causes of Piracy and Counterfeiting in China," *Guanxi: The China Letter*, April 2007. http://www.peteryu.com/guanxi.pdf.

6 Popper, K., *In Search of a Better World: Lectures and Essays from Thirty Years*, 1995. p. 38.

7 Lipman, J.N. and Harrell, S., *Violence in China: Essays in Culture and Counterculture*, New York: SUNY Press, 1990. p. 156.

8 Chien, S.-C., "Cultural Constructions of Plagiarism in Student Writing: Teachers' Perceptions and Responses," *Research in the Teaching of English*, November 2014, 49(2), pp. 120–140.

9 Yang, Kelly, "Expel All Exam Cheats," *South China Morning Post*, June 26, 2013.

10 Yeh, G and Wu, F., "The Transformation of the Urban Planning System in China from a Centrally-Planned to Transitional Economy," *Progress in Planning* 1999, 51. pp. 165–252.

11 Zhang, S., de Roo, G. and Lu, B., "China: What about the Urban Revolution? Rapid Transformations in Chinese Planning and Its

Links with a Slowly Emerging European Planning Theory," *European Planning Studies* 2012, 20(12), pp. 1997–2011.

12 JTP, Changzhi Island, Shanghai, China., A New Settlement: Connecting the Mountains to the Sea, Press Release, jtp.co.uk (accessed March 31, 2016).

13 Trangos, G., "Buffer Zones and Golf Estates: Do We Really Need More Garden Cities?" *The Architectural Review*, September 3, 2014.

14 English Heritage, Conservation Principles, Policies and Guidance, Historic Buildings and Monuments Commission for England, April 2008, p. 9.

15 English Heritage, Conservation Principles, Policies and Guidance, Historic Buildings and Monuments Commission for England, April 2008, p. 52.

16 Sullivan, J., Heroes and Villains, Only Fools and Horses (dir. Tony Dow). BBCTV December 25, 1996.

17 Anderson, R.C., Authenticity and Architecture. Representation and Reconstruction in Context, Tilburg University, 2014: 978-94-6167-217-9.

18 Miao, P, "In the Absence of Authenticity: The Interpretation of Contemporary Chinese Culture," *Nordisk Arkitekturforskning*, 1995, 3, pp. 7–24.

19 Lemaire, R. and Stovel, H., "The Nara Document on Authenticity," *The Nara*, Conference on Authenticity in Relation to the World Heritage Convention, Nara, Japan, November 1–6, 1993, UNESCO/ICCROM/ICOMOS.

20 Schaffer, Simon, "Instruments and Cargo in the China Trade," *History of Science* 2006, 44(2), p. 217.

21 Williams, Laurence, "British Government under the Qianlong Emperor's Gaze: Satire, Imperialism, and the Macartney Embassy to China, 1792–1804," *Lumen: Selected Proceedings From the Canadian Society for Eighteenth-Century Studies* 2013, 32, p. 85.

22 Tingyang, Zhao, "A Political World Philosophy in Terms of All-Under-Heaven (Tian-Xia)," *Diogenes* 2009, 56(1), pp. 5–18.

23 Elliott, M., *Emperor Qianlong: Son of Heaven, Man of the World.* New York: Pearson Longman, 2009.

24 Louis, W.R., Porter, A., Low, A.L., Canny, N.P. and Marshall, P.J., *The Oxford History of the British Empire: The Nineteenth Century*, Vol. 3. Oxford University Press, 1999. p. 149.

25 W. Beasley, *The Meiji Restoration*. Stanford University Press, 1972. p. 81.

26 Palm, Daniel, C. "Chinese Encounters with Foreign Ideas in the Self-Strengthening Movement (1861–1895)," American Association of Chinese Studies Conference October 13–14, 2012, Atlanta, Georgia, USA.

27 Williams, A., "The Origins of China's Copycat Culture," *Global*, 2013. http://www.global-briefing.org/2014/01/the-origins-of-chinas-copycat-culture/ (accessed June 24, 2016).

28 Li, Eric, "How China Broke the West's Monopoly on Modernization," *Christian Science Monitor*, April 28, 2011.

29 James, W., *Pragmatism*. Harvard University Press (Massachusetts, US), 1975. p. 194.

30 Malachuk, Daniel. "Walt Whitman and the Culture of Pragmatism," *Walt Whitman Quarterly Review*, Summer 1999, 17, pp. 60–68.

31 Gu, Edward X., "Who Was Mr Democracy? The May Fourth Discourse of Populist Democracy and the Radicalization of Chinese Intellectuals (1915–1922)," *Modern Asian Studies*, July 2001, 35(3), pp. 589–621.

32 Liu, Fangtong, Huang, Songjie and McLean, George F., *Philosophy and Modernization in China*. CRVP, 1997. p. 103.

33 Quoted in Li, Hung, *China's Political Situation and the Power Struggle in Peking*, 1977. p. 107.

34 Roseland, M. (ed.), *Eco-City Dimensions: Healthy Communities, Healthy Planet*. Gabriola Island, BC: New Society Publishers, 1997.

35 Gongzi, Zhao, "Sinablog, China Hunan's Tallest Building Was Halted," July 27, 2013. http://blog.sina.com.cn/s/blog_5ccd85c20101919v.html (accessed February 22, 2016).

36 Lamb, L., "Can China's Eco-cities Bridge Fantasy with Reality?" *National Geographic*, June 23, 2010.

37 May, S., "A Sino-U.S. Sustainability Sham," *Far Eastern Economic Review*, April 2007, pp. 57–60.

38 Larson, C., "China's Grand Plans for Eco-Cities Now Lie Abandoned," *Yale360*, April 6, 2009. http://e360.yale.edu/feature/chinas_grand_plans_for_eco-cities_now_lie_abandoned/2138/.

39 Lesle, T., "China Green Dreams: A Not-so Model Village," *Frontline World*, January 31, 2008. http://www.pbs.org/frontlineworld/fellows/green_dreams/.

40 Wilson, R., "A Tale of Four Cities: Chapter 3," 2010. http://robswatsonadventure.blogspot.com/2010/12/tale-of-four-cities-chapter-3.html December 8, 2010.

41   Baeumler, A., Ijjasz-Vasquez, E. and Mehndiratta, S., *Sustainable Low-Carbon City Development in China*. The World Bank, 2012. p. 41.

42   Zhou, Yang, "Comparison of Chinese Green Building Standard with Western Green Building Standards, Bachelor of Science Thesis EGI-2014."

43   Pearce, J., "Greenwash: The Dream of the First Eco-city Was Built on a Fiction," *The Guardian*, April 23, 2009.

44   Qiu, Peipei, Lifei, Chen, Zhiliang, Su, *Chinese Comfort Women: Testimonies from Imperial Japan's Sex Slaves*. Oxford University Press, 2014.

45   Sze, J., *Fantasy Islands: Chinese Dreams and Ecological Fears in an Age of Climate Crisis*. University of California Press, 2015. p. 83.

46   Yang, Zhifeng. *Eco-Cities: A Planning Guide*. CRC Press, 2012. p. 373.

CHAPTER EIGHT

Urban Experiments

Rizhao, with a population of around three million, is a prefecture-level city on the coast in Shandong, north China. Prefecture-level cities are not that high up the pecking order but tend to be reasonably large cities with a nonfarming population of more than a quarter of a million and with the authority to administer lesser counties and county-level cities. In November 1999, this seaside resort (the name means "sunshine" and whose motto is "blue sky, green trees, blue sea, golden beach") was officially approved as a National Sustainable Development Experimental Zone. In 2001, the city received official approval to "seriously implement the scientific concept of development, based on the advantages of the sun." The city officials mandated that all houses should incorporate solar panels as standard; a vast majority of homes in the central districts now use solar thermal water heaters. Even the traffic signals, street lights, and park illuminations are powered by photovoltaic solar cells, thus reducing the energy load and cutting down on the need for coal-fired grid power by, some say, up to 30 percent.[1] Admittedly, Rizhao is one of China's largest liquid petrochemical ports and prides itself on its asbestos mines, but by 2008 it had been designated a National Model City of Environmental Protection and Environmentally-friendly National Model City[2] by the Ministry of Environmental Protection (formally, SEPA).

There are many projects and accolades like this throughout China, from the "China Charm City" to the "National Green City" (both titles have been attained by Rizhao). These prized eco-labels provide a variety of standards for demonstration projects and set targets for urban and technical experimentation. Cities like Rizhao—and there are many hundreds of similarly unknown cities like this—are citywide testing grounds for technologies, urban designs, and policy initiatives that are setting the ground rules for China's environmental cleanup. These test sites not only improve the ecological standards of cities but also ensure that they benefit economically from an improved tourism offer, for example, by waving as many eco-certificates as possible on city promotional websites and TripAdvisor.

Way back in 1986, Yichun City in Jiangxi Province was named as the first trial Eco-city in China. By 2011, it was festooned with an almost unsustainable number of paper certificates documenting its position as China's National Sanitary City, China's Garden City, China Excellent Tourism City, National Afforestation Model City, and the First class National Road Traffic Engineering Management City. Yichun has significant mining industry extracting aluminum, tungsten, and zinc, but its lithium deposits have also enabled it to become the Lithium Battery New Energy High-Tech Industry City.

China is clearly using environmental efficiency pressures to innovate, whether it is in battery technology or solar thermal, and there is a new research and development incentive to take these technologies forward. Once again, it is necessary to inject a note of statistical caution since there are many cases of inflated "patent generation" in China (i.e., the technical act of filing a patent is officially equated with innovation). But China's visible strides in implementing innovative technology and the concomitant rapid changes in the economic condition are also manifesting themselves in significant physical urban changes.

Once again the example of Shenzhen is telling. This is where Deng Xiaoping launched his famous southern tour of 1992, turning Shenzhen into the first of four special economic zones and introducing the economic reforms that would transform the region and the nation. In its own terms Shenzhen's urban transformation has been an example in mass acceptance, morphing from a provincial region of small towns and fishing villages in the 1990s to a modern mega city with barely a murmur of dissent. (There have been wage strikes[3] and migrant workers' rights protests,[4] but surprisingly few antidevelopment protests.) Peasants and farmers as well as the fisherman were all caught in the development net for the simple reason that many approve of the infrastructural, commercial, and financial benefits that accrue from a developed city. Many crave progress, many lack a desire to hold onto the past, and many want to make as much out of it as possible. But Shenzhen's transformation is truly astounding all the same. How did they manage it?

To effectively raze an area of over 300 km² and build a megacity in just thirty years, to turf people out to build a city, to metamorphose from 0.3 to 15 million in thirty years, each brings to mind the oft-heard exclamation: "Only in China!" Indeed, in some ways China is one of the very few dynamic market economies in the world where the structured social order gives the state incredible leverage to insist that people do whatever is necessary.

Even though there are only seventy million Party members (surprisingly there are twice as many Buddhists as Communist Party members in this atheistic country), the structure of social order is determined by fealty to the Party. That said, China's government is not the single-minded Communist bloc of popular Cold War imagination but is a modern established system of government that, like many governments around the world, is struggling to find legitimacy. The flimsy narrative of a Chinese Dream is a little intangible for some, and China's hard-nosed nationalist rhetoric worries others. Even so, China has preserved a mechanism of social organization that is unique, one that has managed to ensure social stability—with high-profile exceptions—through turbulent times.

The pragmatism of the ruling administration (discussed in the previous chapter) is framed around a self-preservationist necessity to maintain order, airbrushing out the vicissitudes of China's recent history, primarily through the rhetoric and logic of a "harmonious society." A harmonious society maintains the Party in power and the fact that the Party is, to all intents and purposes, the state is a happy coincidence for some. The army swears to defend the Party and not the country; and the State Council, National People's Congress, Political Consultative Committee, Supreme Court, and Supreme People's Procuratorate all report directly to the Chinese Communist Party's Politburo Standing Committee. Sitting above this, the institutions of the Party, the State Council, and the military are now responsible to President Xi Jinping.[5] By and large, decisions are handed down. It feels like democracy is not going to break out any time soon. The ability of the state to implement fundamental social change that would be scorned in many other countries appears to be accepted here, provided of course that it is seen to produce benefits.

That said, in the first half of 2016, there was a total of 1,456 strikes, up by 19 percent from the first half of 2015;[6] so local activism in China is actually alive and kicking in some ways, but trade unions "are virtually impotent when it comes to representing workers"[7] because they are quasi-government bodies, sanctioned by the Chinese Communist Party. When all else fails, the force of law is used liberally to reassert control. Since late 2016, foreign nongovernmental organizations (NGOs) are legally compelled by the Ministry of Public Security to buddy with a "professional supervisory unit" tasked with approving the NGOs' yearly work plan and overseeing hiring decisions.[8] China clearly has a sovereign right to insist that NGOs do not have carte blanche to operate "sans frontieres," which may shock many activists used to meddling in the affairs of Third World states, but it will be interesting to see how the Chinese Communist Party's intrusive and invasive demands on the operation of NGOs cause them to acquiesce or reconsider their involvement.

Within this type of social framework, it is hardly surprising that many Chinese citizens are resigned to whatever will be. They have a phrase for it, *mei banfa*, meaning "there is no solution." Note that they do not say, "there is no alternative," in the way that people express resignation in the West; they say, "There is no *solution*." Lately, the Chinese government has come to recognize that this erstwhile useful fatalism is now beginning to resemble nihilism, which for them needs to be combatted lest it becomes a problem for social coherence and Party legitimacy.[9]

As we have seen in Chapter 4, China is experimenting with forms of democratic engagement such as participatory budgeting and local elections; however, these are merely the impressions of participation because the real decisions have been premade and participation is usually a technical or rubber-stamping exercise. Disputes tend to reinforce the patrician role of the Party to step in to mediate. One researcher suggests that these empowered village councils, elected by local villagers, "sit in parallel to the Communist Party appointed and controlled Village Committee. In principle, there is no overlap."[10] This research failed to conclude that such a principle doesn't hold water, given that there is almost complete oversight by the state authorities. In reality, China exercises what one researcher has called "consultative authoritarianism."[11] There is clearly an ability to "get things done" in China and a concomitant social acquiescence of Chinese locals to being part of these urban test beds.

The use of sticks and carrots is how so many things get done in China, but genuine acceptance of change is a delicate balance.

There is no civil society in China that is able to mediate, to protest, to criticize, and to develop a positional interest. For the German philosopher Jurgen Habermas, the historical development of the "public sphere" in the UK and parts of Europe meant the public use of reason. It is articulated by private individuals engaged in reasoned argument requiring a "liberal political culture."[12] He speaks of bourgeois society and describes how civil society "came into existence as a corollary of a depersonalized state authority."[13] Any comparison will reveal that these conditions do not prevail in China. In the UK, there are organizations such as the Royal Institute of British Architects and the Town and Country Planning Association; in America, there is the American Institute of Architects or the American Institute of Certified Planners to name just a few. These are independent bodies that represent the interests of architects and urbanists but that also challenge policy direction, criticize interests that run counter to the profession, and put forward standards. By contrast, the Architecture Society of China or the China Association of City Planning or the China Society of Urban Planners and so on are given rein by the Ministry of Construction, which is an arm of direct government.

In a paper written in 1996 but still relevant today (because for all the changes in China, many things stay the same), Rachel Murphy notes, "Rather than pursuing interests in a group capacity, entrepreneurs incorporate themselves into network allegiances with the state, and in so doing, they consent to state authority."[14] In 2006, China established the "Top 1,000 Enterprises Energy Conservation Action Programme" involving predominantly state-owned energy supply enterprises. The authorities mandated an internal cap-and-trade policy from on high, reducing energy intensity by 20 percent (achieved by 2010), and fining and punishing failing companies and errant management. The state penalizing a state-owned enterprise (SOE) is an exercise in masochistic management practices, in which the state brandishes financial retribution and then foots the bill itself.

While the Iron Rice Bowl of state subsidy has theoretically ended, Premier Li Keqiang has told SOEs that "when cutting excess capacity, superfluous workers must be transferred to other jobs instead of being laid off." For example, from July 2015 to July 2016, Wuhan Iron & Steel laid off 28 percent of its workforce—around 16,000 workers—costing 10 billion yuan (UKP 1 billion) in company subsidy. The workers thrown out of jobs are often reemployed in fake jobs in the so-called "zombie industries." In late 2016, the government released plans to address these real economic dilemmas, although, of course, social stability remains paramount.

The third level of society, "the public," deals with things differently, and here Murphy quotes political sociologist Andrew G Walder:

> The diffuse web of purely personal relationships through which most individuals...can bend the rules in their favor...has the effect of giving the average worker the sense of that he or she has "beaten the system" through individual, not collective, action and of reinforcing the propensity to retreat from co-ordinated group action and indeed from "politics" in general.[15]

———

Pingdi Town, Longgang District, is a migrant-staffed industrial zone containing a variety of long-standing, highly polluting manufacturing plants, including metal plating, plastics, packaging, and glass industries.[16] The area is located at a potentially troublesome pinch-point for Shenzhen and Guangdong's urban expansion and so the city cleanup—obeying Central Party diktat—is being used as a means to bring these different provincial cities together by focusing on environmental improvements as a useful, noncontentious way of encouraging collaborative working across erstwhile competing interests. Dutch environmental advocates were contacted to share their environmental experience—experience that was lacking on the Chinese side, in order to develop environmental cleanup solutions. The result is the Shenzhen International Low-carbon Town that is a tried-and-tested model of international collaboration, but is essentially a demonstration of how political integration can be translated into ways that local officials from neighboring local administrations can work together. The Netherlands has long been China's second largest trading partner within the European Union (operating a trade surplus with Guangdong Province)—and as a result of eco-collaborations like this one, trade relations between the Netherlands and China have been further enhanced.

Unsurprisingly, maybe, it is Western architects and urbanists who are the most keen to see China as a place to try out new ideas. In tow, there are the slightly less influential design companies desperate to enter the market by the back door, partly because there is little scope for work in their home countries and partly because they believe that they are changing China for the better. Alan Kell, a previous chair of the UK-China Eco-Cities & Green Building Working Group, is quoted as saying, "A lot of activity is frankly smoke and mirrors...So we've got to get involved...to help the Chinese help themselves."[17]

Some Chinese commentators are concerned at the preferential treatment given to foreign architects in Chinese megaprojects and have described it as a new form of cultural colonialism.[18] This is not yet a dominant opinion but foreign architects' high-minded lack of awareness of this debate only compounds the charge and increases the friction.

For instance, it is common to hear China discussed by foreign experts as an "urban experiment." The phrase "living laboratory" was chosen by Dutch interventionists in creating Shenzhen Low-Carbon City mentioned above. Relishing the authority to completely restructure a large area of the Shenzhen, the Dutch planning advisors admitted that "a nagging question remained...what to do with the current inhabitants?" Drawing on Herbert Girardet's construct of "green collar workers," which requires that locals be shunted into "maintenance, surveillance and personal services work in the green economy"[19] was one way of salving the conscious by portraying menial tasks as somehow environmentally moral. I mention this example simply because China has long been harangued for its blasé approach to local residents and their forcible removal, relocation, and resettlement. Doing similar things but with a "green" badge is often thought to be more ecologically legitimate, almost ethically good.

Let's take one more example of inappropriateness masquerading as the right thing to do. In Daxing Ecological Community in Dongsheng, Inner Mongolia, the proposal by Swedish environmentalists to install dry, communal eco-toilets in a relatively poor community in north China ended in disaster. An eco-toilet is a product that is common in the Third World where a sprinkling of sawdust replaces the normal flushing mechanism—effectively a glorified, technically enhanced bucket. These toilets were installed in homes but the residents suffered years of unpleasantness, odor, inconvenience, and consequent ill-health. However, the Stockholm

Environment Institute saw the farrago as a valuable learning experience; it is worth quoting its version of events in full:

> As the project got under way, the value of coal in China was rapidly increasing and Dongsheng saw a mammoth building boom. The standard of living skyrocketed to levels similar to Hong Kong and Shanghai. Also, a 100-kilometer pipeline was built from the Yellow River to Dongsheng to increase freshwater supply, and fossil groundwater reserves were further developed. As a result, the bases for the project—extreme water shortage and poverty—quickly disappeared, and the eco-toilet project was overshadowed by the rapid development. In fact, an entire new city, Kangbashi, was built adjacent to Dongsheng during the period of the project.[20]

While this kind of low-grade, stopgap alternative technology toilet has been installed in Africa for many decades (a place where development still remains a dream for many), it is actually only in China that the pace of real, meaningful social development could overtake the time required to install such a bog-standard affront. The company sounds faintly disappointed that the residents opted for modernization and that they are now living in a better environment. Some journalists have praised China as "one of the most environmentally progressive countries, rapidly changing from the world's factory to the world's clean-tech laboratory."[21] But actually, many of its simple advances—like flushing toilets and drains—are not politicized environmental improvements; they are simply improvements. No prefix necessary.

Another commentator has said that "the choices made in the construction of China's cities will determine the future of the world."[22] This might be a little extreme but there are definitely lessons to learn, so let's look at a few examples of a range of urban innovations.

————

When I first arrived in Shanghai in 2011, I met a young businessman on a train who pitched for me to invest in his solar panel business. If I invested US$200 million, he could buy a German solar manufacturing plant; or, for a mere US$20 million, he'd set up a plant using American solar technology. When I asked why he wasn't setting up using Chinese R&D technology, he looked genuinely bemused. "Why would I want waste time doing that when I can import it?" he said.

At that time, China's R&D investment had just overtaken the UK's. Eighteen months later in 2013 it exceeded that of the European Union, and in five more years, by 2018–2019, it is scheduled to overtake that of the United States (Figure 8.1). In solar technology alone, Premier Li Keqiang was confident enough in 2015 to condemn many Western solar panels as out of date and to argue for a new generation of solar technology. Responding to the challenge, the Ministry of Science and Technology plans to launch a huge solar array in orbit to beam energy to earth.

Having reached dominance in conventional ecological energy generation—becoming the world's biggest investor in and provider and generator of wind and solar installations, and with plans to produce 30 GW of biogas energy by 2020 (30 percent of the current global total)—China is also looking to other areas of productive and generative efficiencies. Unlike the recommendations of many Western environmentalists, this is an expansive energy plan premised on environmentally friendly production. It is exploring technology gains, resource efficiencies, and land management—to

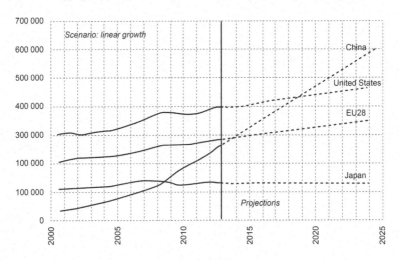

FIGURE 8.1 *Chinese comparative R&D investment*
Source: OECD Science, Technology and Industry Outlook 2014, OECD Publishing, Paris

name but a few—as experiments for a viable transitional economic model. Let's briefly take a look at each in turn.

Technology

In 2004, Guiyang, the capital city of Guizhou Province and home to 4.7 million people, had the honor of becoming China's first pilot Eco-city focusing on the circular economy. By 2012, the city became the pilot "exchange and cooperation platform for national ecological civilization."[23] By January 2016, it became the first Chinese city to become a member of the International Council for Local Environmental Initiatives and the first city in China to propose and implement local regulations on the development of a circular economy. Such powerful firsts have created important business networks that have propelled it into the headlines and further strengthened its economic performance. The city government signed 138 development deals for big data industries to the sum of RMB133 billion (US$21 billion) in 2014 alone, after being boosted by Premier Li Keqiang's statement that "the new generation of technology puts all countries at the same starting line. China should pounce at the strategic opportunity to gain a leading position."[24].

In 2014, China's National State Council launched its National New Urbanisation Plan (2014–2020), which mandated that regions "advance Smart Cities development." Already huge facilities are being built—even in remote Gobi Desert locations —as Smart city centers of cloud computing storage. These are new industrial eco-parks. With no laws directly governing or defining Smart Cities in China, by April 2015, 285 pilot cities were smart enough to give themselves the name.

Since most of China's youth seem to spend much of their time peering into mobile apps, the shrewd growth of eco-urban models combining media-tech facilities, big data parks, intelligent homes, green transportation, smart grids, and other such tech-savvy urbanism is eminently understandable. Many in the West are nervous of data hoarding by private companies, but China has been monitoring people for decades. That said, there is still suspicion of the techno-legitimation of ever more state monitoring and personal data trawling, which is an order of magnitude more intrusive than allowed for private companies in the West. In China, regardless of recent company data protection and cybersecurity legislation, such data is readily available to the state.

Resources

Israel is producing more freshwater than it needs from state-of-the-art desalination plants[25] and is commercially advising California on how to improve its water supply and top up its groundwater resources. China is also commercially applying the same principles but is devising low-energy desalination. If early reports are to be believed, that means that water can be produced at a small scale where needed. A reporter from the *South China Morning Post* suggests that this could help it produce freshwater on remote islands or reclaimed territory, hinting at the military applicability on China's contested islands. Undoubtedly, such a technical advance could "quickly expand habitable areas on reclaimed land or natural islets in the South China Sea,"[26] but taken as technology in itself, that is a remarkable potential to address China's ever-worrisome water problems.

Land use

Tianjin-Binhai is seen as "an exemplary of how to productively and sustainably use environmentally disadvantaged and degraded land."[27] Tianjin is the Eco-city in the Bohai region of north China that is possibly the most advanced and referenced Eco-city in the world. It has been constructed on alkaline salt marshes with some areas contaminated with a toxic sludge including arsenic, cadmium, and mercury. The choice of site was partly inspired by the need to avoid the use of agricultural land, since China is paranoid about the need to feed itself and hence preserve agricultural capacity, and so the use of contaminated land is already heralded as an example of ecological land recovery worthy of praise.[28] The technical wizardry involved has enabled the creation of what they call a "green oasis," meaning that the soil conditions can be engineered to the best possible condition.

After dredging and remediation, some of the heavy contaminants were landfilled but the moderate and light contaminants were used to create a lakeside landscaped mound with new planting and green-landscaped areas.[29] With renewed irrigation the soil has been planted with non-native species, testing the proposition that any plant can be encouraged to grow in this area and in this remediated soil. This is something that fills many Western environmentalists with horror because "native planting" is routinely deemed to be the holy grail of eco-friendliness. The opposite of "native species," for example, is the reproachful phrase "invasive species."

However, early reports indicate that the Chinese use of what it calls "scientific environmentalism" has helped the land to flourish. According to the deputy director of the Sino-Singapore Tianjin Eco-city Administrative Committee, "It means that we can create valuable urban space from nothing." As the urban geographer, I-Chun Chang points out: "By freeing ecological urbanization from place-specific ecosystems, eco-cities can be standardized and replicated anywhere."[30] This is miraculous and akin to a desire to universalize social benefits away from purely local contexts. Already Chinese experts are advising scientists from around the world, from Africa to Pakistan, that desirable rather than just local plants can be grown on engineered soil. While some commentators prefer to report on China's growing desertification, this exciting technology looks at greening the desert. A dream of centuries.

———

In February 2016, China's State Council released a new set of guidelines for the development of cities. These were Central Party–approved interpretations of the Central Urban Work Conference that had taken place a few months earlier in December 2015. An Organization for Economic Co-operation and Development (OECD) report on China published in late 2015 at roughly the same time has many similarities with that Chinese document, hinting that some level of coordinated diplomatic negotiation and statistical information dissemination had gone into both reports.[31]

The truly remarkable thing, much commented on within the Chinese online community, is that the Chinese Urban Work Conference report was the first time that such a group had met formally for over thirty-seven years. They had last convened in 1978, two years after Mao's death in a very different world to the China we see today. During this period, the urban population has leapt from

18 to around 50 percent with the number of Chinese cities rising from 193 to the current level of 653. One of the central concerns in 1978 had been to assess how China's urban expansion was going to come about. Now they are worried about how they manage it!

The State Council's guidance, or instructions, is listed under several headings, from "Improve Public Services" to "Advance Air Quality Restoration." This is not a liberal document and many of the guidelines on better urban planning speak of China's use of satellite imaging to locate illegal construction so that they can be demolished more speedily, tightening the evaluation of violations and illegal settlements, and emphasizing the inviolability of master plans. It also talks about drawing a boundary—effectively a greenbelt, an urban perimeter, within which the "ecological carrying capacity" of a city can be maintained. This is clearly a code for setting population caps to restrict immigration. Proposing an immigration policy as an act of environmental stewardship shows how much China has learned from Western enviro-speak.

What follows is a brief snapshot of some of the main benign points likely to influence China's urban experimentation over the coming period.

Planning

Between 2011 and 2015, Chinese property developers built thirty-two million new apartments. In 2014, China's construction industry "started construction of 7.4 million low-income housing units in urban areas — and 5.11 million of these units were basically completed by the end of the year."[32]

However, while the quantity is impressive, quality has long been recognized as an essential missing ingredient in China's cities. Built at speed, in the same way that most postwar reconstruction in Europe tended to focus on immediate functional need rather than aesthetic considerations, China has been urbanizing in order to accommodate its growing population often with scant regard to the finer points of urban design. The Soviet housing model of relentless block grids served its purpose in providing reasonably decent, much-improved conditions for a vast amount of poor people. The post-1998 generation of housing improved greatly on that prior model, but now China is insisting on introducing some meaningful urban quality (although, admittedly, overcoming what one writer calls the *chabuduo* culture[33]—a phrase meaning, "why complain, it's good enough"—may take some time).

Gated communities

Gated communities are almost universally loathed by planners, but generally loved by people who live in them. In China, these are usually known as *xiaoqu* (小区), referring to a gated residential community that were first codified in Chinese planning policy in 1994. These provided simple layouts that could be constructed quickly and easily by the first generation of inexperienced private developers. In general, they are built on gridded parcels of land, each containing around 5,000 apartment units in five-to-ten-story blocks behind a high perimeter wall with security guards at each entrance.

The Chinese government is now proposing that no new gated communities be constructed, partly because of the detrimental impact on the outward-facing appearance of a 2.5-m-high fortress wall. More importantly, these *xiaoqu* are being phased out because they represent an inefficient use of land for traffic, with cul-de-sacs in lieu of streets. Finally, *xiaoqu* are being challenged because there are some worries about local power groups challenging the on-site Communist Party. One study notes, "Different kinds of homeowners also have different expectations of property management which can easily lead to conflicts."[34] Unsurprisingly, the state prefers that the local Party official sort things out rather than encouraging independent *xiaoqu* community organizers.

Whatever the difficulties, Chinese planners still regard *xiaoqu*s as a necessary stage of development. As such, gated communities are being introduced into rural areas as part of the Socialist Countryside Movement. Their orderliness is seen to be a mechanism to "civilize" communities there.[35]

Architecture

The new planning guidelines insist that developers "prevent a biased focus on a building's outer appearance." This seems to follow President Xi Jinping's exhortation in 2015 that there should be "no more weird architecture." Actually, it is a sensible request, given the poor quality of construction. All too often, impressive-looking buildings have no damp proofing, the metalwork is inadequately treated, steelwork rusts, joints leak, concrete spalls, timber rots, toilets are grim, and condensation and fire risks are everywhere.

Fetishizing architectural form while ignoring the fact that many new buildings are damp and uninsulated, for example, is something that the Chinese government is keen to put a stop to. The next generation of architects are clearly doing better. But once again, a cultural change, rather than merely a technical one, is needed.

Efficiency

It has set a goal that "30 percent of buildings constructed (will be) pre-fabricated" by 2025. If achieved, this could be a transformative impact on its construction speed and quality. The government is keen to invest in this production method and is suggesting that the Jing-Jin-Ji urban megapolis will be the ideal location to try this out. China has the luxury of having new construction sites where new ideas can be prototyped. It is also making great inroads into 3-D printed housing and even earthquake-resistant, printed homes.

Targets

Shanghai and Suzhou are among the fifteen pilot provinces and cities that have set 2020 as the year for peak CO_2 emissions. Ningbo, a key industrial port city in Zhejiang province, has set its peak emission target as 2015. Government policy is pressurizing local officials to ensure that targets are met. In Foshan district, for example, its twelfth Five-Year Plan has revised performance indicators for planning officials. In the past, job promotion and pay increases were based on hitting GDP growth targets but now local officials have to prioritize environmental targets (see Table 8.1).[36] This is undoubtedly as ripe for abuse as were the GDP figures, but it shows that China is driving toward the environmental moral high ground.

TABLE 8.1 *Foshan Performance Management Guidelines; or "Targets for promotion"*
Source: Foshan Performance Management Guidelines in Xiao, G., Zhang Y., Law, C-k. and Meagher, D. (2015). China's Evolving Growth Model: The Foshan Story, Fung Global Institute. May 2015, p34 (redrawn)

	Primary	Secondary	Tertiary
Objective criteria	Economic development (31%)	Economic growth (5%)	GDP growth (5%)
		Industrial upgrading (12%)	Input/output (3%) Industrial optimization index (3%) Industrial supply chain targets (3%) Private sector value-added growth rate (3%)
		Technological innovation (8%)	Innovative city development index (4%) Information development index (4%)
		Developmental outcomes (6%)	Income development index (2%) Local public revenue growth (2%) Tax revenue growth (2%)
	Urban development (19%)	Upgrading (8%)	Urban upgrading three-year plan completion rate (8%)
		Management (2%)	Urban management index (2%)
		Environmental protection (9%)	Fiscal expenditure and environmental protection investment (2%) Resource consumption index (2%) Emissions reduction (2%) Garbage treatment (3%)

Social development (19%)	Public services (10%)		Education modernization (2%)
			Health development index (2%)
			Cultural development index (2%)
			Social security development index (2%)
			Transport and community infrastructure development index (2%)
	Public safety (8%)		Public safety index (4%)
			"Peaceful Foshan" index (4%)
	Democracy and rule of law (3%)		Democracy and rule of law index (3%)
	Social integrity (4%)		Credit system construction (2%)
			Market supervision system construction index (2%)
Governance development (15%)	Managerial innovation (4%)		Managerial innovation index (4%)
	Administration by law (7%)		Openness of information (2%)
			Significant reduction in administrative negligence (2%)
			Honest government index (3%)
	Administrative costs (4%)		Costs as share budget (2%)
			Public finance transparency (2%)
Discretionary evaluation	Social assessment (10%)	Service satisfaction (10%)	Social satisfaction index (10%)

Sponge cities

In 2013, President Xi Jinping announced that cities should become like "sponges."[37] When the president speaks, even if no one really knows what he means, within a short period of time the message will have filtered down through the Party dissemination channels to the local level. Suddenly everyone was talking about urban sponges.

He was referring to sustainable urban drainage, a system of passive drainage absorbers and collectors—like gardens and ponds—on floors and roof surfaces that soak up and attenuate rainwater flow. A green roof, for example, absorbs and slows down the flow of rainwater, whereas if it was channeled directly into gutters, an unregulated surge might cause flood risks. Where once this was seen as a problem caused by inadequate drainage, now the aim is to minimize the flow so that the existing drainage continues to perform adequately. It minimizes the need to constantly upgrade drainage capacity and is a common feature of many eco-construction projects. It helps eke out more life for old drainage infrastructure.

China recently rolled out a centrally administered "Sponge City" pilot program across sixteen cities including Qian'an, Baicheng, Xiamen, Jinan, Wuhan, and Gui'an New Area. By 2018, these cities are scheduled to have functional state-controlled systems to absorb rainwater and capture, purify, and store it. Liu Yubin is the deputy head of the "sponge city" management committee in the city of Fengxi, which is one of four municipalities lying within Shaanxi's Xixian New Area and whose drainage and storage program alone will hold 4,000,000 m^3 of rainfall every year. In reality, using international standards, this would be classified as a large dam.[38] But as we have seen in other chapters, a "sponge city" is a more acceptable phrase than "dam" or "reservoir" with the concomitant allusion to a program of community displacement. Sponge cities are viewed as a win-win, low-technology mechanism by which rainwater can not only be prevented from causing floods but also be retained in order to minimize the threat of water shortage. They are thus being incentivized with a huge budget of between RMB 400 and 600 million for a variety of projects every year.[39]

Innovation

China is clearly aiming at a different conception of "eco." From Suzhou to Qingdao, high-tech centers sit alongside and are integral to the development of Eco-cities. They are charged with experimenting with new ideas and encouraging start-up business opportunities. One such development is the old Baoshan steel works in the north of Shanghai which has been earmarked, since 2000, as a 450-hectare Gucun Living Eco-park[40]: dispassionately predicting the decline of heavy industry and factoring in change. It plans to undergo a significant transformation of its out-of-date industrial warehousing, transforming it into high-tech research facilities, robotics labs, and even a 3-D printing museum.

These are innovative experiments in the *grand project* sense. None more so than Tianjin Eco-city—as one example among many—which is testing on a giant scale. Here data is being mined on a range of technologies and systems that have been implemented as full-scale, as-built testing rigs, rather than as computer models or small-scale trials. Like all cities, it is a real-life social experiment, but here they are also experimenting with environmental techniques, methods, and materials in real time and at human scale, as well as providing training grounds for construction operatives, technical managers, and project supervisors.

Testing out large-scale sponge city technologies, for instance, Tianjin has installed ground filtration systems that have been laid as a citywide infrastructural network of permeable paving to minimize rainwater runoff. Drinking water supply will be partly provided by desalination plants. Bike lanes and boulevards will separate traffic and pedestrians with intelligent traffic management. Solar thermal collectors for hot water generation are being installed as a matter of course. All of this provides opportunities for foreign investors eager to use Tianjin as an invaluable source of information: Philips planning to pilot its latest energy-saving lighting solutions, General Motors announcing that its electric cars will one day be populating the city's streets, and Tesla and Baidu using real highway infrastructure as an automated vehicle testbed.

The UN proudly boasts that most of its millennium development goals have been attained. Those goals targeted poverty, education, gender equality, child mortality, maternal health, disease, the environment, and global partnership, and its former Secretary General Ban Ki-moon stated that "the 15-year effort to achieve the eight aspirational goals set out in the Millennium Declaration in 2000 was largely successful across the globe."[41] It failed to say that without China's urbanization as an economic and social dynamo, the goals would not have been met. Most of the targets for poverty alleviation, housing, hunger reduction, and education were realized in China. Statistically, the magnitude of China's success in these areas—averaged across the world—has simply raised everyone up.

Consequently, when the United Nations Habitat III Summit launched yet another set of UN–mandated environmental guidelines under the imperious title "The New Urban Agenda,"[42] China could no longer be the butt of eco-jokes from the Western nations. One urbanist pointed out, "It's my assumption that these guidelines would have been eye-openers in China 25 years ago (but) most of these recommendations are implemented or on the way."[43]

These improvements are social and arise out of China's desire to create a developed society to rival the West. It is building many Eco-cities that are scarcely "eco" in the way that Richard Register (the inventor of the phrase) had in his mind in the 1970s, but they are attempts at humane urban improvements that will inevitably lead to transformative thinking, regulatory guidance, and new methods of construction.

Many cities—Qingdao, Hangzhou, Hefei, Chengdu, Nanchang, and so on—lay claim to some level of innovative eco-development within their boundaries, and all, to some extent, are trying something new in order to learn valuable lessons about the quality of life as manifested in livable urban environments. The China-wide experiment is something akin to the creation of the British Research Establishment (BRE), an organization that was set up after the First World War to investigate the performance of various building materials and methods of construction. China is experiencing its own version of postwar innovation as it transitions from socialist cities to postsocialist transitional cities,[44] and there is a similar need for efficiency frameworks, social improvements, infrastructural expansion, and urban experimentation.

Coincidentally, the BRE is involved in monitoring buildings at Meixi Lake Eco-City in Hunan Province. This is a city for 180,000 people, which is masterplanned by the American firm of Kohn

Pederson Fox, the architects that gave you the impressive Shanghai World Finance Centre and the risible Automotive Museum in Los Angeles. The Eco-city is being built 8 km outside Changsha and comprises a forty-hectare man-made lake with the usual checklist of urban essentials around the shoreline: high-end residential housing, commercial and a central business district including an obligatory convention center set among parklands, an entertainment district, a cultural island, and two research zones.

Put simply, Meixi Lake Eco-city is an aspiring city. It is designed to be a neat, modern city with high-tech industries, cleanish air, parks and recreation, urban efficiencies, better living standards, social and mobile connectivity with well-designed urban areas, pleasant architecture, and decent transport. Who is to say that these new Chinese cities shouldn't have the "eco-" prefix attached?

Notes

1   Hald, M., *Sustainable Urban Development and the Chinese Eco-City Concepts, Strategies, Policies and Assessments*. Oslo: Fridtjof Nansen Institute, 2009. p. 56.

2   Guo, Xin, "Tourism Summit Opens Rizhao to Development Possibilities," *China Daily*, July 11, 2008.

3   Bontje, M., "Creative Shenzhen? A Critical View on Shenzhen's Transformation from a Low-cost Manufacturing Hub to a Creative Megacity," *International Journal of Cultural and Creative Industries*, March 2014, 1(2), pp. 52–67.

4   Yamaguchi, Mami, "The Voice and Protests of China's Labour NGOs and Their Efforts to Promote Migrant Worker Rights," IDE Discussion Paper, No 508, 2015.

5   Yang, Guangbin, "Xi's Got the Power to Guide the CCP to 2049," *East Asia Forum*, March 1, 2015.

6   Lockett, H., "China: Strikes and Protests Jump 20%," *Financial Times*, July 14, 2016.

7   Metcalf, D. and Li, Jianwei, Trade Unions in China CentrePiece Summer 2006, 2016. pp. 24–26.

8   Mirasola, C. "Understanding China's Foreign NGO Activities Law," *Lawfare*, May 16, 2016. https://www.lawfareblog.com/understanding-chinas-foreign-ngo-activities-law (accessed August 1, 2016).

9   Anon (2016), "Nihil sine Xi," *The Economist*, October 29, 2016.

10 Cabannes, Yves and Lipietz, Barbara, "The Democratic Contribution of Participatory Budgeting, International Development," Working Paper Series 2015, No.15-168, pp. 1–33.

11 Raman, G.V., "Environmental Governance in China," *Theoretical Economics Letters* 2016, 6, pp. 583–595.

12 Habermas, Jürgen, *Between Facts and Norms: Contributions to a Discourse Theory of Law and Democracy*, transl. W. Rehg. Cambridge: Polity Press, 1996. p. 371.

13 Habermas, Jürgen, *The Structural Transformation of the Public Sphere: An Inquiry into the Category of Bourgeois Society, Polity.* 2014.

14 Rachel Murphy, R., "A Dependent Private Sector: No Prospects for Civil Society in China, Asia Research Centre," Working Paper No. 62. April 1996.

15 Walder, A.G., *Communist Neo Traditionalism*. Berkeley: University of California Press, 1986. p. 247.

16 Hooning, K., Lanschot, F. v., et al. "Pingdi Eco-city Research: Research on the Current Status of the Pingdi Area and Case Studies of Similar Eco-cities, China." *Delft, Next Generation Infrastructures* 2010, p. 115.

17 Burnham, M.P., A River Ran Through It. A case study of Yuhuan, a disappearing. Chinese island and aspiring eco-city. Michael P. Burnham, Portland State University, 2011. pp. 1–37.

18 Ren, Xuefei, "Architecture and Nation Building in the Age of Globalization: Construction of the National Stadium of Beijing for the 2008 Olympics," *Journal of Urban Affairs* 2008, 30 (2), pp. 175–190.

19 de Jong, M., Wang, D. and Yu, C., "Exploring the Relevance of the Eco-City Concept in China: The Case of Shenzhen Sino-Dutch Low Carbon City," *Journal of Urban Technology* 2013, 20(1), pp. 95–113.

20 Environment Stockholm Institute, "Doomed Eco-toilet Scheme was 'valuable experience'," *China Dialogue*, August 7, 2012. https://www.chinadialogue.net/article/show/single/en/5088-Doomed-eco-toilet-scheme-was-valuable-experience (accessed May 5, 2016).

21 Liu, Peggy, "China's Green Goddess," *Diplomat*, November 2, 2011, http://www.diplomatmagazine.com/ (accessed March 4, 2016).

22 Peters, Adele, "How Many of China's 200 New Eco-Cities Will Actually Be Built?" *Fast Company*, June 30, 2014. http://www.fastcoexist.com/ (accessed October 30, 2015).

23 News, "Guiyang City Becomes Member of ICLEI," *International Council for Local Environmental Initiatives (ICLEI)*, January 18, 2016.

24 Li Keqiang quoted in New Release, "Nation to Take Off on Cloud Computing, Big Data," *China Daily*, June 7, 2016. http://usa.chinadaily.com.cn/epaper/2016-06/07/content_25641220.htm (accessed June 20, 2016).

25 Jacobsen, R., "Israel Proves the Desalination Era Is Here," *Scientific American*, July 29, 2016.

26 Chen, S., "China's Desalination System May "Tip the Balance" in South China Sea Land Disputes, Scientists Say," *South China Morning Post*, January 15, 2016.

27 I-Chun et al., "A Green Leap Forward Eco State Restructuring and the Tianjin Binhai Eco City Model," pp. 1–15.

28 Anon, Tianjin, Eco-City, China in Operationalizing the Urban NEXUS Towards resource-efficient and integrated cities and metropolitan regions Case Studies, GIZ and ICLEI, 2014, pp. 42–49.

29 Yee, T.W., Lawson, C.R., Wang, Z.Y., Ding, L., Liu Y., "Geotextile Tube Dewatering of Contaminated Sediments Tianjin Eco-City, China," *Geotextiles and Geomembranes*, 2011, 31, pp. 39–50.

30 I-Chun et al., "A Green Leap Forward? Eco-State Restructuring and the Tianjin–Binhai Eco-City Model," pp. 929–943.

31 OECD Urban Policy Reviews OECD Urban Policy Reviews: China 2015, OECD Publishing, April 18, 2015.

32 "China Houses Nearly 40 m in Urban Areas," *China Daily*, February 14, 2015. http://www.chinadaily.com.cn/china/2015-02/14/content_19590172.htm.

33 Palmer, J. "Chabudou: Close Enough!" *Aeon*, October 4, 2016. https://aeon.co/essays/what-chinese-corner-cutting-reveals-about-modernity.

34 Wallenwein, F., The Housing Model xiaoqu 小区: The Expression of an Increasing Polarization of the Urban Population in Chinese Cities? Master Thesis, Ruprecht-Karls-Universität Heidelberg/Heidelberg University Centre for East Asian Studies. December 9, 2013. pp. 1–82.

35 Bray, D. and Jeffreys, E., *New Mentalities of Government in China*. Routledge, 2016. p. 7.

36 Xiao, G., Zhang, Y., Law, C.-H. and Meagher, D., *China's Evolving Growth Model: The Foshan Story*. Fung Global Institute, May 2015. pp. 34–35.

37 Anon, "At Sea in the City: When Building Cities, Someone Forgot the Drains," *The Economist*, August 8, 2015.

38 World Commission on Dams, *A New Framework for Decision-Making, the Report of the World Commission on Dams*. Earthscan Publications, 2000. pp. 404.

39 Anon, "Beijing, China releases Pilot List of 'Sponge Cities' to Utilize Rainfall," *Global Times*, April 20, 2015. http://gbtimes.com/china/china-releases-pilot-list-sponge-cities-utilize-rainfall (accessed March 15, 2016).

40 Li, X. and Jiancheng Pan, J., *China Green Development Index Report 2011*. Springer Science & Business Media, 2012. pp. 339.

41 UN Department of Public Information, "MDG Success Springboard for New Sustainable Development Agenda: UN Report." *The Millennium Development Goals Report 2015*, July 6, 2015. http://www.un.org/millenniumgoals/2015_MDG_Report/pdf/MDG%20 2015%20PR%20Global.pdf.

42 United Nations Conference on Housing and Sustainable Urban Development, Habitat III Revised Zero Draft of the New Urban Agenda, June 18, 2016, 1–17.

43 Quoted in Shepard, W., "Between Habitat II and III, China Changed Everything," *Citiscope*, 2016. http://citiscope.org/habitatIII/news/2016/07/between-habitat-II-and-III-china-changed-everything/ July 15, 2016 (accessed July 20, 2016).

44 Hua, Yu and Wei, Dennis, "Restructuring for Growth in Urban China: Transitional institutions, Urban Development, and Spatial Transformation," *Habitat International* 36 (2012). pp. 396–405.

CHAPTER NINE

Conclusion

As we have seen, there are a number of contradictions and oddities, confusions and controversies relating to Chinese Eco-cities. First, they are not built where there are ecological problems nor even where there are many people already living. Eco-cities are not built for ordinary people or to address everyday social concerns (it is no accident that Tianjin was the city with the fastest growing number of millionaires in 2013). In some preliminary research carried out at Wujiang Eco-city, Maria Oenoto, an environmental campaigner, revealed that 95 percent of those interviewed (people living alongside the new Eco-city development) admitted that they have no "interest or awareness regarding recent environmental news."[1]

Many new Chinese Eco-cities aren't really new but are existing cities with add-ons. Some Chinese Eco-cities are not really cities. Many Chinese Eco-cities aren't even "eco" in any acceptable Western sense of the word. Very often a Chinese Eco-city is a park, or a well-insulated industrial zone, or a waste incinerator— whatever it takes to tick the sustainability consultant's box, get the certificate, and rub eco-critics' noses in it. China knows how to play that system. Chinese Eco-cities are framed certificates. An Eco-city is a license.

But criticism aside, many Chinese cities and Eco-cities are hugely interesting; they are innovative, they are experimental, they are socially challenging, they are quirky, and they are fundamentally necessary urban constructs. Many Eco-cities have improved the physical and infrastructural landscape of China's undeveloped interior, but also many other countries, specifically in Africa, more rapidly than did the various European empires over the course of the last 200 or so years. One Chinese left-wing writer argues that Europe "bemoan(s) Chinese advances into their former colonies in Africa"[2] as sour grapes because China has not consciously enslaved the region in the process. He hints that the critics ought to be a little more circumspect.

Ren Xuefei, author of *Urban China*, says that wherever they are, "Eco-cities are intended to serve as role models for sustainable urban living in the future."[3] Role models is a good way of characterizing the Eco-city phenomenon: China is building places for people to live, work, and enjoy. They are doing it purposively, slowly and, in many instances, badly, but they are building experimental urban centers to cater for the next influx of city aspirants. These are also places where China can try out new land-purchasing deals, liberalize planning constraints, and provide eco-inducements and lucrative commercial deals to foreign investors. Here they can test-bed new technologies, try out new construction techniques, and shake up conventional ways of doing things.

This book has indicated that some Chinese Eco-cities don't work, some are a hodgepodge of accumulated urban elements garnered from around the world, some are naïve or grotesque, some are imaginative, none are boring, most are risk-taking, and all are experimental; but most importantly they are all transitional. Many have made an immediate improvement in residents' quality of life, reflecting a new phase in China's development. Many Chinese Eco-cities are simply bad cities trying to be better.

Whether the Eco-label works, who cares? Eco-city construction might be for purely pragmatic economic reasons but through the process China is making and remaking the urban world into a possibility for millions of poor laboring peasants to be able to provide themselves and future generations with more opportunities. If they have to burn coal, import concrete, or knock something down to construct the Eco-city, then so be it. Even though, as we have seen, Eco-cities could become the philosophical embodiment—and excuse for—an economic slowdown, at the moment they reflect China's newfound appreciation of quality over quantity, while still retaining an admirable appreciation of quantity.

———

In reverse order, China's top three Eco-cities are Zhuhai in Guangdong province, Xiamen in Fujian province, and Sanya in Hainan province. Sanya is a city of half a million residents situated on the southernmost tip of the island of Hainan, an island with over 60 percent tropical rainforest cover and regularly described as the "Hawaii of China." Sanya is the island's second city, a tropical tourism beach resort that performs well in most of China's list of environmentally friendly cities. For the record, the other seven in China's top ten Eco-cities list are Tongling, Xinyu, Huizhou, Zhoushan, Shenyang, Fuzhou, and Dalian. It is a fair bet that most non-Chinese people would not be able to pinpoint more than one or two of these environmental centers of excellence on a map of China, primarily because many of these are third- and fourth-tier cities. These are the grassroots places where, as one journalist claims, "You see the future of China, for better or worse."[4]

Sanya registered highly in all categories in China's Green Book, notably coming top in "New Thinking on Environmental issues" and second in the "Healthy City Index" and is listed as one of China's "Top 10 Charming Cities." It has quietly emerged center stage, under the environmental industry's radar as a result of steady, sensible, unremarkable but carefully planned development. Way back in 1999, the Hainan Provincial People's Congress published its "Decision on Building an Eco-province," and within a year, in 2000, the US Urban Land Institute was drafted in to advise. Its specific brief was to recommend ways in which it could be developed into a world-class resort community: effectively how to manage its transition from a sleepy fishing village into an "international tourism destination of the highest sensitivity."

At that time, Sanya was learning the lessons from European resorts; in particular it was trying to avoid the rapid overreach of developments like Spain's Benidorm and Alicante, for example. In the 1960s, these Spanish resort towns had been transformed from fishing villages to international package holiday destinations almost overnight, and clearly suffered culturally and socially. It was only thirty years later that Spain's 1992 master plan set out to consciously improve urban quality and understand the value of cultural and natural heritage in resort areas.[5] China learns by assessing what others have done wrong so that it doesn't make the same mistakes.

The importance of getting it right is even more significant when you realize that while Spain's southern coastal region of Costa Blanca currently welcomes six million tourists every year, Hainan island caters for six million every month.[6]

The US Urban Land Institute's recommendation that Sanya place "a heavy emphasis on the quality of the environment" has clearly been taken to heart, although a number of core suggestions have been lost along the way in the intervening two decades. The suggestion that all hotel development should be frozen and that there be a core concentration on traditional farming and fishing—a common but unrealistic romantic allusion within environmental discourse—has been paid lip-service only.[7] This is, after all, a modern, aspirational Chinese tourist economy.

Ambitions for a purpose-made Sanya Eco-city Construction Plan for 250,000 residents along the lines of Tianjin Eco-city (originally cited in the "11th Five Year Plan of Building Energy Conservation" in 2009) have effectively been shelved.[8] However, Sanya is content to grow into an environmentally enlightened metropolitan area, gradually accruing the ecological benefits through growth, efficiency, and the necessity to be creative due to its relative geographical isolation; with many difficulties posed by its location, it still manages to provide China with its top-ranked environmental performance city in test-site conditions. At the time of writing, Sanya Eco-city is prioritizing its status as a double-double pilot city: a "Double R" city (prioritizing repair and ecological restoration) and a "Double Water City" (a sponge city and an environmental sanitation industrial park). While drains, garbage, and toilets may not be the sexiest topic of eco-conversation, it has provided a clear opportunity for a radical rethink of wasteful activities. It has just completed a waste incineration plant, all built to European standards,[9] now generating 120,000 MWh of on-grid electricity annually (roughly the equivalent of Munich, which has one of the largest waste-to-energy production outputs in Europe).

Sanya is the poster boy of intelligent development in China, although many of its lessons will not be transferable to the mainland. As a city, Sanya still leaves a lot to be desired, but as an expression of pragmatic management and skilled programming, it is exemplary as model of technocratic urbanization.

At the time of writing, it was announced that US architects Diller Scofidio + Renfro had won an international competition

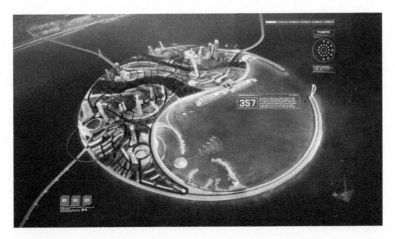

FIGURE 9.1 *South Sea Pearl Eco-Island proposal,* Hainan by UNStudio
©UNStudio

to design a ying-yang-shaped Eco-island off the coast of Hainan on the opposite side to Sanya (Figure 9.1). In typical Chinese fashion, it seems that the project has hit the buffers somewhat. But the groundworks raised from the sea are in place and so something will undoubtedly happen. The intention is that it will add to Hainan's ecological credit rating. Ni Qiang, the mayor of the capital city, Haikou, said that the new island will not only help boost local economic growth "but also bring some of the world's most advanced concepts in urban development to China."[10] China's Eco-cities should merit two cheers at least, that is, if they get built.

Sometimes they don't work. As we have seen in previous chapters, Dongtan failed because of local corruption and misguided ambitions, Huangbaiyu was an all-round cock-up, and city districts like Shenfu Gaokan Eco-city seem to have failed because of what one government official calls "monetary missteps." While Dongtan and Huangbaiyu need to be criticized at every turn, the recent Al Jazeera's documentary about Shenfu is a little sensationalist.[11]

It looked at Shenfu and neighboring Fushun to pillory the city fathers for what it suggested were monumental miscalculations (yet to be borne out) that led to the failure of its Eco-city pretensions.

What isn't explained is that this area was listed in 2009 as one of thirty-two resource-exhausted cities running down its coal industry and trying to mitigate the consequential social and economic problems.[12] Having studied failures in Sheffield, England, and Germany's Ruhr Valley where similar deindustrialization took place thirty years earlier, China was trying to create a new urban dynamic: a clean, parkland-dominated urban zone. In some ways, it was a valiant, misguided, and hugely costly attempt. But China is sometimes damned if it does and damned if it doesn't, with commentators and environmentalists all too ready to demand the closure of dirty, polluting heavy industry and then condemning the regeneration attempts. Such Western hectoring, not to say hypocrisy, must be a little exasperating for Chinese politicians at times.

Actually, China's vast scale sometimes means that the facts are difficult to relate to. For instance, the country is regularly criticized for being the largest emitter of carbon emissions. True, but actually its *per capita* emissions are small, just one-fifth that of Trinidad and Tobago (seldom in the news as a major environmental threat). Obviously, the *total quantity* of Chinese carbon-equivalent emissions is large, but it is fair to say that China is trying to resolve the problem.

Helped by the slowdown in its heavy industries, China started monitoring air quality in a small number of cities only in the mid-1970s and a limited national survey was established in the 1980s, and it placed limits on $PM_{2.5}$ only in 2012, so no one really knows its historic national air quality.[13] Indeed, even now air monitoring facilities are thin on the ground, meaning that pollution data is simply a reasonable approximation. To provide some context, US Environmental Protection Agency Administrator Gina McCarthy, speaking of her trip to China in 2013, said: "What I saw in Beijing was a geology and weather pattern that looked like Los Angeles and the air pollution challenges they were facing in the 1950s to 1970s."[14] In other words, Beijing's—and by reasonable extrapolation China's—air quality is at the same point where a major, not untypical, US city was just fifty years ago. It's a reminder to Western commentators that we in the West have been there ourselves, so casting the first stone is somewhat inappropriate or ungracious and lacks a historical, developmental perspective.

One study reveals that investment in China for environmental protection during the eighth, ninth, and tenth Five-Year Plans (1991 to 2005) accounted for "only 0.74%, 0.88% and 0.99% of GDP respectively. This amount of investment," they note, "is much less compared with the developed countries." Written back in 2009, the Hong Kong-based academics barely conceal their distaste for the fact that much of this money was being used to treat pollution rather than tackling "environmental education and communication,"[15] a *cri-de-coeur* of many a Western sustainability consultant looking for an advisory position.

With falling economic growth figures, China's thirteenth Five-Year Plan (2016–2020) didn't specify environmental spending as a percentage of GDP, but McKinsey estimated that it would now be around 2 percent (in line, they say, with the level that the United States, Germany, and Japan had spent at the peak of cleaning up their pollution during 1970–1980s) but equivalent to a sum "greater than Australia's GDP."[16] Actually, in their thirteenth Five-Year Plan, China commits to an 18 percent reduction in carbon emissions, 15 percent reduction in energy consumed by 2020, with 15 percent of primary energy from nonfossil sources, and a 25 percent reduction in $PM_{2.5}$ particulates.[17] One would have to be particularly churlish not to be impressed at this efficiency drive and its robust environmental cleanup targets. This is, after all, still a major industrialized power—not a deindustrializing one. Yet, unlike most developing capitalist countries, China has suffered pollution for less time and, in fact, it strategically integrated pollution cleanup into its development path.

There are some staggering improvements in the environment in China, given that it started from a grotesquely low base just fifty years or so ago. Within a short time, China has become the global leader in wind energy and aims to provide 100 million homes with wind-generated electricity by 2020 (thus reducing China's carbon dioxide emissions by a further 10 percent). Fly over the coastal regions around Shanghai, the deserts of Xinjiang, or the mountain ranges of Gansu Province and you will see turbines as far as the eye can see. One BBC report claims that China is installing one wind turbine every thirty minutes.

But still China is not known for its environmental credentials. The aforementioned BBC report on wind power still found time to focus on Greenpeace's rhetoric—oft-repeated—that China is building one coal-fired power station every week.[18] Incidentally,

Greenpeace has also said that China was building two coal power plants every week.[19] Actually, China had just implemented a moratorium on further construction for two years.[20] But it is important to clarify the facts from the hyperbole: China was *not* constructing one (or two) plant every week or even month. Indeed, a question tabled by Lord Donoughue in 2013 asking for an assessment of "how many new coal-fired plants are planned by China and India over the next decade" received an official answer: "25."[21] Statistical abuse by some environmentalists, it seems, is intended to make China seem more rampant than it already is. In fact, since 2005, the Chinese government has required that all new large power plants use "high efficiency super-critical coal fired technology"; during 2007 alone, 553 smaller inefficient plants totaling 14.38 GW were shut down.

China has twenty-one existing nuclear reactors, twenty-eight more are under construction with output expected to increase tenfold, to 400 GW, by 2050. But even with such technical expertise (learned from the West), suspicion of China's technical know-how is the order of the day, especially when China starts to sell the knowledge back to the West. The initial debacle over the UK's Hinkley Point nuclear plant being built with the aid of Chinese money was delayed by governmental suspicion of the inscrutability of China's motives, causing Beijing to condemn Britain's "China-phobia."[22] There seems to be always something negative to say about China's environmental credentials. Unsurprisingly much criticism echoes business or political or racial matters rather than environmental concerns.

China is the world's biggest manufacturer of solar panels, producing 30 percent (40 percent if Taiwan is included) of all solar panels globally, and the world's second-largest investor in solar energy with projects scheduled to reach 50 GW of capacity by 2020. And yet China is still criticized for its "over-production" of solar thermal and photovoltaics precisely because it has undercut the cost of Western panels. China has clearly made renewable energy more competitive by driving down costs, but of course at the expense of European markets. If environmental problems are so pressing, you might think that making very affordable remedies would be a good thing.

But there seems to be an ever-present moral opprobrium leveled at China's eco-ambitions. So even though under the 2011–2015

Five-Year Plan, China's hydroelectric power increased from 220 to 280 GW, representing 22 percent of China's total power capacity, there are few voices of endorsement. Hydropower has long been fated as a low-carbon, environmentally benign source of energy, but when it comes to China, most environmental advocates prefer not to identify the Three Gorges Dam as a positive source of electricity generation. It is not looked at in the same regard as, say, the Aswan Dam in Egypt was.

Environmental activists prefer to concentrate on the Three Gorges' impact on 1.2 million people who had to be relocated to allow its construction to commence. The Three Gorges Dam was called a "toxic time bomb"[23] in 2002 and still remains "a model for disaster" in 2016.[24] (For the sake of comparison, one-tenth the number of people were relocated to make way for the construction of the Aswan Dam.) The Aswan Dam has five times the surface area and capacity of The Three Gorges dam but one-tenth of the power generated by the Three Gorges dam. This is surely testament to the eco-efficiency of a more modern facility which is, in fact, the biggest power-generating production facility of any kind ever built. A truly remarkable feat of engineering.

Undoubtedly, relocation—often forced relocations—is an affront to human dignity and needs to be discussed. The consequences of the dam on real lives are explored in Jia Zhangke's movie *Still Life* or Yung Chang's documentary *Up The Yangtse*. But if relocations *per se* are so despicable, then what can we say about the intrinsic nature of China's urbanization drive? According to the "National New-type Urbanization Plan" (2014–2020), China intends to relocate 250 million people to urban areas by 2025; many of them will be rural relocations. This puts the Three Gorges Dam's 1.2 million relocations in perspective. You can either see relocation as a barbaric practice that rips people from their homes, destroying village life; or you can see it as a much-needed social improvement strategy—lifting more people out of poverty in a shorter time than ever before in human history, providing infrastructure and opportunities where none existed before, and raising the potential for the sum total of humanity. But yes, there are undoubtedly inevitable human casualties to this kind of rapid progress.[25]

———

Before embarking on this project, I had read many books, research papers, and articles to get a sense of the subject of sustainability and eco-urbanism, West and East. From Lester Brown's 1981 book *Building a Sustainable Society*, in which he advocates that modern man should adopt "simpler life styles,"[26] to APEC's Low Carbon Society that says that we should reignite our "coexistence with nature."[27] All too often I came across environmental commentators who advocated for the simpler life. The book *Cities and Sustainability* insists that an Eco-city's transportation should be "limited to walking and cycling."[28] Fred Pearce, writing in *New Scientist* in 2006, was pleased to note, for example, that "despite their sanitary and security failings…shanties meet many of the ideals of eco-city designers."[29] Ten years later, the *Atlantic* magazine reported that in the United states, "one family went six months without using soap and raved about the results."[30] Such romanticized paeans to a peasant lifestyle, so common in contemporary Western environmental writings, would suggest that China seems not to be following the West's Eco-script. After all, isn't China trying to escape the countryside for a life in the city?

But I found one Chinese urban documentary that seemed to capture the West's environmental agenda. It is a true-to-life, nonpolemical documentary with limited narration that allows the images to speak for themselves. We are shown a Chinese city with wide pavements with the greenery and boulevards of sustainable streets: what most urbanists characterize as a livable environment. The green canopies of the plane trees open onto relatively empty streets, an unusual feature of modern-day China as only a few cars are evident. Public transport is clearly a popular modal choice as well as a network of bicycle routes. Walking is the dominant mobility option. The film focuses on some elderly people performing Tai Chi in what might be taken as a public expression of well-being, and a much younger group work out as a team, taking personal health seriously and conveying a diligent sense of community. An urban farm producing fresh goods leads directly into the slow food market which is well attended by local people presumably eager to know the provenance of their local and seasonal food source. The documentary shows homes with very low energy use, nonprofligate water use, recycling and waste reuse—a model case study for environmental stewardship. Clearly, there are lessons here for the Eco-cities enthusiasts.

Now for the reveal: I am describing Beijing. I am describing Beijing circa 1972. I am describing Beijing, 1972, as broadcast in Italian director Michelangelo Antonioni's groundbreaking documentary *Chungguo, Cine*, filmed in the midst of Mao's Cultural Revolution. Mao had commissioned Antonioni to document the "New China"; to focus on its successes. But Beijing in 1972 was at a low ebb. Depicted here is not a modern city but a flagrantly backward city: a city of poverty and isolation. It was a regression to more primitive social organization. Sadly it ticks all the boxes of contemporary sustainability. Let's look at the reality in more detail.

The film shows car-free empty streets precisely because no private vehicles existed, and downtrodden workers are seen crammed onto open-topped lorries masquerading as public transport. Walking and cycling was the dominant mode of transport because it was the only proletarian propulsion option available to them. The young people mentioned above were, of course, not a happy *al fresco* fitness class but part of a regimented working party sent to emulate the hard-working peasants, armed with shovels to labor all day in the fields. The urban market was indeed a source of local food, much rationed and fought over, with the urban consumers oblivious to the famine in the rural areas that had subsidized its provision. Water was supplied sparingly by a standpipe minded by the ever-watchful party cadres in the communal living quarters. Recycling was a way of eking more use out of limited supplies rather than it being a happy moral choice. Low energy use was predominant because there was little energy to use and even less to use it on. The childish naiveté of Chun Yu's poetry during the Cultural Revolution captures a sense of the reality: "During winter, it was so cold,/ And there was no heating… after sitting in class for a while,/ I couldn't feel if my toes were still there."[31]

Italian filmmaker Antonioni had been invited to China in the 1970s to document China's success. On seeing the results—footage honestly portraying the dire peasant realities in Beijing, as well as Suzhou and Shanghai—Mao banned the film, and it was rereleased in China only in 2002. Antonioni was so defamed in the process that he became a target of a mass national criticism campaign and was even captured in song: "With the Party the whole world will be red and Antonioni will be mad."[32] But his auteur style showed the Chinese as they really were, their poverty keeping them closer to nature than they cared to be.

For many Chinese people today, their reliance on a bicycle is still very much an indictment that China hasn't delivered.[33] While many environmental campaigners in the West seem to want to renounce the gains of modernity—progress, growth, and consumption— China has maintained a defense of its right to enjoy their fruits. While the West advocates low growth and sustainable development, China still needs and wants material progress and real development.

But things are clearly changing. On the one hand, China's economy is slowing and the environmental legitimization of restraint is appealing to an authoritarian Chinese state needing to close down industries and tighten belts. Lester Brown's almost fifty-year-old concept of "conspicuous frugality"[34]—that he likened to "a means of rescuing spiritual life from the suffocating influence of commercialism"—is becoming a hallmark of environmentally aware, middle-class Chinese consumers. Most people in China, of course, are still delighted with the novelty of having commercial choices, but Xi Jinping's has primed society for a less predictable GDP growth rate and fewer choices.

Indeed, the internal and international pressures on China to improve its environmental record and clean up its act will probably result in the shutting down of many more high-profile, high-employment heavy industries. If Xi can sell the slowdown on the basis that it is a necessary ecological or air-quality-improving civilizational project, it could be a handy patriotic device to keep the peace. As Confucius said: "Even though you have only coarse grain for food, water for drink, and your bent arm for a pillow, you may still be happy."[35]

On the other hand, China, as it becomes a major global player, is wearying of Western environmental jibes. Even as it leads the world in solar, wind, and hydropower, it is still chided. For all the ambition embodied in China's Eco-city revolution, *National Geographic* quoted one North American architect as saying that "China's eco-cities are, understandably, just as consumptive, toxic, and ecologically harmful as other instant cities."[36] Try as they might, China seems not to have done enough to satisfy a Western environmental lobby that is clinging to its moral authority (even as its real authority is being gradually usurped).

One reviewer introduces a note of caution, referencing Europe's relationship with China, that Beijing "does not appreciate being criticized, lectured, or even mentored, and EU efforts to exercise its 'normative power' can lead to friction in Sino-European relations."[37]

From the condemnation of China's environmental record featuring highly in American media outlets[38] to Donald Trump's regular China bashing, China seems to be rising above it all; and on environmental matters it is beginning to play the West at its own game and, to some degree, seems to be winning,[39] with the UN crediting China's "robust leadership" at the G20 Paris climate deal in 2015.[40] At the same time, China is also turning its gaze eastward, finding friendlier relationships with countries that are more sympathetic—or less concerned—about China's internal politics.

We will look at these two points in more detail: the issue of China's environmental explanation and justification (or apologia) for some painful economic decisions to come; and we will explore China's perception of itself and how it locates itself in a globalizing world. But, first, let's look briefly at how China attempts to manage it contradictions, and the success or otherwise of its social-economic structure.

———

In his book *Capitalism, Socialism, and Democracy*, economist Joseph Schumpeter identified the nature of a capitalist entrepreneur as one who innovates in products and manufacturing processes to create progressive improvements in both. However, he recognized that in the process conflicts would arise and obsolete production would inevitably, unavoidably, unconsciously be destroyed. But in "Schumpeter with Chinese characteristics," the state is the producer *and* the entrepreneur, thus removing the hostile nature of competition in the classic capitalist model. Here, the state controls the process of what Schumpeter called "industrial mutation" and "creative destruction" to ensure that social relations are maintained rather than destroyed along with the economic transformation around it. That control, by the way, is not necessarily a healthy thing.

Even in the growing independent sectors, like media and automotive industries, commercial autonomy comes with responsibilities and penalties. Since 2001, Chinese capitalists have been allowed to join the Communist Party, where they can learn which side their bread is buttered. In this patrician protectorate, the business freedom to compete can be removed by government at short notice if the simple market mechanism works against the

Party's plans, as many company bosses know to their cost. This is why nine out of the top ten independent company bosses are linked to the Party and the tenth, Jack Ma, CEO of Alibaba, acknowledges learning how to take tough decisions from studying the communist leadership.[41]

China's economic dynamism isn't fake, of course; it is simply that while its goal is profitability, the continuance of social stability through Party rule is a higher order of importance. So although China knows that it has to embark on what one commentator calls a drive for "ferocious innovation,"[42] the reality of the potential consequences of capitalist competition is a little too unsettling for the Chinese Communist Party. As a result, China is inherently denied the social radicalization that real dynamic capitalism presages.

Marshall Berman sketched out the brutal market reality that China is shielded from:

> Everything that bourgeois society builds is built to be torn down…(from) the firms and corporations that exploit the workers, to the towns and cities and whole regions and even nations that embrace them all—all these are made to be broken tomorrow, smashed or shredded or pulverized or dissolved, so they can be recycled or replaced next week.[43]

This is what real recycling looks like.

Creative destruction requires a fair amount of destruction but China is often afraid to countenance it. As a way of restraining the tendency of capitalism to wreak havoc, the Chinese variant of creative destruction is a completely technocratic controlling mechanism whose main aim is self-preservation through social harmony. Rounds of Chinese capital accumulation are therefore orchestrated by the state, not by rival firms. The shakeout of existing industries is planned and timed to maximize state benefit, not a midnight corporate raid to benefit shareholders. The housing bubble is maintained at an impossible level but some of the more overblown local markets are punctured in a controlled fashion. In many ways, the Chinese state gets to say when the free market rules apply.

Clearly, there is a certainty in this approach, and Western regimes are very taken with China's clarity of purpose, its managerial finesse, and its apparent economic and social success. However, the socially transformative autonomy of Western economics is what gives it its power, its invention, and its creativity, and under its existing social relations China cannot offer this.

Real creative autonomy in China is currently out of bounds, although that doesn't stop discussions and genuine invention in academic, manufacturing, and commercial fields. But in so many ways, China has to restrain creativity—the very prize it seeks so desperately—because of creativity's intrinsic destabilizing character. There are great individual innovators, irrepressible minds, youthful inventors, ambitious thinkers, and insightful educators who all attest to the probability that China will hit its target to be the No. 1 innovative country in the world by 2050. However, creativity for China is something that is fundamentally necessary and yet undoubtedly corrosive.

Environmentalism is clearly one way of providing a philosophical legitimization of austerity, and the West is looking keenly at China's ability to pull it off. Speaking of the economic future, President Xi says: "There are risks, but not that formidable,"[44] which is easier for Chinese authorities to say than the more risk-averse, recession-laden Western world. China is presenting environmental transition as an opportunity for growth and the next round of accumulation, and Xi portrays the closure of many of the heavy industries that launched China's economic miracle as the necessary step to modernization. In that interpretation, Eco-cities are a test bed for some of the new industries, research facilities, innovation themes, quality assurance processing, and ways of working that will lay the foundations for that modernizing rebirth. Ten years ago it was a legitimate question to ask whether China could "afford to threaten a new found economic gains of literally tens of millions of Chinese with environmental reform?"[45] Ten years later and it seems that the answer is a muted "yes," with reservations.

Behind the scenes there are several social forces pulling in different directions. There is the growth of an influential urban middle class openly criticizing consumerism; there are many young people detached from the cohesive authority of the old China; and there are still regular protests in village communities at being left out of the gains of the last thirty years. With all of these tensions, China is finding it difficult to create a new narrative. Currently, China admits to an unemployment rate of around 4 percent, although some analysts assess that this might be three times higher, claiming that "state-backed 'zombie' factories are being kept alive by local governments to keep a lid on any social unrest."[46]

The unifying Communist ideological authority is gone; and the country's economic dynamism is ebbing, so can the abstract reference to a "New Normal" work? Does the rhetoric of sustainable limits, integral to the Chinese eco-dream, help hold it all together, providing growth and yet managing urban slowdown while also satisfying millions of people's "yearning for a better life"?[47]

There are several ways to achieve the transition from the old to a new economy. But will the rhetoric of environmentalism and efficient sustainable practices be enough to help explain and excuse some tough decisions to come? Here we outline a few pragmatic management policies already on the horizon.

Rule of law

The government is bound to maintain and intensify its war on graft whereby, in the name of cleaning out the stable, industries will close for ethically purifying reasons. Such acts appease local anger and more importantly reinforce the role of the party as the arbiter and as the sole legitimate ruling authority to decide on the fate of guilty parties. Emphasizing the rule of law in China is simply a way of emphasizing the rule of the Party after all. Far too many businesses and industries are run illegally or continue environmentally unsound practices, and the Party can relatively easily explain the necessity to shut them down for the good of China, with minimal fallout.

Labor reform

The government will need to take action on the major state- or semistate-owned industries (SOEs) that are overproducing and distorting the market. In the steel and coal industries, where oversupply was the first item on the agenda of the Hangzhou G20 Summit in 2016, there is scheduled to be around 1.8 million layoffs of Chinese workers in the next few years. To sugar the pill, the central government has been forced to promise a 100 billion yuan (US$15 billion) stimulus package for resettlement and other support systems, including reassignment and retraining in Eco-city business parks where old skills are still needed in transitional industries.

The general passivity of the older generation—to eat bitterness— is a necessary precondition for this transition to work, but the younger generation have been less inured to hardship and pose more of a challenge to convince, which is why improving more ephemeral "quality of life" issues—urban value added—is one thing now being tried to win people over.

It's clearly more difficult with workers in minority areas like Xinjiang, Gansu, and Qinghai who are often employed in SOEs due to some of China's positive discrimination rules for ethnic minorities where, in some areas, there are affirmative action policies in employment, tax and family planning, and so on. In some SOEs, minorities can be removed only after making substantial compensation payments. However, as SOEs close, privately owned industries are less obliged to employ them for these liability reasons. In truth, it was never that rosy for minorities as the *China Labour Bulletin* notes, "Even in government departments, discrimination continues to be tolerated."[48] Maintaining stability, one of the core aims of the Party, will be a tricky business in the western regions.

Creativity

China demands innovation. It has long sourced Western expertise to adapt, to co-opt, sufficient now to improve and create its own areas of dynamic production. It is already spearheading a production revolution in robotics, smart technology, space exploration, artificial intelligence, and environmental power generation, including the recent successful mining of combustible ice.

Although a slow starter in the Fourth Industrial Revolution as it is called, China's state spending could speed the catchup. Its ten-year "Made in China 2025" industry strategy announced in 2015 includes billions of yuan for technological upgrades, including advanced machinery and IT, buying one-quarter of all robots made globally in 2015. It helps that many of these smart technologies rely on informational big data that the Chinese government is particularly adept at obtaining, especially through the recently formed Cyberspace Administration of China.

Much of the Western world, caught in economic problems of its own, is looking enviously at Chinese ability to monitor, to data trawl, and to eavesdrop. After all, China has the ability to provide an experimental environment for future growth unimpeded by troublesome liberalism. The real problem is that the data collected by the state usually stays with the state and businesses often have to fall back on old-fashioned autarky. When the state refuses to give unauthorized personnel information like, for instance, detailed topographic maps, or demographic data, it forces companies to use Open Source data and to find out for themselves. In this way, China's development is not as straightforward as some might imagine.

————

Finally, let's explore the changing perception of China. Emerging from a peasant economy to be the largest trading nation in the world in thirty-five years is astonishing; but its shift from Tiananmen Square revilement, to gaining a seat on the UN's Human Rights council in twenty-five years is no less remarkable. From a Communist pariah state to delivering the opening speech at the World Economic Forum in Davos, it seems that we all pragmatists now? This final section looks at how China is seen by the outside world and how it locates itself in a globalized world.

While not jeopardizing its commercial deals and its growing influence in the West, China is looking Eastward for support and alliances better suited to its national character (sometimes classified in terms of Confucian values). These are *inter alia*: social stability over conflict, family duty, educational achievement, and a robust work ethic.[49] China's alliances with Singapore in the construction of Suzhou Industrial Park (Suzhou-Singapore Industrial Park) and Tianjin Eco-city rely on political as well as economic allegiances. However, even though Singapore is not averse to autocratic rule and is China's largest foreign investor, it is actually too culturally diverse to be a simple ally and remains "economically pro-China but militarily pro-United States."[50] Indeed, China's apparent refusal to invite Singapore to the Belt and Road Summit in 2017 appears to have been a diplomatic snub.[51] However, China hopes to grow its large backyard of compliant states—friendly or desperate—willing to not (openly) criticize China's human rights record or its technocratic rigidity. These countries may be more culturally attuned to accept the sanctuary of a modern-day tribute system: the benign authority of a powerful state. Indeed, some have pointed out that the dominance of China in its Belt and Road initiative will result in China offering largesse to supporters or withholding trade from dissenters.

Clearly, China is an integral player in the global market straddling East and West and is increasingly thought of as some kind of central arbiter. At the World Economic Forum in Davos in 2017, WEF founder and chairman, Klaus Schwab, said, "In a world marked by great uncertainty and volatility the world is looking to China."[52] While the West urges greater Chinese leadership, some voices in China are theorizing about how China can firmly establish itself at the heart of global affairs.

China wasn't called "China" ("Zhongguo") by anyone in China until about 1900. Until then, the empire was simply called by the name of its dynastic rulers.[53] In the Zhou Dynasty (1046–256 BC), the belief was that everything under the heavens was the entire extent of the world and the emperor was the representative of heaven on earth. In other words, China was Zhou and the Chinese empire was everything with no limits and no borders.

Professor Zhao Tingyang, Great Wall Professor of Philosophy at the Chinese Academy of Social Sciences, has long argued that the Chinese conception of "All Under Heaven" (*Tian Xia*) is the best philosophy for understanding and governing the world. Professor Zhao argues that it is necessary to reignite this traditional and benign conception of world governance precisely because it is applicable and necessary today.[54] Such ideas have clearly had an influence on Jeanne Marie Gescher's book *All Under Heaven: China's Dreams of Order*, published in 2015,[55] which portrays China's way of seeing as a mechanism for global harmony.

Zhao argues that the Western values typified in Samuel P. Huntington's *Clash of Civilizations*—of imperial domination, competing interests and perpetual inequality—need to be usurped by a unifying philosophy. He is careful to state that the social system of which he speaks is an invention and not a religion. That said, he advocates a universal state (what Wang Mingming has called a "symbolic empire"[56]) in which national concerns are eliminated, claiming that "relations, and not 'essence,' define what something is … (thus) we need a world philosophy that speaks on behalf of the world."[57]

China's first-ever conference on international relations was held in 1987. Ever since, academics like Yan Xuetong of Tsinghua University in Beijing have been trying to assess whether China has the clarity for moral leadership in world affairs and setting a new global ethical standard.[58] Dangerously quirky and unequivocally antidemocratic, Professor Zhao's intentions chime with some of the underlying themes that have been identified throughout this book affecting both East and West. Many people, disillusioned by human history, are increasingly ready to accept the infallibility of a mandate from heaven, or an equivalent secular overlord.

Enter, stage left, China. It happily finds itself in a world where there is a growing global acceptance of technocratic oversight by the so-called benign unelected authorities in social and political affairs (look no further than the visceral clamor for supra-state paternalism by some pro-European Union [EU] campaigners in the UK's Brexit discussion). Secondly, ecological issues have developed an ethical claim to universalism that frequently brooks no challenge (see the frequent high-minded use of the phrase "the debate is over" when speaking of environmental science).[59] Finally, there is a growing disenchantment with national sovereignty in global affairs (as demonstrated in the increasing number of "democracy is overrated" debates whereby economist Thomas Piketty can insist that "we have to overcome our own national egoism").[60]

There is, of course, Thom Kuehls' 1996 book *Beyond Sovereign Territory: The Space of Ecopolitics* that mirrors Zhao's point that contemporary internationalisms are anachronistic. Twenty years on from Kuehl and one writer seeks to appeal to "those who believe in 'earth democracy' and the renewed ethical commitment to ecological global government,"[61] closely resembling Yan Xuetong's proposed "superpower modelled on humane authority."[62] The International Confucian Ecological Alliance says that through environmental Confucianism "we embrace or enable family cohesiveness, social solidarity, national integrity, and world peace. It provides an authentic possibility of transcending selfishness, nepotism, parochialism, ethnocentrism, nationalism, regionalism, and anthropocentrism."[63] Others take a more authoritarian view of world peace. In 2015, environmentalist Eero Paloheimo (the Eco-city idealist who we met in Chapter 1) launched a campaign called "Unite The Armies," that seeks to bring all the world's militarized coercive force of arms together "to save the planet."

Donald Trump (pronounced in China as *Tangnade Chuanpu*)—the US president at the time of writing—has spent considerable time criticizing China. At the time of his election, many Chinese netizens were enthusiastic about Trump's "pragmatic way of thinking,"[64] suggesting that, at last, America has come around to recognizing that Chinese-style no-nonsense rule is the best way forward. Since his inauguration and subsequent diplomatic spats with China and his tendency to inflame passions in China's backyard, Trump's erratic foreign policy has galvanized China's desire to exercise greater leadership in global economic affairs.

Many liberals in Britain marched in defense of the unelected EU. They openly argued that democracy is overrated, that sovereignty is unimportant and caviled against the popular mandate of a referendum. For China, like many liberal commentators in the UK, the Brexit referendum result represents "a failure of democracy," and unsurprisingly an opportunity to refresh arguments against populism. Unelected members of the Houses of Parliament sought to block the referendum result and many liberals casually invoke the patrician oversight of unelected officials. Indeed, in 2011, *The Guardian* newspaper published an article headlined "In defence of Europe's technocrats."[65] With this in mind, China is looking increasingly like a country that we can do business with precisely because Western liberals, worried about a divided nation, seem to want to circumvent difficulties by rising above the ugly, difficult business of democratic engagement. One political journalist noted in mid-2015 that "the EU functionally vetoed the outcomes of Greek democracy,"[66] so how much more likely is it that China will confidently flaunt the idea that China itself is not ready for, or desirous of, democracy.

Indeed, the World Bank points out that one of the difficulties for cities successfully implementing necessary ecological changes lies within the democratic nature of Western society. The World Bank points out that "the election cycle" is a problem constraining authorities from "execut(ing) policies over the long term"[67]—a criticism straight from the Chinese Communist Party handbook. The World Bank report continues: "Change in leadership frequently means a loss in continuity ... it is important that plans compensate for this disadvantage."[68] The World Bank has long endorsed the can-do attitude of leaders who transcend the process of democratic oversight, but in today's climate, China, I'm sure, will be more than happy to advise.

———

In the opening chapter, I favorably quoted Jonathan Fenby's temperate approach to China. Two years later, in his book *Will China Dominate the 21st Century*, he is a little less forgiving and lists legitimate reasons why China is in a far more parlous state than Sinoptimists admit. He quotes commentator Guy de Jonquieres: "China has shown that it can shake the world order. It has yet to show that it can yet shape a future one."[69] While Fenby does incredibly valuable work in this book as usual, I believe that he misses one important point, that is, the coincident collapse of politics and sense of order in the West. This lack of moral, political, and economic legitimacy in the West is important in deflecting attention toward the alleged dominance of China. China may indeed shape the future, but by default rather than by design.

He is correct to note that few people from around the world are choosing to adopt a "Chinese way of life." True. But many are definitely seeing something in the Chinese model precisely because there is little to offer in the Western one. It is China's ability to get things done, its pragmatism, its political stability, its family values, its cultural heritage, its educational rigor, its infrastructural investment, its construction rapidity, its urban transformation, its poverty alleviation, its environmental Damascene conversion, its paternalism, and its lack of democratic hindrance that catches the eye of many. That many people are so blasé about the reactionary aspects in that list is a sign of desperation at the Western project. It is not China's fault that its apparent rise is as much the result of the West's collapse but it is certainly going to take advantage.

At the beginning of the book, I suggested that many contradictions would remain. Dear reader, I hope that I haven't let you down. I hope that this book has sparked an interest in China and its exciting urbanization, its political tensions, and its creative aspirations. I hope too that it has opened up a wider frame of reference and criticism of the Western discourse on this topic, which far too often is governed by restraint, risk aversion, and environmental instrumentalism. This book is not intended to foster support for China's version of events or its social organization, but to open up some critical discourse on environmental matters per se. It exists to question the dominance of a single uncritical position from wherever it comes.

This book has merely used Eco-cities as a prism through which to explore China's fascinating incongruities. Over the coming years we shall see if it manages to resolve—or even cares to resolve—any of its many fundamental underlying contradictions.

Notes

1   Oenoto, Mia, Towards Eco-City: Assessment Report on Ecological Education and Public Awareness in Wujiang Tai Lake New City, CDE201 Environmental Sustainability Assignment II, XJTLU University, 2016, pp. 1–19.

2   Wang, B. and Lu, J. (eds), *China and New Left Visions, Political and Cultural Interventions*. Lanham, MD: Lexington Books, p. 33.

3   Ren, Xuefei, *Urban China*. John Wiley & Sons, 2013.

4   Davis, B., "Why Does China's Economy Need to Change? For Clues, See Smaller Cities," *Wall Street Journal*, September 3, 2015.

5   Mantiñán, M.J.P. and Solla, X.M.S., "Impact of Tourism on Coastal Towns: From Improvisation to Planification," *The Open Urban Studies Journal* 2010, 3 s., pp. 21–27.

6   Xinhua, "China's Hainan Sees Robust Tourism Growth From Foreign Visitors," *China Daily*, April 20, 2016.

7   ULI, Sanya, Hainan Province, China: Strategies for Becoming a World-Class Resort Community: An Advisory Services Panel Report, Urban Land Institute. September 10–16, 2000.

8   World Bank, "Sino-Singapore Tianjin Eco-City: A Case Study of an Emerging Eco-City in China." Technical Assistance (TA) Report, *The World Bank*, November 2009. p. 133.

9   Messenger, B., "China Everbright Completes Phase II of the Sanya Waste to Energy Project," *Waste Management World*, June 7, 2016. https://waste-management-world.com.

10 Sayer, J., "Diller Scofidio + Renfro wins Competition to Design Artificial Island Complex in China," *The Architects Newspaper*, August 31, 2016.

11   Chao, S., "Inside China's Ghost Towns: 'Developers run out of money'," *Al Jazeera News*, September 21, 2016.

12   Li, Qingdong and Cui, Zhixin, "SWOT Analysis of the Fushun Resource-Exhausted City's Transformation," *Canadian Social Science* 2012, 8(4), pp. 120–124.

13   Wan, Wei and Patdu, Kaye, A New Era in Air Quality Monitoring in China, AET August/September 2013. p. 1.

14   Anon, "Smog in Beijing like LA in '60s, US EPA chief Gina McCarthy says," *South China Morning Post*, December 13, 2013.

15   Choi, M.Y., Jiang D., Guo, R., Li, F. and Cao X., *Education for Sustainable Development Practice in China*. Institute for Global Environmental Strategies (IGES), 2009. p. 48.

16   Zhu, J., Yan, Y., He, C. and Wang, C., "China's Environment: Big Issues, Accelerating Effort, Ample Opportunities," *Goldman Sachs*, July 13, 2015. p. 5.

17   Geall, S., "China's Plan for Innovation Could Help It Meet Climate Goals," *Chatham House*, May 17, 2016. https://www.chathamhouse. org/expert/comment/china-s-plan-innovation-could-help-it-meet-climate-goals.

18   Harrabin, R., "China Embarked on Wind Power Frenzy, Says IEA," *BBC News*, September 20, 2016. http://www.bbc.com/news/science-environment-37409069.

19   Myllyvirta, L., "China Keeps Building Coal Plants Despite New Overcapacity Policy," *Greenpeace*, July 13, 2016. http://energydesk. greenpeace.org/2016/07/13/china-keeps-building-coal-plants-despite-new-overcapacity-policy/.

20   Johnston, I, "China Suspends Building of New Coal Power Stations as Electricity Demand Declines," July 13, 2016.

21   Aberystwyth, Lord Bourne of, "Coal Fired Power Stations: China and India: Written question—HL525," *Houses of Parliament*, https:// www.parliament.uk/business/publications/written-questions-answers-statements/written-question/Lords/2016-06-07/HL525.

22   Phillips, T., "Beijing Decries 'China-phobia' after Britain Cools on Hinkley Point Nuclear Deal," *The Guardian*, August 19, 2016.

23   Rennie, D., "Three Gorges Dam a 'toxic time Bomb," *The Daily Telegraph*, March 9, 2002.

24   Anon, "Three Gorges Dam," *International Rivers,* 2016. www. internationalrivers.org.

25   Williams, *Enemies of Progress.*

26 Brown, Lester R., *Building a Sustainable Society*. Washington, DC: Worldwatch Institute (W. Norton & Company), 1981. p. 329.

27 APEC, The Futures of Low-Carbon Society: Climate Change and Strategy for Economies in APEC, APEC Center for Technology Foresight, 2010, p. 11.

28 "Cities and Sustainability: Issues and Strategic Pathways," Springer Proceedings in Business and Economics, p. 9.

29 Pearce, F., "Eco-cities Special: Ecopolis Now," *The New Scientist*, June 16, 2006, Issue 556.

30 Khazan, O., "How Often People in Various Countries Shower," *The Atlantic*, February 17, 2015.

31 Chun, Yu, *Little Green: Growing Up During the Chinese Cultural Revolution*. Simon and Schuster, 2013. p. 63.

32 Schneider, S., China through Antonioni's lens, Masterplanning the Future, www.masterplannningthefuture.org. June 24, 2016.

33 Wetherhold, Sherley, "The bicycle as symbol of China's transformation." The Atlantic. June 30, 2012. http://www.theatlantic.com/international/archive/2012/06/the-bicycle-as-symbol-of-chinas-transformation/259177/

34 Brown, *Building a Sustainable Society*, p. 356.

35 Confucius, Nylan, M. and Leys, S., *The Analects*. W. W. Norton & Company, 2014. Item 7.16.

36 Lamb, "Can China's Eco-cities Bridge Fantasy with Reality?" http://voices.nationalgeographic.com/2010/06/23/china_eco_cities/.

37 Green, C., "Green on Vogt, 'Europe and China: Strategic Partners or Rivals?'," H-Diplo, H-Net Reviews. November, 2012. http://www.h-net.org/reviews/showrev.php?id=36590.

38 Schiffman, J.R., "Mass Media and Representation: a Critical Comparison of the CCTV and NBC Presentations of the Opening Ceremony of the 2008 Beijing Olympic Summer Games." Dissertation, Georgia State University, 2012. p. 80.

39 Wike, R. and Stokes, B., "Chinese Public Sees More Powerful Role in World, Names U.S. as Top Threat: Domestic Challenges Persist: Corruption, Consumer Safety, Pollution," Pew Research Center, October 2016. pp. 1–28.

40 Anon, "Commentary: China Resolved to Fight Climate Change, Pursue Sustainable Development," *Xinhua*, November 18, 2016. http://en.people.cn/n3/2016/1118/c90000-9143644.html.

41 Ong, L., "Richest in China Are Connected with the Communist Party." *Epoch Times*, October 22, 2015.

42 Feola, J. and Pettis, M., "Why China Lacks Creativity," *Observer*, April 15, 2016.

43 Berman, M., *All That Is Solid Melts into Air: The Experience of Modernity*. Penguin Books, 1988. p. 99.

44 Yan (ed.), "Xi's 'New Normal' Theory," *Xinhua*, November 9, 2014.

45 Jones, R. cited in (2007). *Vermont Journal of Environmental Law*, Vermont Law School, Spring 2007 8(2), p. 411.

46 Bloomberg News, "China's Hidden Unemployment Rate," *Bloomberg*, June 6, 2016. http://www.bloomberg.com/news/articles/2016-06-05/china-s-hidden-unemployment-rate.

47 Xi, Jinping quoted in Huaxia (ed) Xi: Chinese Dream Fundamentally about "Making Life Better for Chinese People," Xinhuanet, September 22, 2013. http://news.xinhuanet.com/english/2015-09/22/c_134649177.htm (accessed August 9, 2016).

48 Anon, "Workplace Discrimination," *China Labour Bulletin* 2015. http://www.clb.org.hk/content/workplace-discrimination.

49 Leung, J.C.B. and Xu, Y., *China's Social Welfare: The Third Turning Point*. John Wiley & Sons, 2015. p. 10.

50 Sun, X., "China and Singapore are Distant Relatives at Best," *The Globalist*, December 20, 2015. http://www.theglobalist.com/china-and-singapore-are-distant-relatives-at-best/.

51 Han, A., How China Snubbed Singapore at the Belt and Road Summit, The Interpreter, Lowry Institute. May 18, 2017 https://www.lowyinstitute.org/the-interpreter/how-china-snubbed-singapore-belt-and-road-summit.

52 Barkin, N. and Piper, E., "In Davos, Xi Makes Case for Chinese Leadership Role," Reuters, January 18, 2017. http://www.reuters.com/article/us-davos-meeting-china-idUSKBN15118V.

53 Goodman, D.S.G., "Address to the Faculty of Arts and Social Sciences," *University of Technology Sydney*, May 6, 2009.

54 Zhao, T., "Rethinking Empire from a Chinese Concept 'All-under-Heaven' (Tian-xia)," *Social Identities*, Routledge, 2006, 12(1), pp. 29–41.

55 Gescher, *All Under Heaven*.

56 Wang, Mingming, "All Under Heaven (tianxia) Cosmological Perspectives and Political Ontologies in Pre-modern China," *HAU: Journal of Ethnographic Theory* 2012, 2(1), pp. 337–383.

57 Zhao, "A Political World Philosophy in Terms of All-under-heaven (Tian-xia)," pp. 5–18.

58 Callahan, W.A., "Chinese Visions of World Order: Post-Hegemonic or a New Hegemony?" *International Studies Review*, December 2008, 10(4)), pp. 749–761.

59 Laurance, B. and Ehrlich, P., "The Debate is Over: Earth's Sixth Great Extinction has Arrived," *The Ecologist*, November 18, 2016.

60 Piketty, T., "Thomas Piketty: 'Germany Has Never Repaid its Debts. It Has No Right to Lecture Greece'," *Die Zeit*, August 7, 2015.

61 Westra, L., *Ecological Integrity and Global Governance: Science, Ethics and the Law*. Routledge, 2016, p. 176.

62 Xuetong, Yan, *Ancient Chinese Thought, Modern Chinese Power*, Daniel A. Bell and Sun Zhe (eds), Edmund Ryden (trans), Princeton: Princeton University Press, 2011. p. 9.

63 Tu, W., Confucian Statement on the Environment, Alliance for Religions and Conservation, Trondheim, Norway, July 2013. http://www.interfaithsustain.com/confucian-statement-on-the-environment/.

64 Shih, L., "Trump's China-bashing can't stop Chinese netizens from loving him, China Update." *Mercator Institute for China Studies*, No 2/2016, April 8–May 11, 2016. p. 10.

65 Fisher, L., "Peers Join Forces with Attempt to Block Brexit," *The Times*, August 1, 2016.

66 Mason, P., "Greece Put Its Faith in Democracy but Europe Has Vetoed the Result," *The Guardian*, July 13, 2015.

67 Anon, *Eco2 Cities: Ecological Cities as Economic Cities, Synopsis*. World Bank, 2010. p. 6.

68 Suzuki, H., et al. *Eco2 Cities: Ecological Cities as Economic Cities*. World Bank, 2010. p. 34.

69 Fenby, J., *Will China Dominate the 21st Century*. Polity Press, 2014.

INDEX